THE BOOK OF
JOBS

EXCLUSIVE CAREERS
GUIDANCE FROM INSIDERS

LUCY TOBIN

HERON

BOOKS

First published in Great Britain in 2015 by Heron Books
an imprint of

Quercus Publishing Ltd
Carmelite House
50 Victoria Embankment
London EC4Y 0DZ

An Hachette UK Company

Working Lives of Fabina and Louise published with the kind permission of mi5.gov.uk

A CIP catalogue record for this book is available
from the British Library

PB ISBN 978 1 78429 134 1

EBOOK ISBN 978 0 5705 395 4

10 9 8 7 6 5 4 3 2 1

Illustrations by Nicola Budd

Typeset by Hewer Text UK Ltd Edinburgh

Printed and bound in Great Britain by Clays Ltd, St Ives plc

Thank you to my parents, for setting me on track to the career of my dreams. You are the best and us three Tobnobs are so lucky.

Howard, thank you for being brilliant in this life-changing year – and for cooking and washing up many a dinner while I embarked on interviews for this book.

To Jamie, who grew into a tiny person during the nine months it took for this project to come to life – this book is for you, with all my love.

CONTENTS

Dream Jobs

Odd Jobs

Famous Faces

Tables

Appendices

INTRODUCTION

'When I'm a grown up, I want to be a . . .'. Career chat starts in the playground. But for most of us, our tiny-tot aspirations to be an astronaut, train driver (Thomas the Tank Engine, you have a lot to answer for) or England's top goal scorer don't quite follow through to reality.

That's where the inspiration came for this book. As a national newspaper journalist, I spend weeks of every year interviewing top City bosses, whistle-blowing interns, entrepreneurs and staff about what their jobs are really like – and I always leave them feeling surprised. Because it's not just our five-year-old selves that might be taken aback at what actual careers really entail, or what their future self will end up doing for their long working life. The working world is changing fast – many of the best-paid and popular tech jobs didn't exist a decade ago, while other roles, like some secretarial and manufacturing jobs, have gone the way of the dodo. Job-hopping has become the new normal: the average graduate today will change industries as many as six times during their lifetime. But at school and university, advisors still bang on about us knowing our 'life-long career plan' from the time we can pen a CV.

And that's not the least of their misguided advice. Most people find so-called careers guidance to be more mystifying than helpful. I remember one session where my friends and I were told to log on to the computer jobs questionnaire: the bored-looking careers advisor promised us it would help us to 'find out what we should do in life'. We were, however, left a bit confused when we found out that the program reckoned all of us, whatever our interests or qualifications, would be well suited to life as a farmer.

It's thanks to a frankly enormous dollop of luck that I've ended up doing a job I love – writing for newspapers – because at school, and even at university, my friends and I struggled to work out what some jobs involved, and what others even meant ('actuary', I'm looking at you). I started out studying sciences with the intention of being a doctor, before changing my mind after a traumatic work experience placement in an HIV ward.

So this is the book I'd like to have read when I started grappling with future career options. Back then, I wanted something practical, non-stuffy and filled with horse's-mouth advice to help me work out what the various important or fun-sounding jobs really involved.

And others feel the same: ask the average commuter on the 07.59 train into London, and most of them, too, will admit that their daily work isn't what they had expected it to be. One recent survey of 2,000 Britons found half hate their jobs so much that they think they're in the wrong career, while a quarter said they were poor employees because they were so unhappy. The research, by banking firm Kalixa Pro, found the legal profession was the unhappiest – with four in ten not enjoying their work – followed by manufacturing and then hospitality.

But whether you're a new graduate or a career-changer looking for a totally different working life, unless you're actually doing a job, it's hard to find out what most industries are really like. You can see primary school teachers working 9am to 3pm and ogle over their long holidays, but you might not realise the hours of planning and training that they have do on top. You see TV footage of miners struggling with dark, dank working conditions, but you might not know that the average salary is a healthy £53,000.

At university, big companies host 'milkround' recruitment events, where they erect a bit of bunting and pump out propaganda about how their staff get paid mega-bucks for working a handful of hours a day. But if you're the one person who asks about the real working hours or what staff actually do, or your expected take-home pay in two years' time in your interview, you're probably not going to be the one who will be living out those working hours in a few weeks' time.

Yet these are questions we all want to know the answers to when considering a new post. And there are endless other issues that you might want addressed, too. Do fashion designers need to be business-savvy? Do translators get to travel the world? Do zookeepers spend more time shovelling poo than hanging out with chimpanzees?

Sure, some of these questions are more flippant and easily answered than others, but the truth is, even if you do know which careers might be a good fit with your skills, qualifications and personality – whether you're just starting out in the job market or considering changing what you do – it's not easy to know where to go for advice.

So this is what I went on a mission to find out: what are Britain's most popular careers really like? While other books and websites might give you details about pay and conditions, in *The Book of Jobs* I wanted to go further and give you a feel for what it was actually like do these jobs day-to-day. In these pages, people in Britain's most popular, lucrative and desirable jobs – from academic to zookeeper via web developer and fashion designer, pop star and chef – have shared the secrets to success in their industries: the best way to crack into each industry, what to expect when you get there and how to climb the ladder. Some of their names are hush-hush (all the better for truly dishing up a dose of cold job reality) but they're all successful at what they do, and include some of Britain's most high-profile executives, as well as those working hard behind the scenes.

And, since it's going to be a fair while till most of us get to be the top dog, *The Book of Jobs* doesn't just focus on those years at the pinnacle of your profession, it's also got the career lowdown on those a good few rungs further down the ladder. Interns and office juniors, as well as those in their industries for up to five years, revealed to me just how many cups of tea they had to make before getting their first pay cheque, the day-to-day reality of their work, how fast people can progress, and whether they'd recommend their job to their best friend.

While writing this book I learnt a lot, too. It became clear to me that some of Britain's most successful executives and entrepreneurs took a pretty relaxed approach to their careers, trying out many different industries and learning a lot in the process. It's clear that specialising early isn't always the best move – a broader work experience can make you a better candidate for a myriad of brilliant roles. Most of all, you have to (swallow the cliché and) follow your dream – because that old quote about choosing a 'job you love so that you will never have to work a day in your life' is actually true.

The twenty-first-century job market is wildly different from that of any other time. It's a place where a job interview could see you being told to make up a jingle and sing it, solo, in the next ten minutes. Unlike the old days, when Britons embarked on one job for life, the average worker today has numerous different careers before retirement – a concept which is itself starting to disappear. Yet the job market has become tougher as top workers come to the UK from abroad and the number of jobs available crashed in the aftermath of the recession. Leading employers currently receive about 39 applications for every graduate job. So for *The Book of Jobs* I also spoke to top recruiters and careers advisors about the interview grillings and weird questions you should expect, and what preparation you can do ahead of time.

So think of this book as the honest careers advisor – a bit of a contrast to the coffee-breathed maths teacher at school who did jobs advice on a Tuesday and asked if you'd thought about working in an office. Or on that farm. Pay, work/life balance, any lingering industry sexism or racism, training, effort levels – here you'll find the truth about working in Britain's most popular jobs.

Earnings potential

	Less than 5 years	5 to 10 years	10 to 15 years	15 + years
Local government	£34,000	£48,000	£63,000	£72,000
Charity	£29,000	£41,000	£47,000	£76,000
Accounting	£31,000	£52,000	£67,000	£97,000
Marketing	£32,000	£56,000	£93,000	£121,000
HR	£36,000	£55,000	£102,000	£124,000
Media	£36,000	£66,000	£97,000	£135,000
Legal	£58,000	£92,000	£133,000	£179,000
Finance	£67,000	£152,000	£240,000	£304,000

Source: salary benchmarking website Emolument.com

ACADEMIC

AVERAGE STARTING SALARY – £20,000–£25,000

ENTRY POSITION – Research Assistant or Research Fellow

TYPICAL WEEKLY HOURS – Variable, often temporary

RECOMMENDED QUALIFICATIONS – Teaching experience. PHD. Published work

IF YOU LIKE THIS YOU MIGHT ALSO LIKE . . . author, journalist, teacher

If you love being a student, a career as an academic – that is, a member of a university or college – could be for you. It doesn't exactly mean that you can live in your pyjamas and slurp pasta for the rest of your life, and the *Brideshead Revisited* world of academics living a life cut off from everyday realities is long gone, too. But you can devote yourself to becoming an expert in your subject; whether via hours studying old texts in the library, through hands-on science lab work or by exploring unknown places in the world. Consider academia if you're passionate about research, about pushing the boundaries of knowledge, or inspiring the next generation of undergraduates with a love for an academic subject.

There are three main types of jobs in this field:

- A research-only role, where the vast majority of your time is spent researching your subject and very little, or none, is spent teaching.
- A teaching role, with little time specifically allocated for research.
- A hybrid position, such as a lectureship, where you're expected to both teach and conduct research.

Whatever subject or academic aspiration you have, though, you'll need to have good time management, be hardworking, flexible (able to work weekends and late), an analytical thinker (able to think of research questions and design experiments or studies to answer these), with good attention to detail (particularly in science – you cannot be careless as each piece of data matters), social and communicative and adroit at critical appraisal – that ability to acknowledge the limitations of your own and others' research.

The usual path to working in academia is: first you'll need to pass an undergraduate degree, followed by a master's. Then you'll need to undertake a doctoral degree, or PhD, before embarking on post-doctoral research and/or becoming a member of teaching staff.

You don't, however, always need a master's to get a PhD – those who do particularly well in their undergraduate degree can apply for a PhD straight away, or sometimes embark on a '1+3 PhD', which includes one year of MSc studies (with a stipend). 'It's great because a three-year PhD can be a bit tight and a lot of people end up needing an extension,' says one graduate who did just that. 'With the 1+3, you start planning your project in the first year and it gives you a bit more time.' The typical academia route after a PhD is to become a lecturer, senior lecturer, reader, then professor.

Lots of PhD students who are interested in academia (or just keen to boost their bank accounts) take on extra work teaching undergrads. But it's a difficult industry in which to secure full-time employment: changes to how unis and research are funded mean it can be tough to finance your studies, and there are also far fewer funded, permanent, full-time posts available – even brilliant students with top degrees and stellar teaching and lecturing records can struggle to find tenure – a permanent position. There are also more and more people with PhDs, so instead some would-be academics go into industry (e.g. using their research expertise in the corporate environment, or for pharmaceutical companies or business strategic sectors) or teach (mostly in secondary schools). Scientists who do not want to pursue the academic career path might become a research assistant in a lab.

Other academics who have struggled to get work in this country sometimes try to secure a position abroad, where academic institutions may have more positions available and pay more. Or some diversify by writing textbooks, or becoming media 'talking head' experts on particular subjects.

But first you've got to embark on the career. You'll need to be brilliant at your subject, of course, with an excellent history of scholastic achievement, and have an intellectual curiosity as well as the above skills. A 'capacity for seeing through long-term projects, and being self-motivated and disciplined (especially in terms of managing your own time)' are also key skills, according to one academic. As you go up the ranks of university study, you'll need a record of getting work published in academic journals, with honed research skills, and be good at communicating with a range of audiences – from freshers to experts more senior than you.

The kind of work you do as an academic will obviously hinge on your specialism – a professor of medicine will have a very different existence from a professor of humanities. But as an overview, as a PhD research student you'll have to come up with ideas for original research, write proposals to apply for funding, carry out the research –reading, collecting and analysing data, comparing various sources, etc. – write and publish the research, manage a research budget, speak at conferences, supervise other students and perhaps teach, too.

As an academic member of staff, teaching responsibilities can include the designing of curricula, preparing presentations and notes for lectures and delivering them, instructing undergrads and postgrads in small tutorial groups, marking essays and exams and supervising dissertations. Another facet of academic life is administration – roles like admissions tutor (deciding which students to admit to courses), course organiser, school liaisons officer, subject leader, etc. Academic work often also involves joining committees within departments, universities, or even those formed of particular subject specialists across the UK or the world.

A junior (post-doctoral) permanent position pays around £32,000 a year. An experienced academic can expect up to £60,000, depending on the institution and responsibilities, while a few top professors and vice chancellors of universities will receive six-figure salaries.

WORKING LIFE: Dr Helen Barr is a fellow and tutor in English literature at Lady Margaret Hall, Oxford University.

'There's no such thing as an average day as an academic, because it depends crucially on whether it is in term or outside of it. In term, I usually start marking written work at about 6.30am for tutorials or classes that are happening that day. Once that's done, I check my email for anything that needs prompt attention. Depending on the day in question, I might spend the rest of the day teaching classes (with up to about ten students) or tutorials (one-to-one, or one-to-two), or be working on administration. Lunch is with colleagues, usually in college, so we can discuss teaching and/or admin. But no day follows a fixed pattern; it depends on the outline of teaching, lectures and committee meetings.

During term-time, you can be working as many as 70 hours per week, perhaps more. Outside term, it's more like 50 hours. At Oxford, terms are only eight weeks long, so vacations are also a prime time for supervising graduate students, giving talks in other universities and attending conferences. But even outside of term, there's still administration to tackle, and college meetings, examination marking, long-term college projects or faculty work.

But I try to earmark the early part of the morning for research, especially writing [Dr Barr's most recent book is *Transporting Chaucer*]. If the day is free of external commitments, then is the time to read, preferably in libraries, and to formulate ideas both for existing projects and for future ones.

Working at a university, you've almost always got things to do in the evenings and sometimes weekends, too: there are a lot of functions to attend, and seminars. Evenings are often taken up with marking and tutorial preparation. Outside term, it is easier to claw back some time in the evenings and at weekends, unless there is a deadline for submitting work to publishers.

My career path was fairly standard – after completing my doctorate, I had a few short-term teaching posts, then finally a tenured job. To get that, I established a good teaching record and practice and a distinguished record in research.

My favourite parts of the work remain teaching and writing, but the most boring is filling in official forms to justify what we are doing, which are sent to the people who manage us, and being forced to defend teaching and research in a culture that is obsessed with quantification and outputs.'

WORKING LIFE: Caroline Mzumbo* is a post-doctoral science researcher working in London

'I've devoted most of my research so far to looking at children with ADHD, so my days are different if I'm testing kids for research. I am usually up at 8am, finish off some work from the night before over breakfast, then get to work for 10am. The first hour is dedicated to making a cup of tea, chatting to colleagues about what is happening that day or the night before (gossiping, essentially!), and eventually checking and replying to my emails.

If it's a testing day – about twice or three times a week – I do developmental assessments with toddlers and interviews with their parents. I'll then have a de-brief meeting with colleagues and write up notes. On other days, work includes admin (calling families to schedule their appointments, sending letters for their appointments) or programming (writing scripts to analyse data and meetings). Other tasks can include writing or preparing papers for publication, clinical meetings (to discuss cases seen) and supervision of students and

---

* *name changed for anonymity*

interns who do data entry, or data analyses for their undergraduate/master's project. Once a week I also lecture undergrads.

With research jobs, you don't ever stop working. If I am at home and have my laptop on in the evenings, I'll reply to emails and work on papers or do some reading. But I really enjoy my job – especially getting to know families involved in the studies and assessing (playing with!) the children. The data entry is boring, though, and all the meetings can be SO tedious, long and pointless.

When I embarked on a career in science, I thought it would be quite intense and serious, but in reality most people and university environments are fairly relaxed. I also thought it would be pretty peaceful (and non-political), but there are often work politics and all the issues that you find in other working environments.'

ACCOUNTANT

AVERAGE STARTING SALARY – £15,000–£25,000

ENTRY POSITION – Trainee/Accounts Assistant/Junior Accountant

TYPICAL WEEKLY HOURS – 30–40 hours

RECOMMENDED QUALIFICATIONS – Accountancy qualifications depending on the area that you are interested in

IF YOU LIKE THIS YOU MIGHT ALSO LIKE . . . actuary, management consultant, banker

It might be the most joked-about profession around: Googling 'are accountants . . .' automatically brings up the suggestion 'boring'. But if you're good with numbers and finances, this could be the job for you. Accountants are well paid and always in demand, particularly as new, more complicated tax rules are brought in every year. There are lots of accountants, too – you'll find them everywhere from small high-street 'private practice' firms (meaning they work for lots of different clients and companies) through to government departments and huge special-ist multi-national companies, as well as in-house working exclusively for specific companies.

Work-wise, the job involves calculating how much tax people and firms need to pay, and often how to minimise their legal obligation, forecasting annual profit and loss and costs, advising on deals like mergers, monitoring firms' financial performance, and carrying out audits (independent inspections of a firm's accounts) of annual results and other transactions to make sure they are all above board.

A lot of big business stars begin life as accountants – JP Morgan was a Wall Street accountant, now his name remains on the banking giant he built up, while many FTSE 100 chief executives began their careers as accountants. All of their finance directors, meanwhile, will usually have qualified as an accountant.

To land an accountancy career, you'll need to pass exams – lots of them, which you'll do while working in an office. Smaller high-street firms and a handful of major firms accept non-graduates (see below: working life) with A levels or similar qualifications, but most big companies limit applications to graduates. They're not usually restrictive about the subject: it doesn't have to be maths or finance, but if you do have a degree in a related subject you might be allowed to skip some of the accountancy exams later on. You'll then sign up to one of the several professional bodies offering accountancy training, which usually includes three years of your work being monitored plus two years of professional exams.

Alternatively, another role is an accounting technician: this involves preparing the financial documents that accountants or business managers use. Candidates need good numeracy skills but no specific qualifications to embark on training (which is usually part-time while on the job). Some progress to chartered accountant status later on.

The key skills for the accountancy industry, according to one high-flyer, are: 'communication – being able to listen to clients to understand what is important to them, as well as simplifying technical concepts so they can be understood; relationship management – you need to build relationships and trust with clients; problem solving – finding solutions to the issues of businesses and individuals; management skills – managing a team to achieve maximum efficiency but also ensuring you are approachable and patient for junior members of a team. Plus time management and an ability to grasp and utilise technical skills.'

A trainee accountant can expect to start on about £19,000 per year outside London or £22,000 in the capital, but 'be aware that starting salaries usually include an employer's contribution to training and study leave,' says one who's been through it. A newly qualified accountant can expect to see their pay packet increase to around £40,000, rising with experience to six figures for a top City accountant – whilst a few FTSE 100 finance directors are on multi-million-pound packages which include pay and bonuses.

If you're considering a career in accountancy, 'understanding basic bookkeeping and running a business either by taking on an apprenticeship role or work experience in a local firm will help give someone an insight into the possible career path,' is the experts' advice.

WORKING LIFE: the Big Four accountant

'I'll usually arrive at my desk between 8.00 and 8.30am. If I'm in the midst of an audit, I'll be based at a client site, which means that everything is a little slower – if a client stops by our room, I'm expected to drop whatever I'm doing and speak to them about whatever issue they have.

An increasing amount of my day is sucked up by meetings, but outside of them, I'll be either managing a team of up to ten staff on a major audit, dealing with their questions or reviewing their work, or planning ahead for the next major project – I usually have up to five clients or jobs on the go at a time. I'll also be tackling my own work – following up clients' queries, or writing up meetings and findings from my preliminary work.

If I'm at my office, I will head out to a client during the afternoon for a meeting; if it's near the end of the day, I may go home afterwards to finish work from my living room. The nice thing about this job is that often it doesn't matter where you are, physically. If I have a large team working under me, it's tougher to work remotely, but I can always pick up the phone or send an email.

Home time can be anything from 6.30pm to 10pm – depending on what needs to be done. I'm fortunate that most of my clients are based in Central London, not far from my house, so the commute back isn't too tough.

Working for a big firm, you're well looked after: there's a department for everything – IT, payroll, technical problems – so there's always someone to call. If you want to do volunteering, or go on a career break, that's generally encouraged, too. On the flip side, my department is 900+ people and I barely know a fraction of them, despite working in the same department for over five years. You don't get the same tight working environment that you probably would at a smaller firm.'

THE LOWDOWN: newly qualified accountant

'I didn't follow the route most people do by going to university – I started full-time work after my A levels. Then I fell into working in accountancy rather than actively seeking it out, securing an entry-level job working in public practice for a small firm. After 11 months there, though, I moved to another company, got a training contract and began on my five-year career path to qualifying.

Many people believe that university is the only route into accountancy. From personal experience I know this isn't the case. I went straight from taking my A levels into an accountancy role where I studied towards an AAT qualification – the professional body for accounting technicians – to become a qualified accountant. There can be fewer professional exams for graduates, because if you have a degree you're exempt from lower-level papers.

Now I work about 42 hours a week – although during busy periods, such as before the end of the tax year in April, the working day is much longer. My favourite part of the job is that clients come from all over the world so I am able to meet and work with a wide variety of individuals. It's also really interesting – yes, even in accountancy – to work with a number of different businesses and understand how they operate. The downsides? Administration and paperwork are always involved.'

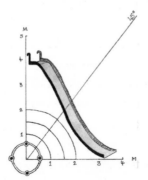

ODD JOB: Water slide tester, UK base, worldwide travel

A British holiday company pays a staff member £20,000 a year to make sure their hotels' water slides are safe, fun and fast. Lots of travel is involved – and you have to be happy sporting a uniform of trunks or cossie.

ACTOR

Some sobering statistics for anyone considering a career in acting:

£60 – Reported nightly pay for a child actor appearing in West End musical *Matilda*

$250,000 – Reported pay per episode for *Homeland* actress Clare Danes to play Carrie

$39 million – Forbes' estimate of Hollywood actor Leonardo DiCaprio's earnings last year

6% – Proportion of Equity members earning over £30,000 a year

52% – Proportion of Equity members earning less than £6,000 a year

11.3 – Average number of weeks per year that UK actors work professionally

10–15% – Average cut of earnings paid by actors to their agents

8% – Proportion of UK actors thought to be in work at any one time

So whilst acting can be one of the most exciting, fulfilling and potentially rewarding careers out there, it's also unpredictable, tough-going and often impossible to sustain without a second career. Hence the age-old depressing joke about 'what do you say to an actor?', 'Big Mac and fries, please.'

Those who do manage to find work are 'interpreting others' words in order to bring a script to life, and to put flesh and blood on the characters they portray,' according to the performers' trade union, Equity. Most actors work in more than one sphere – film, theatre, TV, radio, and perhaps also voice-over work. Some roles demand months of rehearsals and research, others are speedier jobs: some ad work, for example, is wrapped up in a day.

For film work, actors need to be able to learn lines and cues quickly, repeat their performance numerous times as they're shot from different angles, be great team-workers, be adaptable, and get involved with promotional media work. Many of those skills are useful in all kinds of acting, as are networking prowess (to secure more work), auditioning skill, a lack of inhibition and a willingness to be made up, dressed, positioned and directed by others; a good diction and accent mimicry, plus dancing and/or singing skills are sometimes demanded for particular roles. A good memory, confidence and an ability to get on with, and liaise with, all kinds of people from venue managers and tour managers to theatre and film crews are also vital.

Unlike most jobs, there's no general route into acting: some go to drama school, others work their way up by starting as a runner on a film or in stage management in theatres, some may be very lucky with a successful audition for work without training. However, 'nearly all professional actors have trained,' according to Equity. 'Many higher education and further education colleges offer Drama or Theatre Studies courses, as do specialist [fee-paying] drama schools, which usually only accept students who are over 18 years of age, and conduct auditions for places, but offer tailored, vocational courses which are recognised by the industry and which have strong links with agents, casting directors, production companies and broadcasters.'

That can be crucial because networking is so vital to finding acting work: remember that actors spend as much as 90 per cent of their time 'resting', which is why most have a backup or second career. Most would also recommend having an agent, although that is not always straight-forward. Agents receive reams of requests from actors to represent them every day, so you'll need to stand out. Target specific agents who represent actors with the kind of career you have, or want to have; ask for recommendations from fellow actors and drama school teachers, and approach them with a professional toolkit – good headshots, a well-presented acting CV with credits listing your performance experi-ence and training, a showreel, perhaps your own website with clips of your performance, and a prepared range of audition speeches. If you secure meetings, be well prepared and never sign a contract without reading it properly or obtaining specialist advice.

No legitimate agent charges any upfront fees, so watch out for the many charlatans out there, but be aware that most agents demand a cut of between 10 per cent and as high as 20 per cent of your pay – thank-fully, it's usually nearer the former.

WORKING LIFE: Jason Flemyng started acting at school and at the National Youth Theatre before enrolling in the London Academy of Music and Dramatic Art (LAMDA). After entering the Royal Shakespeare Company he got his big break in Guy Ritchie's *Lock, Stock and Two Smoking Barrels*. Since then he's worked on over 50 feature films, as well as numerous TV series and shorts.

'My advice to anybody interested in acting is to perform as an amateur for as long as you possibly can. That's the best sort of experience – and some training can be quite damaging if you start too young. Once you're quali-fied, there's no real way to guide your career, the only thing you're in control of is saying no. I've never had the luxury of being in a position to be able to pick and choose roles and make "wise" choices. Acting is an uncertain profession and you often need the money, so I've always just chosen what's in front of me. I'd like to think I've made some good choices ... I'm not stupid enough to do *Spiceworld*, the Spice Girls' movie ... oh no, wait a moment, I did do that!

My dad was a film director and his advice was to check your wallet before making a decision. If it's bulging then you've got what he called "f**k off money" and you can refuse certain roles, but if not then you just take the first job that pays. Only 5 per cent of actors make enough to have it as their primary living, the other 95 per cent have to have other jobs.

The other thing – and I know it's awful to say this, but it's the truth – is that it is easier to make it as an actor than an actress. It's an old cliché but there are 300 soldiers and only one princess. If a parent came to me and asked me to persuade their son not to be an actor, I'd say I can't do that, he should try because it's the best life you can possibly have. But if it was their daughter, I would feel obliged to talk to her and at least tell her how hard it is and what the odds are. It's simple maths.

The best part of being an actor is the travel. I'm a gypsy (if not exactly like my character in *Snatch*) and acting has sent me to India, the Middle East and Europe. The worst part is the uncertainty about where your next role and pay cheque are coming from, but that's just a part of the career and you have to get used to it, even if your family probably never will.

I think being an actor is the best job in the world. On a shoot day you leave your house at around 6am and get to unit base at 8am. You go through hair and make-up and get ready to work by 9am. You might rehearse a little bit and then you could end up sitting on your behind until 3pm, when they'll finally call you to set. Then they'll probably be running behind because they've spent all morning filming a car going across a bridge, and there'll only be time for two tight shots and one wide shot and that's you done – so you have to nail it first time.

There's no room for excuses, nobody's listening: you've got to deliver under pressure, whatever the conditions are. Acting school trains you in trade craft, but the only way you get the true experience of the job is when you're on set for the first time and you've got to nail it in one take. That's the skill of screen acting.'

Dream Job: Astronaut

Tim Peake, 42, is Britain's first European Space Agency (ESA) astronaut to head into orbit and visit the International Space Station.

'ESA advertised online for a new astronaut selection in 2008. At that time, I was leaving the British Army after an incredible 17-year career flying helicopters. I started the year-long application process with ESA, along with over 8,000 other hopeful candidates.

A selection day included eight hours of computer-based tests, each becoming progressively harder and with only short breaks in between – testing memory, concentration, coordination and spatial awareness – plus psychological questionnaires with hundreds of repetitive questions aimed at ensuring consistency of answers.

The week-long medical was fairly gruelling, followed by several interviews – until I found myself at a press conference in Paris along with five other successful candidates. I never expected to make it that far and it is certainly a huge honour and a privilege to now be part of Europe's human spaceflight programme.

So far my preparation for spaceflight has taken me underwater, where I lived for 12 days in a Jacques Cousteau-style habitat, spent seven nights in a Sardinian cave and multiple trips in the infamous 'vomit comet', not to mention centrifuge runs, spacewalk training, flying spacecraft in simulators . . . the list goes on. To go through all this training has been the most incredible experience of my life. What makes it really special is the people you meet along the way and the enthusiasm of all the training teams and fellow astronauts and cosmonauts who are there to offer help and advice. The worst part is all that training comes at a cost and there is a lot of time spent away from home.

There is no one route into becoming an astronaut. Astronauts come from all walks of life: engineers, scientists, pilots, schoolteachers, to name just a few. It is fair to say that a solid understanding in the core sciences will stand you in good stead. But more important are things like good communication skills, psychological profile, an ability to work well in a multi-cultural team, and, of course, to be able to work under pressure!

Many of the most vital skills are those that cannot be taught, which is why I always advise anyone interested in becoming an astronaut to choose the route that suits them best and be good at what you do. I left school aged 19 to become a pilot and follow my passion for aviation and only later in life completed a degree in flight dynamics – certainly not a conventional route but it worked best for me.'

ACTUARY

AVERAGE STARTING SALARY – £30,000

ENTRY POSITION – Student member

TYPICAL WEEKLY HOURS – 30–40 hours

RECOMMENDED QUALIFICATIONS – Third class or above if the degree is maths. First or Second class if the degree is unrelated. Minimum of grade C in a maths A level

IF YOU LIKE THIS YOU MIGHT ALSO LIKE . . . accountant, hedge fund careers, management consultant

It's famously one of the best-paid jobs around – and that's true of actuaries in almost every country in the world. The average 'basic' salary of a senior partner in an actuarial firm is £209,300, plus an £80,000 bonus, according to the Institute and Faculty of Actuaries; even a student actuary pockets an average £39,000 a year. But it's also seriously complicated. So, what does an actuary actually do?

Basically, they're experts in working out risks, using top maths expertise (plus statistics and investment theory) to help measure the probability and risks of possible events. Many actuaries specialise in insurance and in pensions – working out the value of pensions funds by considering things like how long members are likely to work for and live for, and how much their investments will rise or fall in value – but other industries that use actuaries include healthcare, banking and investments. An actuary might analyse past trends in death rates, inflation and investments to work out how much a life insurer should charge in premiums to be able to provide for its policyholders' payouts, for example.

Becoming an actuary involves tough exams – it takes an average of three to six years to qualify, and that's after securing a degree. Most begin with an A level (or equivalent) in maths and/or further maths, then go on to study a degree and achieve at least a 2.1. Those who are already certain about pursuing an actuarial career might study actuarial science as an undergraduate, but 'numerate' degrees like maths, economics, stats, engineering, chemistry or physics are all liked by employers, too. Then you have to find a training scheme at an actuarial firm. (There's a directory of firms that offer work experience or graduate trainee positions at tinyurl.com/actdirectory.)

The profession also gets a fair number of career-changers who sign up later in life; the Institute of Actuaries recommends first undertaking one or two of its exams independently, to assess your skills, adding: 'your experience in your current career may be valuable to an actuarial firm, and you may wish to contact actuarial employers directly to discuss your potential.' Next up, to become an Associate or Fellow of the Institute and Faculty of Actuaries you have to pass its exams, as well as securing 'a satisfactory level of work-based skills.' This is the bit that normally takes three to six years. You study by distance learning (many employers offer support for study, like paid leave before exams). There are as many as 15 different exams to tackle, and they're tough: the pass rate is about 50–60 per cent for intermediate exams and about 30 per cent for finals.

'Degree courses are available which lead to exemptions from certain exams and therefore significantly shorten the time to qualification,' says part-qualified actuary John Fitzgerald (see below). 'However, these can be an expensive option (if done as a master's degree) and won't necessarily lead to a higher starting salary, since employers typically value practical experience over exam progress.'

Skills-wise, numeracy is key, and you'll also need to be adroit at communicating, so you can make complex issues sound simple. An understanding of general business issues is really important, too, and you'll need to keep up to date in developments in your profession, the financial markets and the wider economy.

WORKING LIFE: John Fitzgerald is a part-qualified actuary working for Mitchell Consulting in Manchester

'My job involves advising employers and trustees on a variety of pension-related matters. Simple queries can often be dealt with by a quick phone call or an email, but we discuss more complex questions as a team to ensure we provide the most appropriate advice. I then prepare a draft report which will usually be quite detailed as it needs to explain our methodology and any assumptions we've made, as well as comply with any relevant legislation and professional guidance.

I became interested in this career early on – my school maths teacher actually recommended becoming an actuary. I was fairly sure I wanted a job in finance after university but I also wanted to leave my options open, so I chose to study 'Mathematics with Finance' rather than a degree in 'Actuarial science'. For the past five years, I've been working full-time and taking professional exams with the Institute and Faculty of Actuaries at the same time.

It's a lot of effort to juggle work and study but I really enjoy the job; I've been surprised at how much responsibility you can have at an early stage. Within only a couple of years you'll know more than most, if not all, of your clients. And whilst naturally there are busy periods where you work harder than usual, the work/life balance is generally good and it's noticeably better than in some other professions, such as law.'

Related roles: Insurance

Insurance might not sound like the sexiest career around, but it's a big area. The sector employs some 320,000 people in the UK alone, according to the Association of British Insurers – the biggest insurance industry in Europe and the third-largest in the world. Some of the key roles include insurance broker – people who act as the go-between link between individuals or businesses who need cover and insurers – and underwriters. The latter work closely with actuaries to decide whether to offer insurance cover based on the risks involved and, if so, at what price and level; the aim is always to minimise the insurer's losses and maximise its profits.

Insurance brokers will normally either work on the retail side – nothing to do with shopping, but this involves arranging policies covering things like homes, travel, or business disruption for people or (usually small) companies. Commercial insurance brokers, meanwhile, arrange pricier policies for more complex things – airlines will insure against crashes, for example, so if one does take place, they're not liable to pay out compensation, and so on.

Most workers in the insurance industry specialise in a particular area, such as life insurance (which covers death and injuries or sickness), general insurance (car, household, pet, travel policies), commercial insurance (for firms) and reinsurance – when insurers take out policies with other insurers for big cover policies in order to spread their own level of risk.

Pay in the insurance world depends on the nature of the role and the size of the company: working for a major Lloyds of London commercial insurer, for example, will obviously be more lucrative than being a claims handler, and will require a commensurately higher skill set. Graduates on insurance training schemes usually start at around £25,000; qualified, experienced brokers will receive pay in the region of £40,000 to £90,000, plus bonuses, although some are on commission-based pay with a lower basic salary.

ADVERTISING

AVERAGE STARTING SALARY – £18,000–£25,000

ENTRY POSITION – Junior

TYPICAL WEEKLY HOURS – Variable

RECOMMENDED QUALIFICATIONS – Portfolio or relevant degree according to the area you wish to enter (creative, admin., etc.). Work experience

IF YOU LIKE THIS YOU MIGHT ALSO LIKE . . . author, graphic designer, PR

However much they jazz up the job titles as 'executive account manager' or 'copywriter-in-chief', every job in advertising is about the same thing: making people buy or believe the stuff the campaign is promoting. So if you're good at coming up with catchlines (the slogan in an ad) or enticing creative ideas, this could be the industry for you.

Most ads are made by advertising agencies, so if, say, a fast food chain wants to make a new campaign about the fact that its meals are really pretty darn good for you, it will pay an agency to brainstorm, make and get an ad out there on bus shelters/newspapers/TV channels/websites/milk bottles or anywhere else. In the average agency, there are lots of confusing-sounding roles, which are:

Account management – the go-between who has most of the client contact and conveys their wishes to all of the different departments in the agency.

Account planning – responsible for the research behind the campaign: polling, focus groups, etc.

Creative department – teams of art directors, copywriters, sometimes digital specialists and graphic designers and designers, who work on coming up with ideas for ads and making them.

Production – liaises between the creatives and the director, for TV or video ads, or the photographer, for print/online ads.

Project managers – work with all departments to make sure ads are made on time and deadlines are met.

UX – user-experience experts who work on digital ads.

Media – responsible for planning and buying the slots during which the ads will be shown.

Huge agencies have many people in all these departments; in boutique ones, a few people may cross over the roles.

The skills involved depend on what area you're targeting: account executives, for example, would simply need to be well organised with great communication skills; those targeting the creative jobs, such as an art director, would need lots of visual and creative skills, and perhaps a background in graphics or art, whilst a copywriter needs to be imaginative, good with words and able to come up with memorable slogans, jingles and text (aka copy) for printed ads.

Female graduates and career-changers might be wary about some advice from an ad agency boss, who says: 'The industry at large does not hire enough women – they are marginalised – and very few women find advertising to be a lasting career. It doesn't stretch or bend to accommodate personal life or family needs and sadly few women in the industry reach the highest roles.'

Traditionally, advertising didn't demand specific qualifications, but nowadays most new entrants do have degrees. 'Students still need to be educated to learn what a good idea is, what a bad one is, how to think, how to sell, what is appropriate, what is not and to learn the history of the business,' says Steve Dunn, whose working life is described below. 'So an advertising college or degree is the best place to start.'

Most universities offer related degrees, whilst D&AD, the trade body of advertising, offers courses and workshops. 'See their annuals,' Dunn adds. 'All the best work from around the world is printed in them and they are great reference books of what is "good/great" and who did that work. And read [ad industry magazine] *Campaign* once a month. It's always got the same news, but at least you'll become familiar with the names of agencies and who does what. *Creative Review* magazine also shows some of the best new work around the globe and covers advertising, illustration, design and film making.'

Pay-wise, most ad newbies start on £18,000–£25,000 a year and see promotions every few years. It usually takes about five to seven years to become a manager in advertising, whilst at the highest levels an executive creative director at a big agency earns between £250,000 and £350,000.

WORKING LIFE: Steve Dunn was executive creative director of ad giant Ogilvy & Mather before setting up his own agency, The Assembly Network, whose clients have included Cadbury, Budweiser and Coca-Cola

'I was at art college when a very confident man wearing a purple suit appeared and gave a talk saying "try to work in advertising in London, that's where it's at". I had no clue what advertising was and not much more clue about London, but I liked what I saw so I quit art college, sat in my bedroom for a year and tried to learn the arcane art of advertising, putting together my own portfolio of ideas and regularly setting off to the big smoke to be abused, criticised and mocked by the blue-blood of the London advertising world.

After one year of unemployment benefit and three hundred "sorry, this isn't good enoughs" later, I got hired by Tim Delaney, a renowned industry figure. Working with him, we won every award going. Fame, fortune and a Porsche came my way – as did failing personal relationships and ill health through stress and a bad diet as we worked days, nights and weekends to make the best ads.

When I started my own agency, I took all the bad bits I'd learnt and witnessed from advertising over the years and removed them – the red tape, the slowness, the lack of responsiveness, the complete lack of caring about clients, the way people would show up for the pitch and you'd never see them again, the lack of contact with creatives. My favourite of all the taglines

I've come up with is, "There is only one Harrods. There is only one sale" – it's still used years later.

I think now is a depressing time in advertising – most of the great ideas seldom see the light of day because of diminishing client bravery and budgets. But in what other job can you get paid for thinking of new and great and alternative ideas to help other companies and businesses thrive?

There are many facets of jobs and skills required for them, but to thrive in the creative side of advertising you need to have a huge capacity to learn – and to absorb films, social trends, gossip, media issues, news, art, design, photography, writing and music. Creative people create a depository of ideas in their head. And every now and then when briefs come up these get synthesised together and become a shiny new original idea. That's my favourite part of the job, solving complex and challenging business issues through creativity.

To anyone interested in advertising, I'd say the opportunity is there for the 10 per cent who really want it. At the end of the day it's about hard work. The best are not born the best – they're the ones who have worked harder than the good, and twice as hard as the average.

If you're doing it because you can't think of anything else to do, or you think it's all rock and roll and mad fun, or you think you're a creative genius, you'll fail. But for those that reach the highest positions in this industry, there are few jobs more stimulating and that will challenge every neuron in your brain the way advertising does.'

Dream Job: Interior designer

Kelly Hoppen, 55, is a celebrity interior designer whose client list includes David and Victoria Beckham, as well as luxury homes and hotels across the globe. She was also an investor on the BBC's Dragons' Den.

'I started small, getting jobs by word of mouth, and when I began to realise how popular my design work was becoming I made it an official company – Kelly Hoppen Interiors – by hiring in specialists and accountants. From there, the company grew into an international success, with my team and I working on projects all around the world, and I started creating different ranges of products in the 'Kelly Hoppen Style' such as wallpapers, paints and shutters.

I usually start my day with a good workout at home – it helps to clear my head. During a healthy breakfast I check emails to get the nitty gritty out of the way, then head into the design studio around 9.30am for a catch-up with my PA all about the day's plan – meetings, interviews, and I like to spend at least 2 to 3 hours a day with my design team in the studio working on projects; we have around 50 projects worldwide all at once.

Around 1 o'clock I always insist that my team take an hour's lunch break, and then my day can go one of two ways – back-to-back meetings with clients, my PR team, potential clients and filming, or I may have to visit a project's site and ensure everything is running smoothly. I usually keep going till around 6pm, and often have events or dinners to attend in the evenings.

Nowadays, there are a lot of successful interior designers out there which means you do have to work that little bit harder, but it is all about drive and that fight to the top. I definitely recommend it as career – provided you are passionate, creative and talented in this field.

The best way to start is to approach a designer that inspires you for work experience and become a sponge; soak up everything you hear, observe and learn during that time. First-hand experience is key. Also believe in yourself, otherwise how do you expect anyone else to believe in you? Find a mentor that you can go to for advice on all subjects; someone that has been there and done it all before, so you can avoid making the same mistakes creating a shortcut for yourself.'

ARCHITECT

AVERAGE STARTING SALARY – £17,000

ENTRY POSITION – Trainee

TYPICAL WEEKLY HOURS – 35–40 hours

RECOMMENDED QUALIFICATIONS – Degree in architecture. A year of experience, followed by a postgraduate degree, another year of experience then an exam

IF YOU LIKE THIS YOU MIGHT ALSO LIKE ... engineer, graphic designer, surveyor

If Lego or Meccano was your favourite childhood toy, then a job that involves designing and constructing buildings might be your ideal.

Architects help home-owners, councils, developers, builders and others to design and build new or enlarged/adapted buildings, as well as advising on faltering and listed historic ones. To do so, they have to consider the myriad restrictions, planning and building laws, environmental and energy efficiency issues that govern construction – as well as the basic physics of structure and what is actually possible. As well as planning the construction work, they also manage the building process, are in charge of budgets and liaise with officials about planning issues.

Nowadays few architects make drawings in the traditional sense – they use computer-aided design software to come up with designs based on existing measurements, projections, information from clients, engineers and specialists. The top skills, according to one newbie architect, are: 'artistic ability, excellent communication skills, unshakable self-belief, a thick skin (the profession is viciously competitive), an analytical approach, meticulous attention to detail and a comfortable relationship with mathematics.'

Some architects specialise – such as working with listed buildings, sports stadia, schools, private homes, and so on; others work in general practice. But to get there, you'll first have to tackle one of the longest training periods of any profession – five years of study at university on a course validated by the Royal Institute of British Architects (RIBA). The first stage is a three-year undergraduate degree, which provides students with a graduate qualification even if they do not continue with architecture as a profession.

Next up is the hugely competitive task of securing practical work – usually 12 months' work in an architecture practice, under supervision, although some choose to work for more than a year to earn money for the next stage – which is two more years of university study. Then it's on to stage 2 practical experience – a minimum of one year of further supervised and recorded professional experience, followed by the final qualifying exam – with a written part and oral part – testing professional practice and management. Only after all that can you register with the Architects Registration Board (the title 'architect' is protected by law, so that the public know that they are dealing with a properly qualified architect), and become eligible to become a Chartered Member of RIBA.

Why does it take so long? RIBA says: 'The reason why the path to becoming an architect is so long is that architecture is a wide-ranging discipline based on a large body of design, technical and professional knowledge, in which students develop a high level of skill. This prepares students to make sound professional judgements in difficult, often pressurised situations.'

Pay-wise, first-year trainees can expect to earn between £18,000 and £22,000, depending on the size and location of the practice; part-two graduates can expect £28,000 to £32,000, newly-registered architects can expect £31,000 to £34,000. After that, salaries can rise fairly swiftly with experience, to around £43,000 after five years' work, then beyond.

Securing architecture work experience: RIBA's top tips

Write to architects in your local area. Many architects will take school or college students for one or two weeks' work experience to help in career and university course decisions.

If you look in the RIBA Directory of Practices you will find names and addresses of practices, plus a short description of the kind of work they do (www.architecture.com/useanarchitect). There is no centralised list held by the RIBA of architects who may be able to offer work experience, so you need to approach practices directly. Your RIBA regional office may be able to advise you. When you approach an architectural practice, try to make your letter stand out – you could include a drawing or photograph which shows your interest in architecture. Remember that architects are very busy so it is worth giving them plenty of notice and following up a letter with a phone call. Ask your careers teacher or advisor to help you prepare a letter.

WORKING LIFE: Soaad Islam is an architect at Populous, the firm that created London's 2012 Olympic Stadium, the 2014 Fisht Olympic Stadium in Sochi and Wembley Stadium, amongst others.

'I specialise in stadiums, arenas and other sporting facilities, as well as "mixed-use complexes" and temporary event overlays. I'm currently working as the on-site architect abroad on the overlay for the Gymnastics and International Broadcast Centre for the 2015 European Games in Baku, Azerbaijan. When I'm not on site, most of my days are spent attending meetings, presenting designs, coordinating design strategy with various consultants and the construction team, choosing products, creating and amending drawings, schedules and reports, as well as overseeing the drawing support team, and making sure all documents are where they need to be. It's a very busy job – even when you're not at work, you're constantly aware of potential details and ideas, plus with works going on site seven days a week, you are constantly on hand to react to any issues.

Before I started in architecture, I hadn't realised how much of the job was working out costs and programming, dealing with real budgets and with stakeholders concerns. The worst part is definitely endless meetings – with consultants talking on and on, in order to justify their roles. But I've got to where I am now by doing every task you can get your hands on in a company – within every department. My top advice is to consider what the overall goal is in every task undertaken, and take full responsibility for every task, no matter how menial.'

AUTHOR

AVERAGE STARTING SALARY – £6,000–£8,000 as an advance for a novel
ENTRY POSITION – Author
TYPICAL WEEKLY HOURS – Variable
RECOMMENDED QUALIFICATIONS – An agent and experience/creative writing course
IF YOU LIKE THIS YOU MIGHT ALSO LIKE . . . advertising, journalist, PR

J.K. Rowling famously had her first Harry Potter manuscript rejected by a whopping 12 publishers before it was accepted by Bloomsbury – and even then only at the insistence of the chairman's eight-year-old daughter. Judy Blume, Gertrude Stein and D.H. Lawrence all received several 'no, thanks' letters from publishers before any said yes. But if becoming a published writer isn't easy, making a living out of it is even tougher.

There are always a few stand-out success stories – YouTube vlogger Zoe 'Zoella' Sugg whose first book, which she later admitted to having 'help' writing, enjoyed the highest-selling first-week book sales in history, or the accountant awarded an advance so big she could quit her job that day and focus on writing – but they're unusual. Most authors squeeze their writing into spare time alongside their full-time job and/

or family, whilst those who can earn enough to spend all their time tapping away at a laptop will often juggle their fiction or non-fiction book/poem/scriptwriting alongside commercial work, journalism, author workshops, readings, etc.

The majority of writers are also self-employed, so incomes can be unreliable and on top of working away quietly at your work, time will be spent researching, interviewing, perhaps applying for prizes and grants, talking to publishers, agents and editors, and staying on top of admin like contracts, invoices and tax returns.

You'll need to be seriously self-motivated: most authors don't have a boss sitting nearby telling them what to do, whilst deadlines from publishers might be many months or even a year away. You'll need a healthy dose of luck, too: some books simply meet the right agent/publisher, come out at the right time and hit a zeitgeist; others don't. You'll also need to be dedicated – to keep tapping away at the keyboard after those rejection letters mount or all your friends take you aside to quietly ask, 'shouldn't you think about getting a proper job now?', or to work into the early hours then still make it to your day job.

Some would-be authors attend creative writing schools – those in Bath Spa, East Anglia and Oxford are particularly popular and have been attended by a host of successful writers. They can be a good idea for anyone who decides to be an author early, or career-changers, as they provide advice on writing but also practical advice on contacts and the publishing industry – plus graduates leave with a group of fellow wannabe authors who can read your work critically and support you through the tough times.

Now, how to get published. It's a good idea to start small: if you're a poet, try getting a few poems published in magazines or online, building up a portfolio before you approach a publisher. If you're a fiction writer, do the same with short stories, and enter contests (*The Writers' & Artists' Yearbook* lists many, and there are hundreds listed online, too); if you're a scriptwriter, try some five-minute films or radio sketches. Do all the networking you can – at literary events and publisher parties, or try to contact editors and agents and get your work around. Learn to accept rejection and take on board any criticism.

The money side of things is tricky. Latest statistics show that the number of authors able to make a living from their writing has plunged dramatically over the last decade, and the average professional author is now usually making around just £11,000. That's a fall of 29 per cent since 2005, according to the Authors' Licensing and Collecting Society. Their study also showed that just 11.5 per cent of professional authors – those who dedicate the majority of their time to writing – earned their incomes solely from writing. Back in 2005, that figure was 40 per cent. Which is why this career is partly about the love of writing – to the extent that you might have to do something else, on the side, to pay the bills.

The way most wannabe authors boost their chances of publication is to nab an agent (see previous chapter) to negotiate on their behalf. Many big publishers refuse to read work that isn't 'represented', but in order to grab an agent's attention, you'll need to do some research. Find out which agents specialise in the kind of work that you write (a rapid way to do so is to read the 'thank you'/dedication pages of books in your genre – inevitably authors thank their agents, and if they don't, perhaps they weren't too helpful!). Bigger agencies might have more muscle in a range of fields, and even countries, whilst smaller or one-man/woman agencies could devote more time to your work. Again, *The Writers' & Artists' Yearbook* lists all of the UK's agents.

WORKING LIFE: Tracy Chevalier, 52, is the bestselling author of *Girl With a Pearl Earring* and six other novels including *Falling Angels*, *Remarkable Creatures* and *The Last Runaway*.

'I get up about 7am, get my son up, make coffee and have breakfast. An hour later, I've turned on my computer and start to answer as many of the emails that are lurking in my inbox as I can stand. At about 8.30am I have a sneaky peek at Twitter and Facebook – and usually get sucked in for half an hour. Then at 9am I start "real" work: either writing, or editing, or researching. If I'm writing, I'll re-read what I wrote the day before as that kind of jump-starts me into the current day of writing. I write longhand, or mark up printed manuscripts, and often I take this to the kitchen so I stay away from the computer and internet. I'll have lunch and a walk, then from 1.30 to 4.30pm there is more writing, broken up by phone, Twitter, and a lot of staring out of the window. Then my son comes home and kicks me off the computer so he can use it. By then I'm tired of writing, so I read for research or do admin or reread what I wrote earlier. I stop working at 6pm, but I'm never done, because I'm still thinking about the book while I cook, watch TV, go out, drive, or am in the bath – everywhere.

I try not to write during the evenings or weekends – it's important to keep boundaries. And I don't bring my phone or iPad into the bedroom either; only books.

You have to be good at being alone to be an author – you have to like it, want it. I like nothing better than to sit in the British Library with a book about 19th-century apple grafting or pioneer journals and take notes all day; it's bliss. I also love rewriting. It's a lot easier fixing something that exists than facing the blank page to fill up. It's a great feeling when I work out how to make a piece of writing better. Writing is really about editing

– questioning every word, asking why it's there and how it could be written differently.

But quite a lot of the process is boring! I hate writing descriptions of people and places. Also the bits where you have to get characters from A to B – I cut those right back so the reader doesn't get bored.

Before I became a full-time author, I was an editor for a reference book publisher and wrote short stories on the side. I decided to become a freelance editor to give me time to do an MA in creative writing at the University of East Anglia. Once I wrote *Girl with a Pearl Earring* I dropped the editing and became a full-time writer. You don't really become a writer for the money – but if you do publish a book, be sure you sign up for the Authors' Licensing and Collecting Society (ALCS) and also for Public Lending Right (PLR), as these will supplement your income. Apart from that – anyone who wants to write should read everything. Read genre fiction, read classics, read non-fiction, read poetry. The key is to read a lot, and to WANT to read a lot. If you don't have a book on the go all of the time, then you probably shouldn't be a writer.'

BANKER

AVERAGE STARTING SALARY – £24,000–£45,000

ENTRY POSITION – Trainee analyst

TYPICAL WEEKLY HOURS – 45 hours

RECOMMENDED QUALIFICATIONS – 2:1 in relevant subject (economics, accountancy, maths, business). An MBA is helpful but not essential

IF YOU LIKE THIS YOU MIGHT ALSO LIKE . . . accountant, actuary, hedge fund careers

Conjure up thoughts of a career in banking and you're probably thinking of a sharp-suited exec swigging champagne and rolling around in cash. That, however, is investment banking, which is only one side of the vast banking industry. The largest employers in the UK's financial services sector are banks and building societies, and many of their staff work in local branches earning only a fraction of that cash, helping people and businesses to manage their money and savings and access loans.

The jobs:

- *Retail bankers*: They work in high-street banks and building societies or online banks, keeping track of money movements through the institution, approving loans, mortgages and overdrafts, setting up saving accounts, dealing with customers, creating and launching new banking products and hitting sales targets. Those working in private banking will do the same but with fewer, usually very wealthy, customers. Starting salaries are about £25,000, rising to £60,000 with about a decade's experience.
- *Investment bankers*:

  Analysts – They run the numbers, make spreadsheets and models (mathematical predictions) to help with deal-making, stock market listings (known as initial public offerings), helping firms to raise cash and advice on buying and selling shares. For more details, see below and check out the tongue-in-cheek YouTube video 'A Day in the Life of An Analyst'.

  Traders – They buy and sell financial products ranging from shares and bonds to more complicated assets, seeking to make the highest possible profit. Most specialise in a particular product and execute trades either electronically or on the phone; they're constantly analysing and predicting the market to forecast future price movements. Salaries tend to start at about £40,000 and can rise as high as £150,000 with a few years' experience – with bonuses that can be as much as 200 per cent of the salary. Hours are often better in trading – usually 7am to 6pm, or 6.30am to 5pm for foreign exchange traders.
- *Financial planners and independent financial advisors*: They help people (and firms) to secure mortgages or finance, invest their cash

and plan their financial futures. They research and explain all the latest financial products and charge clients for their advice. Pay usually starts at £25,000 and rises with experience, and success, to around £60,000; a minority of top advisors may receive more than £100,000.

- *Pensions and investment industry*: Fund and asset managers try to make sums of money grow by investing them in particular stocks or funds. For more details on investment roles, see 'Hedge fund careers'.

Getting a job at a retail or investment bank isn't easy – thousands of graduates apply for every job, and the few schemes open to non-grads or apprentices in banks can be even more over-subscribed. 'Most people simply go through the campus recruiting process,' says one City suit. 'Though a not-so-small percentage have an in [a contact connected in some way to the firm, such as a client or relative]. Despite that, very few of my colleagues seem underqualified. Even with a contact, you've got to be good.'

In investment banking, most graduates work their way up, joining as an analyst, then spending about three years at that level before being promoted to an associate – although a lot of future bank bosses actually enter at this latter stage, after getting an MBA at a business school. Three years after that, the best are promoted to being a vice president, then comes executive director and managing director. Most bankers face two phases of career progression: a rapid rise through the ranks, then having to wait to fit the age and image to reach the top. 'Promotions are not automatic,' the City slicker adds. 'You need to be a top performer. If not, you will not get promoted on time, which is a strong sign that you need to be brushing up your CV . . .'

At a junior level, the top skills are an ability to work long and hard, good numeracy, coherent language and grammar, and adroitness at Excel and PowerPoint – although banks do train up their graduates, especially in the required software skills. Starting out, most graduate interns are set one of two tasks: building financial models in Excel (usually to show expected returns to the client in a variety of scenarios) and putting together PowerPoint presentations (based largely around the models).

With experience, more of the job will involve actually presenting to clients and deal-making. 'Most of the skills in investment banking are learned on the job, but understanding the business beforehand and showing that in interviews would give a candidate a serious leg-up,' says one City recruiter. 'It is amazing how few candidates can answer the simple question, 'What does an investment banker do?' Read the *Financial Times* and *The Wall Street Journal*, and watch the markets and big deals. Studying, say, macroeconomics, corporate finance or accounting at university will make it a much easier task than getting a BA in English.' Professional qualifications, such as the Chartered Financial Analyst programme, boost employability, too, though some employers offer this to bankers as on-the-job training. Quantitative studies (in maths, statistics, econometrics) are also in demand.

First-year analysts at an investment bank can expect to earn about £50,000 or £60,000 a year, with perhaps a £10,000 to £30,000 bonus. In the second year, that can be bumped up to £70,000 to £80,000, with a £30,000 to £40,000 bonus; a VP could earn a £120,000 basic salary plus bonus – and so it keeps rising. Long-term potential varies greatly from firm to firm. At a bulge bracket, managing directors might receive a salary of £300,000 and in all but the worst years (for them personally or for the firm), they make close to £1 million with bonuses. For a handful of 'superstar' bankers, with great clients or enormous deal-making prowess, pay is almost limitless – some top bankers have pocketed £20 million or more for a year's work. London-based headhunters whisper that Goldman Sachs, JP Morgan, Morgan Stanley and Credit Suisse offer the highest salaries to their junior bankers.

THE LOWDOWN: Timothy Westbrook* is a graduate intern working at an international investment bank

'Hours-wise, I'm pretty lucky, as I was put in the leveraged finance department. The hours are tied to the markets' opening and close, which means I mostly avoid the 3am finishes that some of the people I joined with who are in other parts of the bank have to endure. My average day goes something like this:

7am: arrive at office for morning meetings.

8–9am: run through remaining emails, finish off anything needed for the morning (often responding to comments from the previous day's work), briefly catch up on news in the *Wall Street Journal/Financial Times*.

9am–12pm: try to cut through as much of my to-do list as possible before more work is piled on. Work on models, presentations, or various deal execution tasks (legal documents, internal memos, etc.). Might have an internal

---

* *name changed for anonymity*

meeting to discuss future presentations, client calls or meetings to pitch business, or deal-execution tasks – things like due diligence calls.

12pm: go out to get lunch and bring it back to eat at my desk.

12.30–6pm: continue my tasks from before lunch.

6–7pm: go to the gym in the office.

7pm: order dinner (provided for free by firm, it's delivered and I eat it at my desk)

7pm–12am: continue punching through my to-do list; by now it will entirely be making models or presentations, unless we're in live-deal mode, to accomplish anything that must be done that day.

12am: take firm-provided taxi home.

Work is pretty much 24/7, weekends included. With the exception of reasonable sleeping hours (12–6), you run the risk of seriously annoying someone important if you do not respond to emails within an hour of receiving them: it's expected to be instantaneous, and, frankly, an hour would not be tolerated as a regular occurrence – you'd be fired. The system does work both ways, though: senior people tend to respond very quickly as well and make sure they are, under normal circumstances, accessible at all hours.

I've made close friends amongst my fellow grads – even though I went to a top private school and university, my colleagues are the most impressive people I've ever met; the sharpest, hardest working, most driven ... But whilst some of the bosses are supportive and great teachers, others can be completely adversarial and create a miserable work environment. Occasionally, you might face an "are you a complete moron?" type of question, but the thick-skinned environment means that virtually everyone immediately brushes off that type of thing. The bigger problem is the degree of politics at the big firms – you never know what people are saying behind your back.

The culture is also male-dominated. It's aggressive, outwardly competitive – a day on a trading desk could, at least at some firms, be confused for a night at an American college's fraternity house. By contrast, in classic investment banking and analyst roles, the work environment is much quieter, more relaxed, and refined. My firm makes a concerted effort to hire and support women, and there are loads of initiatives for retaining and promoting female talent, but the most successful women are those with the thickest skins.

The best parts of the job are pitching for new business and doing a deal. You have to wait a year or two before managers will let you get involved in a pitch, but I've really enjoyed learning what works well with clients and what doesn't – and winning that first piece of business is a great feeling. Deal execution is also fun – even if you're not the one doing the speeches, watching a presentation you worked on turn into a live process and eventually be closed is exciting. But anything involving databasing or record-keeping is painfully boring. And when you start, most of your time is spent doing the computerised equivalent of filing. It is not enjoyable.

Everyone swallows that for the perks, though – free dinner every night, free cabs home from the office, a free mobile, nice pension. But the top perk is pay. You forgive a lot of s*** at the office for that.'

WORKING LIFE: Alain Nahmany is the lead financial controller at one of the largest private banks in Europe

'Private banks are like normal banks, but exclusively for rich people. We help our clients by managing their assets, providing investment services, research and strategy, and finding tax-efficient vehicles to do so, while providing a safe and sound platform to custody their money.

I usually arrive at the office between 7:30 and 7:45am and my day is usually spent in meetings with different members of the team, checking on the progress of projects, meeting clients (usually to present the finance side of our business and tell them how safe we are) and presenting our financial performance to senior management. It's about a 12-hour day; I leave the office around 7pm, but I receive my work emails on my smartphone and tablet when I'm home. I tend to respond to emails once my kids are in bed.

I got into the banking world after qualifying as an accountant in London. I worked for a large US broker, then moved to Geneva in 2003 when my firm acquired a Swiss private bank. I've been there ever since.

For any big job in banking, product knowledge is essential – our customers are usually sophisticated and deal with a huge range of financial products. A deep understanding of how these instruments work and the risks attached to them is essential. On a personal level, you also need to be quick-thinking and have stamina and an ability to deal with pressure.

People think of banking and then associate it with the extravagant, ostentatious behaviour of *The Wolf of Wall Street* – well, that's not been my experience. My job is all about controlling risk, being safe and delivering performance. And my employer is a 220-year-old institution, deep rooted in Calvinism, so rather than being a 'fun' job, any satisfaction derives from performance and keeping your clients happy and safe.

The worst part of the job is explaining to your client why his or her investments have not performed well – plus, since the 2008 financial crisis and the excess that preceded it, the image of the banking profession has been seriously tarnished and that can be tough.'

ODD JOB: Pet food taster, worldwide

Well, someone's gotta do it. Most people employed to taste-test cat and dog food (to make sure the flavours are delicious) say they spit out the food afterwards . . . and keep some chocolate on hand to take away the taste.

BEAUTICIAN

AVERAGE STARTING SALARY – £50 an hour

ENTRY POSITION – Make-up artist

TYPICAL WEEKLY HOURS – Variable (by the hour)

RECOMMENDED QUALIFICATIONS – Relevant qualification (media make-up or equivalent)

IF YOU LIKE THIS YOU MIGHT ALSO LIKE . . . hairdresser, optician, nurse

Beauty is booming: already the industry employs more than one million people and is worth £17 billion, but it's forecast to grow 16 per cent in the next year. When times are tough, a facial or makeover is regarded as a cheap-ish pick-me-up; when times are booming, they're an essential part of monthly grooming.

Make-up artistry is a particularly popular area. You might work with brides before their weddings, Hollywood stars before they go on set, or models and performers, and you could be making them look their best, or worst: it's not all glamour – you may be creating monsters with special-effects make-up.

Make-up artists generally work alone when on small-budget ad campaigns or doing wedding/special events make-up, whilst at major events such as the Oscars, or behind the scenes on the BBC's *Strictly Come Dancing* or big fashion shows, there'll be teams working on make-up from assistants through to senior make-up artists. Big stars often have their own beauty team working just for them, too.

The job is basically about keeping the client happy, but that can be tricky: an A-lister being made up for a magazine shoot, for example, might have different demands from the editor of that magazine. Most make-up artists are freelance; the few employed positions on offer are generally working for cosmetic companies or on beauty counters in shops, or for a college as a tutor.

For self-employed artists, though, alongside the actual cosmetic work there's lots of organisation, admin and travel planning to secure enough work and get to clients. It's usually not just the on-the-day work, either: a bride, for example, will have a trial session ahead of her big day, whilst ahead of film or other make-up sessions, artists will have to liaise with others (director, lighting experts, etc.) about their design ideas, sketch out looks, perhaps make sample prosthetics, have a sterile, well-maintained make-up kit and update their portfolio. Running a business also has its own demands – such as marketing, networking and social networking/online promotion work.

There are plenty of training courses for the beauty industry, but make sure any you investigate are reputable. Well-regarded tutors will be able to provide contacts for work experience and this is another career in which networking is the key to smashing through. Many make-up artists and beauty therapists start out via 'testing' – hooking up with new models, photographers and stylists on unpaid photo shoots to create or boost your portfolio, or offering free treatments to build up a client list. You'll also need to be fairly confident – you're going to be entering people's personal space and touching their face or body so you need to build up some rapport with them.

Most make-up artists work pretty long, and irregular, hours – perhaps a manically busy fortnight then nothing on for the next week. It can be helpful to be trained in hair and prosthetics as well as make-up to boost your chances of securing work. That's true, too, of beauty therapists: the more strings to your bow, the more chances of work. As Britons demand treatments before and after their working day, you might find your daily working hours stretching from early morning to late evening, too.

Most beauty work is freelance, so the pay depends on how much work you manage to secure. Becoming a famous-name make-up artist or therapist means you can charge much higher rates, as well as launching lucrative spin-off cosmetic or beauty ranges. The Producers Alliance for Cinema and Television (PACT) and the Broadcasting Entertainment Cinematograph and Theatre Union (BECTU) set out minimum pay on TV and film sets. With experience, some artists charge £250 a day, while the top names make several thousand for a day's work, but remember most won't have work every single day.

WORKING LIFE: Geraldine Shaker works as a make-up artist in New York, London and Los Angeles, with clients including Al Gore, Drew Barrymore, Raquel Welch and Bruce Willis

'As a freelance make-up artist, my day is tied to the clients' requirements – sometimes I'm up at 4am for a 6am call time and sometimes I won't be needed on set until 10am or later. Usually, if I'm shooting an ad campaign,

I'm typically on location from sunrise to sunset; fashion shoots start later but go on until late in the night, relying heavily on studio lighting, whilst a red carpet event can literally only take a few hours of work but the pressure is intense because the actress is usually quite anxious.

Anyone can learn basic make-up application and hair styling, but you have to have an eye for colour and form, be interested in trends, work hard and have amazing people skills if you're going to compete and succeed. I started out by training as a hairdresser at Vidal Sassoon in London, and worked in that role for seven years. Then I started assisting on ads, before deciding to leave to study make-up at the London College of Fashion; from there I launched my career as a freelance artist.

My favourite part of the work is travelling and meeting new people. I've also lived and worked in many cities around the world. I control my own schedule, I make great money and I don't work every day.

On the flipside, dealing with difficult clients can be tough. Sometimes you have more than one client to please – say, on an editorial shoot – with opposing ideas on how the model should look. You become a mediator and people pleaser, and that's really hard to navigate. As a hairdresser, you quite often work as part of a team, but as a make-up artist you tend to be solo.

Being a freelance artist means it's feast or famine, and that can be difficult to deal with, too. Even when you're not on set, your phone can and will ring at any time – it's up to you to establish the boundaries of when you'll accept work. I leave my phone in the living room when I go to bed.'

CHEF

AVERAGE STARTING SALARY – £13,000–£16,000

ENTRY POSITION – Trainee

TYPICAL WEEKLY HOURS – 30–40 hours

RECOMMENDED QUALIFICATIONS – Apprenticeship or qualification in hospitality or catering

IF YOU LIKE THIS YOU MIGHT ALSO LIKE . . . hospitality, military, teacher

'There's more than one way to peel an onion.' That's the view of one chef when I asked about how best to start on the road to becoming a chef. And he's right – just look at Gordon, Nigella or Jamie. Whilst Ramsay and Oliver started out on the lowest rung of busy kitchens (Jamie in his parents' pub), Lawson began her career as a journalist, becoming a newspaper restaurant critic before having the idea of writing a cook book after watching a dinner party host dissolve into tears because of an unset crème caramel . . .

The important thing to remember, though, is that whilst these and other TV chefs are the handful of first-name stars of our kitchen cook-books, there are a huge number of kitchen roles: from restaurant food preparation work to sous chefs (assistants), pastry chefs and head chefs; then there's cooking work on cruise ships or as a private chef for the super-rich, catering for big functions, for children at schools, staff at offices, the NHS, Armed Forces and many more – everyone has to eat.

Most chefs' responsibilities include menu planning, recruiting, training and timetabling staff, ordering food and equipment, and making sure the kitchen is kept well prepped, clean and hygienic, as well as cooking and presenting meals. In big restaurants or establish-ments, you'll likely be part of a large team; in smaller ones, there could be just a handful of people, or you might be working solo.

There are a few qualifications that would-be chefs can work towards (see below), but the kitchen is still pretty hierarchical and newbies (unless they've picked up a seriously impressive amount of work place-ments, weekend work and other experience) still tend to start as a kitchen assistant or trainee – or 'commis' – chef, learning skills in one part of the kitchen, or as an apprentice.

There are two types of catering and professional chefs' apprentice-ships: intermediate level, where you train in roles like school cook, kitchen assistant and commis chef in a local restaurant; and advanced level apprenticeships, where you train in jobs like sous chef in a fine dining restaurant, hotel or gastro pub; or a pastry chef. You learn prac-tical skills on the job, and many top chefs in some of the UK's best restaurants started out as apprentices.

The next promotion is usually to a station chef (or section chef or chef de partie), running one part of the kitchen, say food prep or desserts or meat, for example. With experience, the role of sous chef, basically deputising for the head chef, is next: in big restaurants or well-staffed establishments this might involve more supervision than cooking. The head chef (or chef de cuisine) position is the top of the kitchen, making menus and organising supplies and budgets as well as cooking.

You've got to seriously love cooking and being in a kitchen to get involved in this career, because the hours are long; shifts are usually the order of the day, often including weekends and bank holidays, and can span 24 hours a day, especially in hotels. The profession is famously masculine, but one (woman) sporting a chef's hat says: 'There's an equal ratio of men to women in the kitchens I've worked in, and I've never experienced any reason for it not to be a fine environment for a woman to work in. You've got to be thick-skinned and ready to be shouted and sworn at but I don't think whether you'll put up with that depends on your sex.'

Pay-wise, if you start out as an apprentice you could be earning as little as £2.70 an hour. But the pay jumps with experience (and pastry chefs tend to earn a little more, as the skills are more niche) and each promotion will bring you up into a higher bracket. Most junior positions pay no more than £15,000 per year, but a head chef in a top hotel or restaurant would expect to be on around £50,000, and the few 'big names' in cooking can be taking home serious multiples of that.

Qualification-wise, there are lots of part-time and full-time courses run by colleges, some offering certificates in hospitality and catering principles or professional patisserie and confectionery; others with diplomas in professional cookery. But apprenticeships remain the common route into this career: 'In this industry you can only get ahead by practice,' says one insider.

As well as kitchen working experience, he recommends: 'using

YouTube to watch how specific techniques are done and try them at home – there's only so much reading you can do about it, this job is all about being practical, so do some experimenting. And food is such a massive industry – go and soak it up. Eat at pop-up markets and try new exciting foods – Twitter and Instagram are great for finding out about one-off or free foodie events. You don't have to go to the most expensive restaurants in the country to eat great food (especially on an apprentice's wage), and remember, if you take friends you can order lots of different dishes and try a bit of everything. Food blogs are a really great way to spot emerging food trends and read about new restaurants. Social media is also a great way to talk to and follow those you admire – most chefs are on Twitter these days and tweet pictures through service, making the whole industry more accessible.'

WORKING LIFE: celebrity chef and restaurant owner Antonio Carluccio

'I didn't go to catering school, I just learnt through cooking and cooking some more – I was helping my mother in the kitchen, then when I was alone as a student in Vienna, I wanted to have the food that my mother used to prepare, so I taught myself.

I never imagined that I would become a professional cook: my first job was as a wine merchant, importing Italian wines to London, then I was offered the chance to become manager of [Terence Conran's] Neal Street Restaurant in Covent Garden. After a couple of years I bought it, turned it into an Italian restaurant, focusing on mushrooms and truffles, and then publicity started to accumulate. I participated in a 'best cook' competition in the *Sunday Times*, got through to the final and the press had some sympathy for me, being Italian, loud, loving mushrooms and all of that, so I had quite a lot of attention.

Soon after, a publisher got in touch and asked me to write my first book, then a few years later the next-door shop to my restaurant became free, and I opened it as a deli importing very good food from Italy – that was the origins of Carluccio's. I found some investors and together we decided to do Carluccio's cafés, a delicatessen brand. Today there are 100. My advice is, everyone should stick to what he or she does best. I've focused on food and publicity and brand, and I delegate everything else to other experts, giving them responsibility and shares – so they are all very interested in Carluccio's succeeding – whilst I am free to do exactly what I wanted to do: to teach the staff, create recipes and the brand.

My other advice to someone who wants to start a restaurant is to remember the importance of quality. You have to have done good things for the press and customers to recognise you as good, and not just whimsical – pursue perfection, and don't do anything that could damage that image of quality. That's why I've always refused to do publicity for supermarkets. Be selective and build up a career based on that. And be a specialist – I was adamant about specialising in real Italian food, not a mock-up, or tempted to use cheap ingredients. Today, TV chefs have recognition and some of them become rich as well, so everybody believes "work in food" and you will be rich. No, no, no!

You have to start to cook well, you have to be passionate about it, then slowly, slowly, if you do those things, somebody will recognise that. You have to want it. It's a very heavy job, people think it's easy, but you have to work hard and long hours, produce very good food, all the time, and be wary of ever risking your reputation.

Never be arrogant – I see many people starting up saying 'I am the best, I can do everything.' No. If everybody else is saying that you're good, that's fine, but don't look for praise. That's what I do, which is very unusual in Italians, I must say!'

THE LOWDOWN: Chloe Ride is an apprentice on the River Cottage Café scheme, currently working as commis chef at a hotel restaurant in Bristol. She writes a food blog, The City Girl's Kitchen.

'Kitchen life is very busy. There's a lot of shouting, mostly because it can be quite noisy – there are pockets of calm in the pastry kitchen. It's a very high-pressure environment in the mornings and evenings, because we always want to make sure the customers have great food. We work shifts, and most chefs work very long hours. I think tiredness is a massive factor in why chefs seem so angry all the time! But although it's very fast paced we really look after each other – I was nervous of Gordon Ramsay types when I started, but everyone on the team was really keen to make me feel at home – they all started out once, and know what it's like.

My shift starts at 7am, so I normally wake up at around 5.30am. Once I'm in my chef whites I have a handover from the previous chef, then get busy prepping the hotel buffet and cooked breakfasts. Once that's done and cleared away, we prep for any private functions – after-noon tea, a celebratory meal or a wedding, for up to about 350 people if it's in one of our conference rooms. I get a thirty-minute lunch break in the staff canteen then prepare the lunch service station. In the afternoon, I head to the pastry kitchen to assist our head pastry chef with decorating cakes for afternoon tea – scones, carrot cakes, lemon cakes and gluten-free cakes. At about 5.30pm I head home, picking up something tasty to cook on the way. By 9pm I'm asleep!

That's one kind of day, but my shifts can also be 3pm to 11pm and 11pm to 7am. We also don't have set days off, and we work through all holidays as the hotel never shuts. The team is really sociable, though, so more likely than not, if you're working a late shift on a weekend, you'll all go out together after.

I got into the job after studying for a degree in English language in 2009 at Edinburgh University. Moving out and becoming independent, I soon fell in love with cooking, having plenty of students around me to feed. I used my long summers to gain experience in the industry, working as an editorial assistant intern at *delicious.* magazine, moving to Paris one summer to work as a baker in a wedding cake shop and eventually became a kitchen assistant and baker for a café in Edinburgh called Brew Lab. I knew I'd need some sort of formal training, but I just couldn't afford to put myself through another expensive course after university, so I entered myself into the River Cottage Rising Star competition and ended up getting onto their apprenticeship scheme and being placed at the Royal Marriott in Bristol. I also visit River Cottage HQ for two days a month for intense training as well as being at my placement.

I love my job but I would tell would-be chefs that the industry is not easy! You need to be prepared to work long hours, cut and burn yourself a few times, and get shouted at. You miss out on a lot of Friday and Saturday nights with your friends, and you're usually working when everyone else is partying. But if you've got that passion, you'll love it.

Working under pressure is hard but rewarding, and once you get in the zone it's great.'

Dream Job: Chocolate-maker

Amelia Rope, 44, is the founder of Amelia Rope Chocolate

'I became a chocolate-maker by accident – I am not a qualified chocolatier or patisserie chef. My past jobs were PA, massage therapist and doctor's practice manager. Then I went on a five-day course at [chocolate-school] Valhrona – which opened my mind to the incredible scope that chocolate has – and started off making my own truffles and crystallised rose petals, mint leaves, violas and pansies which I then dipped in hand-tempered chocolate and decorated with gold leaf.

Nowadays, I'm usually up at 6am. First thing is checking on emails: enquiries, overnight orders, etc., plus check my bank balance to look at the ever-dreaded cash flow. Days can be filled with meetings, visiting my production unit, creating new flavours (I do this at home: it's top secret), designing new packaging, in-store tastings, PR, sending out samples, talking to producers about a documentary I want to do . . . No day is ever the same and days tend to lead into nights and weekends. For the first three years, I barely took a weekend off or went out. Now I am strict on balance and make sure I have at least a day off each week.

If you want to be a chocolatier, test yourself by doing a good part-time course or short course and then train up either as an apprentice or by going to a chocolate school such as Valrhona or Callebaut.'

DENTIST

AVERAGE STARTING SALARY – £30,000

ENTRY POSITION – Dentist

TYPICAL WEEKLY HOURS – 30–40 hours

RECOMMENDED QUALIFICATIONS – Dentistry degree

IF YOU LIKE THIS YOU MIGHT ALSO LIKE . . . Doctor, nurse, beautician

The very word may make some shudder, bringing to mind noisy-drill memories or the heartbeat-raising verdict: 'you need a filling'. But working as a dentist – or hygienist, dental nurse, orthodontist or other mouth-related specialist – means being part of a well-paid, secure industry with regular hours (some do emergency and weekend work, but the vast majority of dentists still work nine-to-five days) and a huge variety of opportunities. You could work in a high-street dentistry practice, or in hospitals or the community, or even in industry or as part of the armed forces.

So who are all those masked, scrubs-sporting, 'open wide'-demand-ing people at the dentist's office?

Dental hygienist: Rather than treating problematic teeth, the dental hygienist (sometimes known as an oral health practitioner) focuses on helping kids and adults to keep teeth healthy. Hygienists do things like scale and polish teeth, remove plaque, and apply fluoride and fissure sealants. Hours tend to be around 9am to 5pm, though part-time work is common. Pay in NHS practices tends to be between £21,000 and £28,000, but can be as high as £35,000 for experienced or specialised hygienists. To get the job, you'll need five GCSE subjects graded A to C, plus two A levels, or a recognised dental nursing qualification, and have passed a course approved by the General Dental Council. These are either a three-year foundation degree in oral health science or dental therapy and hygiene, or a two-year diploma of higher education in dental hygiene, or dental hygiene and dental therapy. The courses cover topics like anatomy, preventive dentistry, dental health education and the management of patients. You'll also need great 'people skills', and be confident handling dental equipment, good eyesight, steady hands and a good concentration span.

Dental nurse: Usually the person found working alongside a dentist, the dental nurse sterilises and organises the instruments, prepares materials such as fillings, operates the suction device to remove saliva from patients' mouths, and carries out stock control and similar jobs. Some may also help in reception in smaller practices. Pay scales in NHS jobs tend to range from £16,000 to £23,000 a year. Some dentists take on trainee dental nurses without any qualifications, but many demand certain GCSEs including English, maths and science. You can then train on the job, or take a full-time college course in dental nursing, but ultimately all certified dental nurses must have a qualification approved by the General Dental Council, such as a Level 3 diploma in Dental Nursing or Certificate of Higher Education in Dental Nursing.

Dental technician: This job involves making, repairing and adjusting dental devices such as crowns, braces and dentures for people who need corrective work in their mouth or who have lost teeth. Most dental technicians work in a dental lab and carry out work for a large number of dentists in the surrounding area, but some are based in hospitals, designing devices for oral surgeons working on patients with facial injuries. Pay usually ranges from £22,000 to £28,000 but can be as high as £35,000 for very specialist or experienced dental technicians. You need to be registered with the General Dental Council to do the job, so you'll need one of its approved qualifications, such as a BTEC Level 3 diploma, or a foundation or honours degree. Some study part-time whilst training on the job in a private dental lab, others study full-time first.

Dentist: The most qualified of the high street dental surgery staff, a dentist checks patients' mouth and teeth, then diagnoses and treats any problems. You'll need to be good at team-working in this role – the professionals above are just some of the people you'll be sharing a surgery with – as well as having good manual dexterity and people skills. The industry is very competitive, so you'll need to be brilliant at science to get onto the training: a Bachelor of Dental Surgery (BDS) degree at university, which usually takes five years, followed by a year (or more) of postgraduate training. Most dentists are self-employed, and many take both NHS and private patients. Work could include treating patients' fillings, removing teeth, whitening them, taking X-rays, injecting anaesthetic, and fitting dentures and bridges.

One of the top benefits is that the hours, unlike other areas of medicine, are usually pretty regular – you're unlikely to be disturbed at three in the morning, unless working as a hospital's on-call dentist. Part-time hours are often possible. The average dentist's pay depends on the amount and nature of work carried out, but a self-employed dentist entering the profession in a training year will usually earn about £30,000 a year. That tends to rise, for a dentist covering both private and NHS patients, to between £40,000 and £150,000 a year, depending on the number of patients seen and the area covered. The higher salaries are usually reserved for those who have specialised knowledge.

Training-wise, before you can tackle those five years at a university's dental school, you'll almost always need to have As in all subjects at A level, including maths, chemistry and, preferably, biology. Some schools, however, offer a one-year pre-dental course to those without science A levels. Many dentist schools also insist applicants take the UK Clinical Aptitude Test (UKCAT).

The first year at dental school is predominantly theory, then from the second year onwards you'll be seeing patients while being supervised by qualified dentists. After those five years, all dentists must complete a one-year training in general dental practice, known as Dental Foundation Training. You can then do a further one year of optional training, known as Dental Foundation Year 2, to focus on a specific aspect of dentistry, such as oral and maxillofacial surgery, paediatric dentistry, restorative dentistry or special care dentistry. Those considering a career change, who already have a good degree in biology, chemistry or a biomedical subject, can apply for an accelerated four-year dental degree course. All dentists must be registered with the General Dental Council.

THE LOWDOWN: a newly qualified dentist

'I spent all my time at school studying to get As and get into one of the top dental schools, then at university I worked so hard on aceing my exams that I barely went out and left without many friends. But despite all of that, I'm really struggling to find work. It's been nine months since I graduated and I've applied to endless positions, but first of all there aren't that many cropping up, and second of all it seems to me that you need to 'know someone' to get ahead. I'm hoping my luck will change soon, but I want to say that it's not as easy as you might think to get a job in dentistry.'

A dentist's average day

8.30am: Arrive at surgery and get dental scrubs on. Check the day list to prepare for treatments . . . and check if there are any difficult patients on the books.

9.00am: Patients start arriving. Each morning and afternoon usually consists of a mixture of check-ups and treatments, ranging from 20 minutes for a filling to an hour-plus for a root canal treatment.

1.30–2.30pm: Lunch, and catching up on writing notes from the morning's patients plus general paperwork, including writing referral letters to specialist dentists.

2.30–5.30pm: Similar to morning, but generally seeing more children with after-school appointments. The day varies a lot depending on whether you are an NHS or private dentist – an NHS day can consist of seeing around 30–35 patients, and provide a variety of general dental treatments. Private dentistry is less fast-paced, allowing for more time with each patient. Most specialist dentists are in private practice, performing complex dental treatment that requires more time, so they see a smaller volume of patients.

Most dentists have no connection to work in the evenings. If you own a practice, though, as with almost all business owners, you'll have recruitment, admin and finance work to get through. Many dental practices are open on Saturdays but not on Sundays. There are also emergency dentists available out of hours, both on the NHS and privately.

If you're interested in becoming a dentist, it's worth spending a week working in general dental practice and another in a hospital looking at how specialists work, if you can. It might seem tedious – all you can do is watch – but it will provide a good insight into the profession. Be aware, too, of the current topical issues in dentistry and be up to date with these, such as the evolving NHS system, what the General Dental Council does, the fluoridation issue and the British Dental Association.

WORKING LIFE: Aniksha Patel is an NHS and private dentist

'The thing I like about being a dentist is that there is always scope to learn things and go on advanced training courses to better your skills. On top of everyday dental work, you can learn how to carry out treatments that you might not think are related to dentistry, like Botox and dermal fillers. You can also dip your hand into areas of dentistry which need specialist qualifications, such as orthodontics and implants, without needing to train as a specialist.

Another good thing about the profession is that the job is basically finished for the day when you have seen your last patient, so it's relatively civilised hours. As the majority of dentists are self-employed, the hours are flexible and you can choose how many days you wish to work.

I love meeting new people; seeing my patients over the years, they become like family. You can get to meet famous or interesting people, too. But it's not easy to get a job. The lack of funding in the NHS means that the profession is saturated and there are not as many new jobs on the market in general dentistry. When a dentist leaves the industry, it's usually due to stresses and strain from work.

I got my job via a contact, but there are lots of dental recruitment websites where people advertise posts. It's now near to impossible to set up a new business from scratch. There are opportunities to buy out existing dental businesses – but prices are really high because demand exceeds supply.'

DOCTOR

AVERAGE STARTING SALARY – £22,000–£30,000

ENTRY POSITION – Doctor

TYPICAL WEEKLY HOURS – 50 hours

RECOMMENDED QUALIFICATIONS – Medical degree and specialist training

IF YOU LIKE THIS YOU MIGHT ALSO LIKE . . . Dentist, nurse, vet

A memorable scene in the medical drama *ER* saw some wannabe doctors being interviewed for jobs. Why, they were asked, did they want to embark on a career in medicine? The answer came in a montage: every single one of the 30 or so candidates said the same thing – they wanted to 'help people'.

So it might be a good idea to come up with another answer if you plan on embarking on a career in medicine and face a similar question at interview. The truth, however, is that this *is* the motivation for many of the clever students who embark on decade-long training schemes to become a doctor. The money can be lucrative – top NHS consultants earn more than £100,000, and pay is higher for those who supplement it in the private sector – but that's on a par with other careers where the training is shorter, hours are less punishing and the responsibility is considerably less.

Becoming a doctor, as even the NHS recruitment site warns, 'isn't an easy option – it takes years of study and hard work.' But there are few more rewarding or respected careers. It's seriously varied, too: there are more than 60 different specialities in medicine, from working in the community as a GP to being a surgeon or psychologist.

Skills-wise, you'll need compassion and must be quick to learn, have good teamwork and communication skills, and a hefty dose of patience. 'You can either have thick skin or you can have fantastic friends and family who support you,' says one hospital doctor. 'And there are all kinds of doctor roles – I have friends who aren't great with people, but they make great pathologists [inspecting dead bodies to determine the cause of death] and radiologists [analysing images like X-rays and scans].'

Being a GP, says one parent in the role, is particularly popular for those thinking of having children: 'It goes well with having a family,' she says. 'Part-time work is considered normal, and there are no weekend or night shifts, unlike hospital medicine.' Hospital doctors, by contrast, face antisocial shifts (although there are lots of days off to compensate), but tend to have the opportunity to specialise in areas like surgery, psychiatry or particular branches of medicine.

In general doctors have great job security. 'There will always be sick people, and people will always need doctors to care for them,' points out one consultant. But there are downsides to the job such as boring paperwork. 'If you want to show commitment to medicine, work as an office assistant before you apply,' says another in surgical scrubs. 'Half of my day is writing, typing, collating, reading, transcribing and deciphering.' And in this career, you can't have an 'off' day. It is a huge burden of responsibility. Some people like that, some people never think about it, and some find it too much.

Salary-wise, NHS doctor pay is tiered: a first-year, newly qualified doctor currently earns £22,600 plus 'banding' for out-of-hours work. Depending on the number of evenings, nights and weekends you work, that could be 40 per cent or even 50 per cent more. A newly qualified doctor working nine to five Monday to Friday, will earn £22,600 a year no matter what job they do, but that same doctor working regular night and weekend shifts will earn £34,000. This increases every year. An NHS consultant can expect to earn between £75,000 and £101,000 per year. But there are professional costs, too – the annual registration fee to the General Medical Council is about £400, whilst optional union membership is about £200 a year. Specialists may have to pay other fees and insurance costs.

To become a doctor, you'll have to get into medical school. 'This is the hardest part,' says one doctor: you need excellent A-level grades (usually including chemistry plus other sciences and/or maths) plus lots of evidence of your passion for the career – work experience in hospitals, nursing homes or GP surgeries, for example – and you must do well at the UK Clinical Aptitude Test, or UKCAT. Some people choose to do biomedical sciences or similar degrees, then transfer onto a postgraduate medical course. 'All medical degrees are equal, regardless of what people might tell you,' says a senior house officer. 'Your chances of a great job are exactly the same if you went to Cambridge as if you went to any other medical school.'

After graduating, doctors face two years as a foundation trainee or newly qualified doctor, in a hospital, where they have to make a portfolio of cases and assessments to demonstrate progress as well as undertaking practical assessments (where someone senior observes them taking a patient history, examining a patient, performing a procedure or explaining something to a relative).

After all of that, doctors are eligible for speciality training – someone who wants to become a paediatric consultant, for example, will face another eight years of training, and becoming a GP involves working in various specialities such as paediatrics and psychiatry that are useful for future work in general practice. When you then start at a GP surgery, you are a registrar for your first year – effectively working like an apprentice and learning on the job with a mentor. You also have to take professional exams during this year to become a member of the Royal College of GPs.

WORKING LIFE: The newly qualified doctor: Nick Schindler is a trainee paediatrician

'In a month, I work as many night shifts and long days as "normal" nine-to-five days. On a weekday shift, my day looks like this:

8.40am: Arrive at work – gives me time to check my hospital email and make a coffee before handover.

9am: Handover from the night team to the day team, to keep everyone up to speed on what is going on with each patient. There is a computerised list of all the patients who are currently on each of the wards we cover, as well as a jobs list for outpatients who may have tests to chase or something that requires organising. This normally takes 30 minutes and is followed by 15–20 minutes of teaching from one of the senior doctors.

10am: The ward round starts, led by a consultant. This varies hugely depending on how many children are currently inpatients with us. Kids get sick quickly but they also get better quickly.

11.30am: Time for getting 'jobs' done – organising investigations, blood tests, scans, discussing children with specialists in other hospitals or writing discharge summaries, which are sent to a patient's GP. If this isn't written and sent within 24 hours of a patient being discharged then the department is fined.

Lunch should be around now, but whilst nurses are pretty good at ensuring they have breaks regularly, doctors are not. We tend to have a long break if all the work is done and no breaks if the place is busy. Sometimes, four doctors can be sat twiddling their thumbs all afternoon only for the two doctors working past 5pm to be run off their feet between a sick child on the ward and a premature baby born in the delivery suite.

Early afternoon: if a child is admitted to the children's ward, you have to find out why – taking a history from their parent or carer, or from the child if they are old enough. You examine them and try to find the signs of the illness that you suspect from your history. The biggest problem might not always be the one that the child or parent complains about. Then you have to come up with a plan and explain that plan to the child and the parents in a way they can understand, then write it up.

4.30pm: Afternoon handover. The evening team need to be told about what has happened in the day. If I'm working a 'normal' day then I go home at this point. If I'm working a 'long' day then it is back to work until 9.30pm.

9pm: The night team start and there is another handover, organised by the on-call consultant who will still be in the hospital from the morning. If I'm not sure every test on a child is complete, I normally ask the night team to check – that way I can get to sleep.

My rota involves working one in every six weeks on a night shift, one in every six weeks on a weekend, and one in every six weeks on a weekend night shift. It can be as much as 78 hours' work in seven days – but then the following seven days I work no hours at all. I leave on Monday morning and don't return until I start again the following Monday morning.'

WORKING LIFE: GP – Ellie Cannon

'Clinics start at 9am, so I usually get to work 20 minutes earlier to clear any urgent letters or emails before patients arrive. We see patients every ten minutes, for three hours – mostly face-to-face consultations but sometimes phone calls. There is no set lunch break, but there is usually a gap of two hours before the next clinic.

Lunch is time to check blood results, do all paperwork, referrals and, crucially, home visits for patients too ill to come in. Clinics re-start in the early afternoon, and again you see patients at ten-minute intervals. Since ten minutes is not really long enough to have a proper consultation, it's usual to be running thirty minutes late by the end of the day. I leave the surgery around 6.30pm.

I'm not at all connected to work when I've left. Most GP surgeries are closed out of hours, but GPs who are involved in managing a surgery usually have paperwork spilling over into the weekend. Some also work extra hours either in walk-in centres or emergency departments. That means seeing a different side of medicine, and making some extra money.

As a GP, you have the chance to build fabulous friendships with colleagues – I really enjoy the teamwork. But general practice is stressful – resources are constrained and bureaucratic processes are difficult. The medicine can also, of course, be upsetting and harrowing – you may be dealing with serious diagnoses, and traumatic life events such as child abuse and domestic violence. It can be hard not to take that emotional burden home with you.'

ODD JOB: Flusher, UK

If you're one of the UK's sewer flushers, your office will be stinkier than most. Your role will be to spend days surrounded by rats and vomit-inducing smells, clearing blockages of 'fatbergs' (huge lumps of drain-blocking lard), tampons and poo.

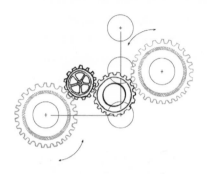

ENGINEER

AVERAGE STARTING SALARY – £17,000–£25,000

ENTRY POSITION – Engineer/Apprentice

TYPICAL WEEKLY HOURS – 35–40 hours

RECOMMENDED QUALIFICATIONS – Engineering degree

IF YOU LIKE THIS YOU MIGHT ALSO LIKE ... architect, graphic designer, surveyor

To 'engineer' literally means to 'arrange for something to happen'– which helps to explain why engineers are crucial cogs in a massive range of industries, from tunnel building on train lines to designing robots and tools, working on new football stadia to designing under-water hotels ... Their job is basically to solve technical problems, so engineers are much in demand. Engineering can be a vocational calling

– many in the industry reckon they were born asking 'why' and wanting to know how things work.

There's currently a shortage of engineers in Britain (especially left-handed ones, apparently!), so the job prospects are bright.

Confusingly, though, a whole lot of jobs have the word 'engineer' tagged to the end of them. There's a very wide variety of roles in the sector, including:

Aeronautical, or aerospace, engineers: work on building and developing new aircraft (for passengers and the military), on weapons, satellites and space shuttles. The work is extremely technically advanced, using the newest materials to try to improve flight safety, make jets more fuel and environmentally efficient, cut costs and make flying more pleasant.

Automotive engineers: design and improve cars and other vehicles. Help make the likes of Aston Martin's DB9 as fast as possible, ensure motorbikes are stable, decide the best materials to use for parts, test cars, vans and bikes before they hit the road, study their energy, environmental and safety aspects and try to improve them, work out costs and check for faults.

Biomedical engineers: work on the best materials and technology to use in healthcare, making anything from knee replacements to robots that carry out surgery on patients to rehab equipment, and arranging clinical trials of medical products.

Civil engineers: plan and help to create key building projects, from massive city bridges to airports and roads; and analyse tasks from managing traffic to organising how and where a whole country's rubbish gets sanitised and disposed of.

Mechanical engineers: this is the part of engineering which employs the most people, who work on manufacturing the machinery used in everything from biscuit-making to construction, water and energy, transport and aerospace – but most people specialise in one area. Work includes surveying existing machinery and equipment to see if it's functioning correctly, and using computer-aided design/modelling programs to design new products.

Structural engineers: design buildings and other construction projects in a way that ensures they will withstand environmental conditions and the impact of humans – which basically means making sure houses, sports venues, hospitals, offices, oil rigs, bridges, ships and other structures stay stable and safe and secure throughout their lifespan. Work includes selecting the materials that best meet design demands, inspecting construction work, advising builders and testing structures to ensure they are safe.

That's just some of the options for engineering jobs, but if you're interested in any of them, you have to be good at problem solving and have 'a logical brain and be pretty good at maths,' says one British engineer who has just been lured to New Zealand on a big work contract. 'You have to be good at thinking on your feet as things sometimes don't go to plan. You also have to be a good communicator.'

Qualification-wise, the majority of engineers are graduates who have studied one branch (such as mechanical engineering or civil engineering) at university. To get there, most unis demand three good A levels, with physics, maths and chemistry sometimes singled out for requirement. A lot of degrees offer a year in industry, where you can secure valuable experience and make contacts to boost your chances of getting a job on graduation. After that, many engineers work towards professional qualifications to become a chartered engineer.

But it's not just a profession for graduates: apprenticeships where you work and study on the job are very popular with contractors. Equally, many engineering areas offer access at technician level, where people with GCSEs or diplomas are paid to work on development and design projects at a lower level, and/or can study on the side to progress.

Pay-wise, most engineering graduates earn around £25,000. Lead engineers with several years' experience take home around £35,000–£50,000, whilst exceptional senior engineers on major projects may well earn more than double that. But salaries vary – some sectors attract higher pay when there are skills shortages. On-site engineers say their hours are long, but that does mean generous overtime packages. Depending on the size of the job or project they're working on, engineers can rise up the ladder every two to three years.

WORKING LIFE: tunnel engineer Leah Jacobs' recent projects include King's Cross Underground Station upgrade and Crossrail Western Tunnels in London

'When I am on site I start the day at 6.30 (in the morning or evening, depending if I am on a day or night shift). I catch up with the previous shift's workers for the first half hour, then I head down on to the site and brief the construction staff on the work for the day. The main task is ensuring quality and safety is maintained. Depending on the type of tunnel work I am on, I might be reviewing its direction or the thickness of the lining. On a day shift, lunch is at 2pm, then we continue with excavation until 7pm, which is handover time to the next shift. If I am not on site, but working in the office, my hours are usually from about 8am to 5pm. My tasks involve planning works and procuring materials and machinery, and ensuring that the method for the next tunnel is correct.

The hours aren't regular – all tunnelling works run through 24 hours a day, sometimes also seven days a week. On a London Underground project, for example, we often work on weekends and nights.

I was recommended to try out engineering because I loved Lego but was awful at art, which ruled out architecture. I also loved maths. And after a spell shadowing an engineer, I knew at the age of 17 that I wanted to embark on this career. The parts of the job that I find most fun are building things and going behind the scenes to places that normal members of the public don't get to see. The worst part is having to work on Saturday nights and the hours in general. The winter is pretty tough on shift, as on a regular basis you don't see daylight, having gone into the tunnel before it gets light, and come out after dark. But despite that, the people you work with are great and there is a laughter and food (tea and biscuits are a huge part of a tunnelling job).

As one of relatively few women tunnel engineers, I can say there is definitely a macho climate, although it's not as bad as people think it would be. On the whole, people are very kind and thoughtful. The tunnelling community has more of a family feel because there are so few of us and we all work insane hours. Plus in the UK we all seem to know each other. People accept you as an engineer if you prove that you know what you are talking about and are happy to jump into the mess.

I love my job – there is no better feeling than using a Tube station or tunnel that you had a role in creating. Very few other careers give you that real, tangible sense of completion and satisfaction – you can actually see what you have achieved at the end of the day.'

Dream Job: Crossword compiler

Sue Purcell works at Puzzler Media, making crossword puzzles for national newspapers as well as its own magazines.

'I have always loved words, even as a child. I just can't see the word mangetout without thinking "man get out", or think of "desserts" without seeing "stressed" spelled backwards. When I was growing up my parents used to buy two newspapers, so they could each do a crossword, so I guess the love of crosswords is in my genes.

I used to be a teacher in adult education, which involved a lot of evening work. As my children got to the stage where they needed me at home in the evening I looked around for a daytime job. I answered an advertisement in the local paper for a part-time copy-editor and began working at Puzzler Media. The publishing director immediately recognised my nerdiness and offered me a full-time job. That was 13 years ago.

No two puzzles are alike so there's always something new to challenge or entertain me – the English language is constantly growing, new words are being coined all the time and words change in meaning over time.

The key to the perfect crossword is fairness. For cryptic crosswords, the solver should be able to get one answer from the words in the clue – there shouldn't be anything extra or irrelevant in the clue. The clue "Yellow tropical fruit" could lead to BANANA or PAPAYA if you are presented with _ A _ A _ A, the clue European river could be RHINE or RHONE in RH _ NE. A good crossword editor will ensure that there is no ambiguity, so would use clues such as "Yellow crescent-shaped fruit" or "German river".'

ENTREPRENEUR

AVERAGE STARTING SALARY – Variable

ENTRY POSITION – Whatever you want it to be

TYPICAL WEEKLY HOURS – 24/7

RECOMMENDED QUALIFICATIONS – Leadership and management skills

IF YOU LIKE THIS YOU MIGHT ALSO LIKE . . . CEO, management consultant, online entrepreneur

More than any other kind of career, being an entrepreneur is seriously tough to categorise, because what's involved, the rewards you could achieve and the risks you face are much more extreme and diverse than in any other job. Unlike the average graduate career, starting your own business could turn you into an overnight millionaire, but far more likely it will involve years of hard slog, chasing investment, and blind hope that you're on the right path.

If you're considering setting up a start-up – be it a new invention, service or idea – you'll need to do lots of research into whether the idea will work, whether it already exists (and, if so, if you could better it) and whether it's likely to succeed. You might need to register your idea to make sure no one else steals it, and/or write a business plan to help you to seek out funding from a bank, angel investor or family and friends.

You don't have to do everything yourself – it's very rare to find someone who is good at all aspects of starting a business, from coming up with the idea and skills to the finance, planning and accounting sides – but you do have to be good at finding people who can fill your gaps. Much of the success of a start-up lies in finding the right people to complement your own skill set. Being an entrepreneur is an increasingly popular option – the number of new graduates who've opted to start their own business rather than climb a traditional career ladder is up from 2.2 per cent in 2007 to 4.8 per cent today, meaning graduate entrepreneurs now make up a sizeable chunk of the UK's four million-plus self-employed people.

That's partly because the cost has come down: the accessibility of creating an online start-up means the average expense of starting a business from scratch is now £632, according to research by PeoplePerHour. But the earnings could be anything from negative (you may have to plunder your own savings) to zillions, and the skills vary wildly depending on what industry and idea you're tackling. Here's one entrepreneur's average day and tale of success.

WORKING LIFE: Thea Green founded nails brand Nails Inc. in 1999: it now has an annual turnover of £22 million and employs 400 staff

'I wake up at around 6am most mornings and whilst my three kids are still asleep, do a quick scan of my emails to see if anything has come in overnight from the USA or Asia. Once they're awake, it's a mad scramble to get everyone washed, dressed and fed before jumping in the car – I do the school run three times a week. Then I begin my series of daily update calls with managers to get the latest sales figures.

A typical week could involve discussing the campaign for the next season's collection, meeting with manufacturers and distributors, presenting to retailers and meeting with PRs. If I'm in the office, I will have a salad at my desk between meetings, and about two or three times a week I have either a breakfast meeting or a dinner with contacts.

Once I'm home and have given the kids dinner, I tend to work into the evenings as we do a lot of work in the US and their day starts as ours is ending. So I am online most evenings. Although I do try to make sure the weekends are time exclusively for my family, I usually end up checking my email on Sunday evening to catch up on things that I didn't get around to during the week.

I think I always knew I wanted to run my own business but it wasn't until I started regular trips to the US in my previous job – as a magazine journalist – that I discovered the idea for Nails Inc. I've always loved fashion but I realised early on that I couldn't draw well enough to be a designer, so I focused on writing, taking a course in Fashion Journalism at the London College of Fashion, before getting a job at the *Daily Mail* and then *Tatler*.

When I'm creating new products, I still get the same thrill as I did on day one. Overall, I think the key skills for being an entrepreneur are vision, determination, a passion for what you do . . . and a good sense of humour. You never know what the financial reward is going to be – as an entrepreneur you need to be willing to invest in the business, particularly in the early stages, with new products, premises and people – and sometimes that can come at the expense of your own pay packet.

I'm a big fan of vocational training, apprenticeship schemes and entrepreneurial learning as an alternative for those who don't think university is right for them. And I'm definitely putting my kids on a coding course. When you think how much technology dominates our lives – from the cars we drive to the phones we use, and even to the nail polishes we manufacture, it seems a good idea to have at least a basic understanding of how code is used so that you can develop apps and software. Technology is no longer a distinct sector; it has become a layer within every business. Whether you work in fashion, retail, food or sport, technology influences them all.'

ODD JOB: Fake bank robber, international finance centres

The insiders' term is 'penetration testers' – they're on the payroll of banks who ask them to try to beat their security systems, be that attempted hacking or acted-out hijackings (Robert Redford played one in the 90s film *Sneakers*).

ESTATE AGENT

AVERAGE STARTING SALARY – £12,000–£16,000

ENTRY POSITION – Administrator

TYPICAL WEEKLY HOURS – 35–40 hours

RECOMMENDED QUALIFICATIONS – Apprenticeship/Experience in customer service work. Good people skills and sales skills

IF YOU LIKE THIS YOU MIGHT ALSO LIKE . . . advertising, surveyor, PR

Nearly everyone in Britain has an opinion about estate agents – a recent poll put the job only just below traffic wardens and bouncers in a list of the nation's most-hated professions. But good estate agents – who help people to buy, sell or let residential or commercial properties or land – have a role in one of the biggest purchases of people's lives. And although the hours are long, the pay is usually based on commission, so it can mean a salary of six figures for top agents.

On a day-to-day basis, estate agents inspect properties (they act for sellers, not buyers), compare them with others in the area to value them, market the land and buildings and negotiate on sales to try to secure the highest price for their client. Towards the end of the deal, they often also have to talk to lawyers, banks, mortgage brokers and surveyors to try to ensure an exchange of contracts. In Scotland, though, different laws mean more of the transaction is organised by lawyers.

Residential agents only work on houses, flats and sometimes also land, whilst commercial agents deal with business properties ranging from offices, shops and restaurants to leisure sites and major developments. Many agents are also involved in auctions.

Most work for local estate agencies, or branches of national chains, although there are some companies who will 'rent a desk' to an aspiring agent, meaning they work on commission only and pay a share of that commission to the company where they are renting the desk.

On average, estate agents start on a basic salary of between £10,000 and £14,000, plus the all-important commission. With experience, that base salary might rise to between £20,000 and £35,000 plus commission. Different agencies run different commission structures: it could be a flat 10 per cent on house sales, or it might be a sliding scale that depends on negotiators hitting certain targets. Managers usually secure a percentage of the office's takings. It usually takes between two and five years for an estate agent to become a manager.

Estate agency doesn't demand any formal qualifications, but there are college and university courses you can now take, as well as joining professional bodies such as the ARLA (the Associated of Residential Lettings Agents) or the NAEA (the National Association of Estate Agents). Most agents recommend anyone interested in the career should get a weekend job to see how it works, or a holiday job shadowing a negotiator or manager. The number of actual jobs available hinges completely on the state of the property market; in the depths of recession few people buy houses, so agents tend to cut jobs rather than hire any new blood. But when the housing market booms, so too do estate agent job opportunities – and commission potential.

WORKING LIFE: Mark Newton is an estate agent at Winkworth

'I get to the office for 8.30am, make a coffee and have a quick scan of the newspaper headlines to look out for any property stories. I'll check emails from the night before and send responses where needed, then go through the sales enquiries and split them between myself and my colleague, to keep things fair. I then see if I can arrange some viewings or, if someone who lives locally wants to sell, arrange a valuation.

Between 10am and midday, I follow up on any viewings or valuations from the previous day and then give feedback to our sellers: constant contact is very important in our industry. If you don't let the client know what's going on, even if there's nothing going on, then you could lose the instruction. This way at least they know they're important and you're working on their behalf.

After a quick lunch, it's time to phone buyers about any properties that may be new to the market, or reduced in price, and arrange viewings. The afternoon is split between phone calls and going out on viewings, then home time is around 7pm – although it can be later if there are late viewings or valuations to carry out.

I started in estate agency when I was 21, and have worked as a negotiator, manager and now as sales manager in the West End of London, Broadstairs in Kent, north and north-west London. I can pretty much fit in anywhere. In this industry, you've got to be passionate, enthusiastic, professional, trustworthy, a good listener and have an outgoing personality.

What can be tedious is chasing sales, and trying to deal with lawyers who don't want to talk to estate agents. If the market is very quiet, it can seem like there's nothing to do, but any agent worth their salt will always find something – be it canvassing or chasing old valuations.

You have to watch out so you don't work for a charlatan – there always seem to be new agents opening up thinking that they can earn some quick money from selling or renting property. Unfortunately, in the UK anyone can open an agency and doesn't need to be qualified. Too many people enter estate agency thinking it's a fast route to quick money – but many can't handle the long hours and possible months without earning commission. My advice is to work for an agent that's accredited to ARLA, NAEA and the Property Ombudsman Scheme.'

FASHION CAREERS

AVERAGE STARTING SALARY – £18,000–£22,000

ENTRY POSITION – Design assistant

TYPICAL WEEKLY HOURS – Variable

RECOMMENDED QUALIFICATIONS – Relevant degree (foundation/Higher National Diploma) in fashion design

IF YOU LIKE THIS YOU MIGHT ALSO LIKE ... hospitality, interior designer, photographer

Britain's fashion industry is a seriously big deal. Whilst most of the clothing manufacturing industry that the country was once famous for has now been exported to cheaper, foreign lands, there's still a huge range of mostly creative and design jobs in the UK's fashion industry – ranging from buyer (see working life, below) to designer, fashion writer or PR (see the relevant chapters). At last count, the UK's fashion industry was estimated to be worth £26 billion to the UK economy, supporting 797,000 jobs.

Getting a foot in the door is infamously difficult and even a little scary – especially if you imagine starting out in fashion to be a little like the put-upon interns immortalised in the film *The Devil Wears Prada*. Trends change fast and the industry demands fashion-forward people who can work well under tight deadlines.

Fashion internships are where a lot of people start out: most are unpaid, involve folding clothes and/or making coffee, and are deadly dull. It's a tough start, especially if you don't live in London, where most of the roles are. But even for those who have studied fashion-related degrees or courses, most jobs do demand real-world experience.

So what are the key roles?

Designers – They're the ones who first conceive ideas for new clothes, shoes and accessories. Most are specialists, working, say, for high-street brands on men's footwear, women's coats or kids' T-shirts; some focus on haute couture (spectacular, expensive one-off creations); others work for top-end designers on their 'ready-to-wear' ranges, or for high-street fashion brands to incorporate new trends into affordably priced clothes. Some designers are independent, and hired sporadically under contract for either famous designers or retailers. Designs can be turned around seriously fast: technology and speedy factories mean a design can be on a hanger in a store in less than two months. The job involves trend-spotting; sketching designs by hand or using software; selecting patterns, materials, embellishments, etc.; planning ranges; working with buyers (see below) and the media, as well as sales and manufacturing teams; and making protocols and patterns. Independent fashion designers will do other jobs, too –such as sourcing manufacturers, budgeting, sales projections, etc., whilst those working for big brands or high-street chains will work with other teams of people who take on those roles.

Buyers – They work for retailers, planning and buying in the clothes and accessories, etc., to sell in shops and online. The buyer takes into account the findings of customer focus groups, trends, the image of the store and budget of its shoppers in a bid to keep customers loyal and wares flying out of the shops. They often have to travel to the major international fashion weeks (New York, London, Paris, Milan, etc.) to pick up on the upcoming trends, as well as to manufacturing plants to find and manage relationships with suppliers.

Merchandisers – They work with the buyers to make sure the right amount of stock is in the right shop (or online warehouse) at the right time. They aim to work out how many lines should be bought, deal with suppliers, set prices and decide mark-downs, as well as matching up supply with demand (e.g. getting more coats in stores ahead of a big freeze, analysing stores where larger sizes are more popular and organising stock deliveries accordingly, etc.). A good merchandiser is crucial for a retailer's profitability.

The normal route into the industry is to do a fashion-related degree – sandwich courses, with a year in related employment, can really help you secure a job on graduation. But plenty of fashionistas study totally different subjects, or don't go down the university route at all; it's a sector where a CV full of work experience and networking can be as important as your qualifications. A weekend job on the shop floor of a clothes shop shows that you have fashion experience and awareness of what customers want, whilst work experience in a buyer's, designer's or merchandiser's office shows that you're learning about the business. Reading all the fashion magazines and following on-trend bloggers is a good idea, too.

Rather than securing the dream job immediately, lots of people in fashion work their way up, be it from workie [work experience] or an entry-level job like a buyer's clerk. The latter role mostly involves admin but can be the first step on a ladder to becoming an assistant buyer (where pay is usually in the region of £20,000 to £25,000), then a junior buyer (salary usually around £30,000, or up to £40,000 at some high-street chains), then, with a lot of experience, a senior buyer (with pay around £50,000 to £60,000) or even head of buying (pay up to £100,000). These strata don't exist in every business, though – smaller stores might just have one buyer–merchandiser who runs the whole process. 'There are a few really well-paid jobs in fashion, but not many,' says one insider. 'I'm not sure people go into the industry for the money. It's more because they love it.'

Another point to note: fashion isn't always as glam as it looks. Going to the Paris catwalk shows, for example, can mean 16-hour days travelling from one show to another, whilst a trip to see suppliers in the Far East might see dozens of meetings squashed into a visit lasting just a couple of days. 'But,' one merchandiser adds, 'even when you're staring at spreadsheets for days on end or visiting a store somewhere in Slough, if you love fashion you feel like you've got the best job in the world.'

THE LOWDOWN: Top tip for breaking into the fashion industry from Superdry's resourcing boss Simon Amesbury

'Fashion is an incredibly popular sector and competition can be fierce, with only the very best people standing out from the crowd to be offered that valuable first step on the career ladder. So how can you make sure that person is you?

- Put together an eye-catching CV and portfolio. A plain black and white CV for a fashion designer role won't catch the eye. Don't just have a dry list of qualifications and experience – bring it to life with examples of your work and talk about your successes and achievements. Have a portfolio of your very best work ready to send, but make sure that you tailor your portfolio to the style of the company you want to impress – you wouldn't send the same work to a Savile Row tailor that you would send to Superdry.
- Build a network. Get a LinkedIn profile, add as much detail as you can, make yourself sound interesting, and start connecting with people. Research which companies you would like to work for, find out who the key people are in the recruitment team and the department you want to work in, and send personalised invites to connect. The more connections you have, the more people you will have access to, and you can build a great network of contacts. Go to fashion shows, read blogs, read the trade press, see who inspires you, and reach out. Be brave and don't be afraid of initiating contact.
- Secure work experience, internship or volunteering experiences, even if it's unpaid. Ask everyone in your network for referrals – a personal recommendation will usually pay dividends. Any job within the industry will

help – it shows that you are building your personal brand by seeking out relevant roles in the industry.

- Work for a retailer. Getting a job in a fashion store is not all that hard – there are thousands of jobs in fashion retail. Great performance in a store job can lead to opportunities at head office, and access to the people who can help you make the leap in your career. One of our brightest young fashion designers started off working part-time in our Newcastle store while a student.

- Think about how you come across. You can make a massive impact in a week's work experience: work relentlessly, introduce yourself to everyone, speak up, generate ideas, be memorable (without being annoying). One intelligent comment in a meeting might just make that decision maker remember you when they have a vacancy.'

WORKING LIFE: Emma Roback is an assistant buyer at River Island

'Our weeks run to the same structure – for example, Monday we have a trade meeting to discuss what sold well, and what didn't, in the past week. We also have fit sessions twice a week, where a model comes in and we fit the garments on her to make sure they're perfect for the customer to wear. The rest of the day I'm dealing with suppliers, answering their questions and making sure all the clothes are going to arrive in stores on time. There's also cloth sourcing – meeting cloth suppliers and seeing their new ranges, including prints. This is one of my favourite parts of the job. Prints are so beautiful, it's hard to think with your head and not your heart! There are also sign-off meetings with the senior bosses, where we propose what we want to buy for each season, then we go ahead and book them.

Working in the fashion industry, the key skills are organisation, time management, creativity and passion. I'm always connected to work – on evenings and weekends I'm not necessarily checking emails or at my computer, but I'm always going to the shops, seeing what is new out there, what our rivals are doing, looking at blogs, seeing what the celebs and bloggers are wearing, and looking at the latest fashion shows. I do have a lot of clothes . . . Especially jackets. I love them because they always fit even if you are having a fat day! I often have to sneak shopping bags past my boyfriend.

I kind of fell into my job – I studied psychology at university then did work experience at River Island, and I loved it so I applied for a job. I joined on the trousers team three years ago and now I'm an assistant buyer on dresses.

My favourite part of the job is when the dresses you have spent a lot of time and energy on sell really well – that's an amazing feeling. The top perk is definitely our discount card – we get 50 per cent off. And being ahead of the game, knowing what everyone will be wearing in a year's time. The people are great, too – fun people work in fashion. By contrast, sometimes styles you've spent ages working on arrive in store and the girls don't like them. It feels personal, like they don't like you!'

WORKING LIFE: Nisha Grewal is a freelance fashion and celebrity stylist, working with stars including Girls Aloud and Goldfrapp

'Since most stylists, like me, are freelance, your schedule is based on the volume of work you take on. Usually I'm either having prep days – where I'm researching, calling in samples, answering emails, liaising with PRs and show-rooms and attending appointments or client meetings – or I'm on set.

Days on a shoot can really vary – you might be working anything from four hours to 16, depending on how the photographer or director works and the nature of the project. The atmosphere is usually fast-paced, with a tendency to be dramatic. Music videos always have extremely long hours, whilst commercial campaigns can span several days; editorial shoots, for magazines, websites or newspapers generally last just one day. For red carpet events and celebrity appearances, there is generally a fitting in advance, plus you work on the event day.

Some projects give you a lot more preparation time than others – I've prepped for a shoot and done fittings frantically in one day, followed by working on it for 15 hours the next day, but equally I'm sometimes given the luxury of a week's notice.

Even when I'm not officially working, on evenings and weekends I'm constantly checking emails and am on social media. Most of my jobs come via word of mouth, which is why networking is so important. Ditto editorial work – it's low paid, or sometimes unpaid, but you do it to keep your port-folio fresh and your name known.

A career in fashion is a lifestyle choice – you make a lot of connections networking, so I spend some evenings attending events to help build relation-ships. It's an extremely competitive industry, so dedication plays a large role.

Everyone's route into this career is different – I have an art foundation and a degree in textile design – understanding colour, shape and texture is essential for a stylist. I then did work experience at various magazines and with freelance stylists, and assisted a stylist full-time for three years before going out on my own. Work experience is the best way to learn.

Many others start out in a fashion journalism, design or PR. It's a career that a lot of people switch into – you just need to have a creative mind and a passion for art and design alongside superb organisational skills, time management and personality.

As a freelance stylist you can never guarantee the amount of work you'll receive and there is a lot of talented competition out there – it can become daunting. But if you crack it, it's such a fun job and the pay can be good. You're mostly paid a day rate – I have been paid anything up to £1,200 a day, but you're unlikely to have a job to do every day. There's low-paid editorial work or commercial work which has much higher rates. You also have expenses such as agency fees, office rent and taxes to come out of that. You do, though, get great fashion discounts and amazing gifts from PRs and designers.'

FIREFIGHTER

AVERAGE STARTING SALARY – £21,000

ENTRY POSITION – Trainee

TYPICAL WEEKLY HOURS – 42 hours

RECOMMENDED QUALIFICATIONS – Good standard of education and physical fitness. Over 18 years of age. Must pass background checks

IF YOU LIKE THIS YOU MIGHT ALSO LIKE . . . military, police officer, tradesman

A sample episode of *Fireman Sam* or *London's Burning* might suggest otherwise, but the average firefighter's working week doesn't actually involve extinguishing flames. Alongside fighting fires, their job is to protect the public from a range of emergency situations, from terrorist attacks to car crashes, chemical spills to flooding, and rescuing people and animals from a range of dangerous situations.

There are also a host of more everyday tasks: promoting fire safety in talks to schoolchildren, office or council workers and others;

inspecting commercial properties and homes for fire safety equipment, carrying out practice drills, checking and maintaining vehicles and equipment and training. Firefighters in management roles will be the ones deciding what to do and making a plan for use during emergency situations, writing up incident reports and running recruitment and budgets.

Being a firefighter can be dangerous and traumatic as well as stressful, but the job can also have one of the highest rates of satisfaction – you can be regularly saving individuals' lives. Most work from fire stations, usually full-time, but in some remote rural areas 'retained firefighters', who live very near the fire station, only attend it during a call-out or for scheduled training, and usually have another full-time job. Some firefighters, however, work in specific settings, such as at airports or ports, in particular industries such as for chemical or nuclear power firms, or for the armed forces.

It's a competitive industry – most fire brigades receive hundreds of applicants each year. Although there are no specific academic qualifications required, candidates face a long and tough selection process, including interviews, physical tests (which may involve using ladders, hoses and other emergency equipment), psychometric and written exams. All trainee firefighters (who must be over 18, with good eyesight and hearing) face initial training (often a three- to four-month residential course), then have a minimum two-year probation period before their job is confirmed. After that, there's ongoing training for all firefighters.

Some people have additional jobs alongside working for the fire brigade (for shift details, see 'working life', below) because the average firefighter's hours are compressed into long shifts. 'It's no different to someone having evening work to supplement their income,' says one firefighter.

The starting salary for a firefighter is almost £21,600, rising to £28,800 on completion of the development process, plus overtime. Managers could take home about £41,000, whilst supervisors of several fire stations could make as much as £55,000 a year. An extra premium is paid for those working in London. Retained firefighters are paid an annual sum – starting on about £2,200 a year – plus a fee for every incident they attend.

WORKING LIFE: Fred Howden* is a London Fire Brigade firefighter

'Major fires don't happen as often as you think: we attend more road traffic incidents these days, which can be more horrific as we are only called when there is someone confirmed as trapped in a vehicle. But you keep on doing your job, and that overrides any trauma you're facing – normally you don't process it until later on. Often we will have a debrief afterwards, back at the station, to talk over the incident and make sure everyone is feeling all right. The team camaraderie is great – working with the same people you really get to know everyone's strengths and weaknesses and it creates a great bond.

The situations that really get the heart racing are when you turn up and the fire is punching out the property's windows. There are so many things to think about in those first few moments, from how to deal with the fire to

---

* *name changed for anonymity*

checking the inside of the premises for people, and where to get the water from. It takes great teamwork to be able to deal with a fire efficiently.

Many of our calls are for automatic fire alarms in business premises or flats; although these tend to be false alarms, they need to be treated with caution until we find out the cause of the alarm. We do go to some interesting call-outs: "there's a phone book alight," "my neighbour's barbecue is annoying me," and yes, every now and then a cat up a tree, although there isn't much you can do with cats – they are very capable at getting down themselves. Normally when you get up there, they jump down before you get a chance to grab them.

Since one of the most important parts of being a firefighter is responding to emergency calls, you never know how a day is going to pan out. But regular duties include a morning roll-call when we inspect our fire gear, detail riding positions and are told about duties for the day. We also test breathing apparatus sets, vehicles, vehicle inventories and all equipment. Later in the morning we'll have station activity, sometimes including training drills and Home Fire Safety Visits – fitting smoke alarms or inspecting premises, either for familiarisation, planning purposes or to check the risks held within a building, for example gas cylinders. We also have lectures on policies and procedures, topography [maps, surroundings], training for drivers and gym time. But that doesn't include emergency call-outs, requests for emergency visits, off-site training and standby duties at local neighbouring fire stations. You have to be very adaptable in planning a day's schedule, as well as willing to cancel or move any appointments at the drop of a hat.

We work two days on, two nights on, and then four days off. The days are 09:30 until 20:00 and the nights 20:00 until 09:30.

It's a fantastic job and I would recommend it to anyone. The best parts of the job are the emergencies, as they get the adrenaline pumping, but as these are often the worst day of the victim's life, it's a tough balance. Making a positive difference to someone's life by reacting to a 999 call makes the job worthwhile.'

Dream Job: Test pilot

Simon Sparkes, 48, is a Rotary Wing Test Pilot at Nova Systems

'Almost all qualified test pilots start off as officer pilots in the military; in the UK, candidates for test-pilot training are required to have at least 750 flying hours – including significant frontline experience – and be rated as above average for pilot skills and management qualities. Typically, the Ministry of Defence trains nine test pilots a year; the training takes one year, flying up to 25 different aircraft types and simulators. The secret to a good test pilot is someone who can fly well, is level-headed, and can clearly express themselves both verbally and in writing to a high technical standard; some students have a real difficulty in producing the latter.

Once trained, most test pilots return to work on their original aircraft type, either at MoD Boscombe Down, RAF Brize Norton or RAF Coningsby. Many test pilots go on to have successful senior management careers in the MoD, or working for the major aircraft manufacturers or engineering firms.

A typical day as a test pilot begins with a meteorological brief, then meetings, conferences and flying all mixed in; all test-flying activities require substantial planning: the scientists and engineers will sit with the crew and discuss any specific risks and issues. Once airborne, we build up to the difficult, and likely more dangerous, stuff, and fly the test sequences, often with a direct link back to the engineers who have real-time displays of the aircraft instruments so they can see if there are issues. Then the crew come back and conduct a thorough debrief; the test pilot has to write an extensive report, often very quickly, to the designer or safety authorities. Test pilots can be unpopular with these teams because we "say it as we see it"– it's a job where honesty and a desire to protect those flying the aircraft are always at the forefront. Being a pilot was always my childhood desire and being a test pilot has certainly been the most rewarding flying role I have ever undertaken – and one that I would recommend without hesitation.'

GRAPHIC DESIGN

AVERAGE STARTING SALARY – £14,000

ENTRY POSITION – Designer

TYPICAL WEEKLY HOURS – 35–40 hours

RECOMMENDED QUALIFICATIONS – Relevant degree

IF YOU LIKE THIS YOU MIGHT ALSO LIKE ... advertising, photographer, TV producer/director

Whole swathes of our world would look a lot duller without graphic designers – they're the creative types who use fonts, images and computer wizardry on posters, ads, packaging, websites, films, magazines, TV, exhibitions, corporate logos and more to make items stand out or be more appealing.

Graphic designers are usually given a brief directly by their client, or they work within or in collaboration with ad agencies; the nature of the job will totally depend on each brief. If a big corporate company wanted a new logo, it might call in a team of graphic designers to come up with prototypes, choose typefaces, imagery, colours and layouts, and work out how to use them in a clear way to help the company to communicate the brand idea it wants to beam out to the public. Part of the brief might also be to consider how the new design(s) would work in a range of places – from petrol forecourts to business cards.

A good designer will need a raft of creative skills – attention to detail, an eye for colour and lighting, good spatial awareness and a distinct style (if the work calls for it), as well as highly practical ones such as good time management, excellent communication and self-motivation and adroitness with the latest computer-aided design software like Photoshop, InDesign, QuarkXPress, 3ds Max, FreeHand, Illustrator, Acrobat, Dreamweaver and Flash. Many graphic designers are self-employed, working on a range of contracts for different clients, but even those working within agencies have to come up with their own ideas and pitch to win briefs.

To break into the industry, most graphic designers have a degree in a related visual arts subject, such as illustration, 3D design, fine art, or indeed graphic design; often these courses demand a foundation degree or BTEC qualification for entry. Some firms will offer apprentice-style roles based on a candidate's personal portfolio, with on-the-job training, but these are becoming more unusual. Either way, try to secure work experience where you can help out on real-life projects to start building a portfolio, and/or come up with your own briefs for mock clients to show off at interview.

'An amazingly graphic-designed CV is one way to stand out,' says one designer, 'and this is the kind of industry that appreciates something out of the ordinary. But be careful of screwing up – a typo in your CV doesn't exactly suggest you're good at the kind of proof-reading and detailed work most jobs will require of you.'

Pay-wise, a junior designer can expect to earn anything from £15,000 to £20,000. 'This will be based entirely on the company, as well as any prior experience you might have,' says designer Ben Revens (see below). Depending on which part of the industry and particular role you end up in, salaries can hit the heights of £50,000 to £60,000 for a top designer and are often much higher for creative directors and supervisors. Freelance day rates can start anywhere between £75 and £100, but can build all the way up to £400-plus per day.

WORKING LIFE: Ben Revens is a 3D and visual effects artist

'I started out in graphic design, but now my specialisms are in 3D and visual effects – creating and integrating computer-generated objects into photos or footage. So I will do the modelling, animation, lighting, texturing and rendering of 3D models, as well as 2D compositing and colour grading to sit them into the footage on films, adverts, campaigns and TV shows.

Being a designer definitely changes the way you see media, from picking apart posters and recognising fonts, to understanding how CG sequences are created in films.

The parts I enjoy most are working on high-profile projects – like event graphics for the *World War Z* film, artwork for Sea Life aquariums, and an ad for O2 – and using new technologies and exciting new software. Seeing your work in public, on TV or your name in credits is always a proud moment, and being able to name-drop campaigns, adverts or films you've worked on is a nice ego boost, too!

Although the design industry itself is very competitive, the office culture is typically very relaxed. In a good team environment everyone has things they can teach others, and there is often a good sense of camaraderie when deadlines are tight. Like a lot of people in the industry, I sometimes freelance from home or work on personal projects, so the work spills into the evenings and weekends.

I got my first job as a designer through someone I knew, but during my career I've gone through various recruitment agencies and been contacted by companies through social and professional networks, as well as seeking out and approaching companies directly for work.

The industry is a lot smaller than I'd imagined it to be. Also, people are generally a lot more approachable than I thought they'd be. As a junior, it's easy to put senior designers and creative directors on a pedestal, but they all started the same way as you, and are usually very keen to impart their knowledge.

The best advice I could offer would be to spend some time looking into your preferred area, long before looking for jobs. Read design magazines and websites, play around with the software you are likely to be using, or follow online tutorials. Showing that you've invested time and have a genuine interest in the field can go a long way in an interview, even if you have no real experience.

Also, first impressions are extremely important in the creative industry – your personality can often be as important as your skill level. You'll almost always be working with other people on a project, so employers will be looking for someone who will fit well into their team and get on with others. The industry is surprisingly small, and you'll very often end up working with familiar faces in other companies, so it's all about who you know and who will vouch for you.'

HAIRDRESSER

AVERAGE STARTING SALARY – £14,000

ENTRY POSITION – Trainee/Hairdresser

TYPICAL WEEKLY HOURS – 40 hours

RECOMMENDED QUALIFICATIONS – Training in hairdressing

IF YOU LIKE THIS YOU MIGHT ALSO LIKE . . . beautician, nurse, photographer

'Have you got any nice holidays lined up?' 'Your hair looks sooooo stunning!' As a hairdresser, you'll need to be as good at chit-chat and schmoozing people as cutting. And it's not just cutting, either – most hairdressers can tackle anything their clients want, so although there are a few specialists, as a junior you'll learn to be adroit at cutting, dying, highlighting, styling, straightening and perming hair. Some hairdressers focus on men or on women, whilst others become expert at Asian, Afro-Caribbean or another hair type, or specialise in wedding or occasion hair.

Hair and beauty courses are amongst the most popular in the UK: recent government figures show that 94,000 students undertake further education in the subjects in one year. But when they graduated, there were only 18,000 vacancies. So it's seriously competitive.

Junior or apprentice hairdressers might start out in a salon and steer clear of formal qualifications, beginning by sweeping and cleaning up, then washing hair, perhaps taking bookings and manning the front desk, before the salon owner or experienced hairdresser trains them to gradually start cutting, styling, and more. Others head to college for a course in hairdressing (such as NVQ Levels 1 to 3) or barbering. Some combine formal education with part-time salon work or a Saturday job for the experience.

Many hairdressers are self-employed, so you can earn as much as you can work – and some top stylists in London salons charge several hundred pounds per cut. But starter salaries can be as low as £11,000 for a trainee.

WORKING LIFE: Jamie Stevens, salon owner and X Factor hairdresser

'If you're keen on cracking hairdressing, my top tip is literally to work hard – stylists notice the juniors who are there early, eager to watch and learn all the time, help clean up the salon and develop their skills in any spare seconds. You might not think your hard work is being noticed, but it will be.

Life as a celebrity hairdresser isn't all that glam. I wake up at about 5am to check emails, my diary and the news. My work schedule varies – I can be out of the country for weeks at a time teaching students, filming or doing the hair for shoots. But when I am in my London salon, I start seeing clients [who include Kylie, Nicole Scherzinger and Leonardo DiCaprio] and usually have between 15 and 18 appointments each day. A lunch break is a luxury.

With appointments all afternoon, I'm very lucky if I get home at 8pm, but often I have to work on red carpet events, premieres or award ceremonies, so it'll be the early hours of the morning. My job never stops on the weekends, either – whether I'm working on shows, shoots or TV – and I'm always checking social media for upcoming trends in my spare time.

This is not a job for me, this is my life. It started back when I was 12; my mum ran a salon in Somerset and I worked there, first clearing up then going to SCAT, a hairdressing school, at the same time to get my NVQ Levels 1, 2 and 3 in hairdressing. It's hard starting out in hairdressing – ten years ago I was working in a small salon in Somerset earning £30 a week.

Hairdressing is thought to be one of the worst-paid industries – even today kids start on £400 a month as a junior or assistant on an apprenticeship. But you can work your way up, and the harder you work the more money you earn. I know hairdressers who earn six-figure salaries.

A Saturday job in a salon is a great way to experience the salon environment and how it works – you'll need people skills, knowledge of current trends, patience, passion and determination.

If you want to crack hairdressing, keep an eye out for fashion trends in *Vogue*, *Elle*, *Marie Claire*, etc., and read hji.co.uk, which has trends and celeb hair news. Also, most good salon websites will have blogs and social media entries which are great to look at for job news, plus more trends and styles.'

HEDGE FUND CAREERS

AVERAGE STARTING SALARY – £100,000–£200,000
ENTRY POSITION – Equity analyst manager
TYPICAL WEEKLY HOURS – 60 hours
RECOMMENDED QUALIFICATIONS – Experience in investment banking
IF YOU LIKE THIS YOU MIGHT ALSO LIKE . . . accountant, actuary, banker

It's a role that most people have heard of, usually because of its 'ker-ching' factor, but few actually understand. So what is a hedge fund? It's an investment vehicle that pools together capital (aka money) from a number of investors and puts that money into a range of different places. Hedge funds differ from, say, pension funds or other more straightforward investment vehicles because they're only open to certain 'accredited' investors (usually, those who are seriously rich). Their job is to make money whether financial markets fall or rise, so portfolio managers can 'hedge' themselves by going long (investing in something you think is going to become more valuable) or short (predicting it will fall in value).

Investors receive a set cut of the profits and give the hedge fund a carte blanche to invest their pooled cash. The fund then takes a juicy cut – say, 2 per cent of the total funds under management each year. And that cut is why working in a hedge fund is regarded as one of the most lucrative in financial services – itself one of Britain's best-paid industries.

As with jobs at investment banks, there are lots of different roles at hedge funds, including analysts, portfolio managers and traders, as well as support jobs. Six-figure salaries aren't unusual, and you even hear of the occasional hedge funders in their twenties pocketing multi-million-pound pay cheques for a year's work at one of the major firms. They will, however, have stomached one of the most stressful working environments: if you start losing money for your hedge fund, it won't be long before you get sacked.

Competition for jobs is tough, too: think Premiership footballer-tough. Some hedge funds receive hundreds of CVs a week and don't even have any openings. 'It is highly unusual for anyone to go straight from university into a hedge fund,' adds one insider. 'They don't usually run internship or graduate programmes, so the most junior roles usually require two to four years' work experience at an investment bank – with salaries that reflect that.' Skills-wise, you'll need a sparkling numerical ability, good communication skills, and you must be personable and a very slick networker: hedge fund jobs are rarely advertised – it's about who you know. 'Posts are not easy to find even if you are a perfect match,' says the hedgie. 'The best way into it is by starting your career at an investment bank and then building up a dialogue with someone working in the industry – preferably lots of people.'

The roles within a hedge fund – and the number of people filling those roles – vary according to its size, but the general positions are:

Portfolio manager – Their job is to pick the investments and, under serious pressure, to make the best possible return. They will often use the work of the analyst(s) to pick investments – ranging from shares, currencies and bonds to commodities, bundles of mortgages, and so on. The most successful managers can become 'names' in the industry, with journalists and industry figures tracking their actions. A big fund will have several portfolio managers, each of whom might formerly have worked as a trader, analyst or risk manager. They will also have some, or in small funds all, of the responsibility for schmoozing clients (investors), getting new ones and keeping current ones on-board.

Middle office – These roles are mostly in accounting: running the books of the fund with intricate records of all transactions according to the regulator's principles.

Analyst – This job involves researching and reporting – aka analysing – a potential investment's level of risk and reward to help portfolio managers decide whether they're worthy of the fund's cash. Most analysts are Microsoft Excel wizards, with fingers flying across the keyboard with shortcuts. Some focus on working out projections from a company's financial statements; others use software to predict prices and spot trends in a particular industry, area or asset, from equities (that's shares) to commodities (you're going to have to Google these if you want to work in a hedge fund), bonds (ditto) and more.

Trader – Some funds will have traders whose job it is to buy and sell products – again, it could be shares, commodities, futures, or others – on the financial markets according to the manager's demands.

Marketing/sales manager – The official schmoozer: there to ensure the hedge fund has enough cash to function. They need to have the confidence and networking skills to secure new clients and manage existing ones – and if performance slips, this role is one of the first to be axed.

Pay-wise, a newbie with a few years' banking experience behind them might be lured to a hedge fund on, say, £200,000 a year; fixed salaries won't rise much beyond that, however much experience they get. Bonuses, however, are another matter: they're tied to the performance of the fund – i.e. they are a percentage of the fund's return – and can be on a Lamborghini-buying scale . . . Or, in a bad year, they may not even cover a 20-year-old Fiesta.

WORKING LIFE: Rupert Lendl* is an equity analyst at a London-based hedge fund

'I am an equity analyst working for a portfolio manager (PM). That description alone is usually enough for people's eyes to glaze over at parties, but what it means is that I try to tell the portfolio manager which stocks to invest in and which to stay away from.

Since I'm relatively new to this role – I used to work for a City investment bank – for now I mainly investigate stock ideas that my PM has suggested and, once I've made a decent start, I'll pass on my work and we have animated discussions about what I've found.

My working day usually starts on the way to the Tube at around 6am,

---

* *name changed for anonymity*

when I skim all the equity research put out by investment banks for interesting reports. I'm normally at my desk by 6.30, and have 10–15 minutes until things get busy – that's when my boss gets in, and she has usually spotted something on her way into work that she wants me to investigate. I then spend the morning reading reports, speaking to sell-side analysts (that's people doing a similar job to me but for an investment bank, and we buy their reports and advice), listening to conference calls with company executives and building and updating financial models.

There's no real lunch break – we tend to grab a sandwich and eat it at our desks. Unless there are management or analyst meetings to participate in, the afternoons are usually quieter, so I delve deeper into ideas that have sprung up in the morning. Whole hours might be spent building or refining an Excel model on a particular division or aspect of a company that my firm is considering investing or trading in.

Then I usually knock off around 6pm, unless it is a particularly busy day. But I've never spent a weekend day in the office, which is in stark contrast to equity analysts at demanding banks such as Goldman Sachs, where a Saturday is like a normal working day. Whilst I'm working just shy of 12 hours on a regular day, it mostly flies by so it doesn't feel like long hours.

I really enjoy learning new things, so any day that I get asked to look at a company or industry I haven't looked at before is a good day. I also like discussing opinions with my boss or with sell-side analysts; it is a very friendly, collaborative and surprisingly relaxed environment. That is, unless you are losing the firm money . . .

You also get taken out for dinner, football games or gigs by your sell-side contacts – you're their client so they want to keep you 'on side'. Though I'm told entertainment is not as lavish as it used to be, as the finance sector has tightened its belt and regulation has become more stringent.

There are boring parts of the job, though – particularly results season. These are the few weeks, four times a year, when most companies update the City about their financial performance. It means I have to spend hours updating models that I've previously built, which becomes tedious.

Hedge funds vary massively in size – the larger ones have a multitude of roles on the investment side, including scores of PMs, analysts and traders, as well as those in support functions (accounting, IT, HR, compliance, etc.) and in compliance and legal, as hedge funds are coming under increasing scrutiny from regulators.'

10 of the UK's best-paid roles

1. CEOs or managing directors
Average pay: £107,703; annual change: down 8.4%

2. Aircraft pilots
Average pay: £90,146; annual change: up 12.5%

3. Marketing directors
Average pay: £82,962; annual change: down 2.4%

4. PR directors
Average pay: £77,619; ; annual change: up 23.8%

5. Transport associate professionals (air traffic controllers, ship captains, flight planners)
Average pay: £64,889; annual change: up 6.7%

6. Medical practitioners
Average pay: £63,677; annual change: up 4.4%

7. Corporate lawyers
Average pay: £63,484; annual change: up 10.2%

8. Senior police officers

Average pay: £57,664; annual change: down 2.2%

9. IT directors

Average pay: £55,426; annual change: down 11.5%

10. Senior officers in the armed and emergency services

Average pay: £54,539; annual change: down 1%

Source: ONS

HOSPITALITY AND EVENTS

AVERAGE STARTING SALARY– £19,000

ENTRY POSITION – Trainee or assistant

TYPICAL WEEKLY HOURS – Variable (shifts)

RECOMMENDED QUALIFICATIONS – Apprenticeship or a relevant degree

IF YOU LIKE THIS YOU MIGHT ALSO LIKE . . . HR, life coach, PR

If you're the crazily organised one out of your friends – always planning holidays or nights out and having a spreadsheet or to-do list on the go – working as an events planner or running a hotel or restaurant could be just up your street.

Hospitality is the catch-all term used to refer to the entertainment, events, hotel, food and drink service industry – everywhere from a theme park or cruise liner to a pub or hospital, with roles ranging from waitressing to management. Events planners, for example, are responsible for having the ideas, creativity and contacts to organise and put on dos ranging from weddings and parties to conferences and extravaganzas such as the Olympic opening and closing ceremonies. They are in charge of the whole shebang, from the first planning meetings with organisers to running everything on the day. It's a lot of responsibility, but a lot of fun, too, according to those who do it.

Some of the major hotel chains and restaurants run graduate schemes which give a fast-track to management roles as well as regularly changing experience in a range of jobs; career-changers with relevant experience might also be able to switch into senior roles in hospitality.

The nature of hospitality jobs depends massively on where you're working, but whether you're managing a local restaurant or a five-star hotel, tasks are likely to include running or overseeing a budget, being responsible for staff and guests/diners, planning and supervising services (potentially including food and drink, health and safety, complaints, reception, bookings, site inspections, housekeeping, concierge and marketing). In big hotels the role will be more overseeing other specific managers (such as front of house, housekeeping, food and beverages, etc.) with perhaps less guest contact. Usually, though, the top staff, managers and owners at five-star institutions have worked their way up and spent time working at smaller firms.

In the events management world, the job will include constant networking with both potential clients and other suppliers in order to get new business, as well as talking to clients about their requirements, conjuring up great themes or ideas for the events, securing the best suppliers and venues, negotiating prices, organising any extra requirements from security to time-keeping, and ensuring the whole event goes as it's supposed to on the day – including problem-solving anything from dress repairs to a no-show, or a deluge of rain at an outside event. Some planners embark on qualifications like diplomas in events management (such as the Level 2 Certificate in Event Planning or in Live Events and Promotion) or degrees in hospitality or hotel management, others work their way up via work experience and promotions.

In hospitality, starting salaries (say as an events assistant or assistant to a hotel manager) tend to be around £14,000 to £21,000 a year for unqualified new-starters, rising to £30,000 to £45,000 a year with experience. Top self-employed planners or hotel managers can hit six-figure salaries. Freelancers in the events industry usually pocket £100 to £200 per day depending on the company, industry, type of contact and event. Amongst hotel and restaurant owners, the earnings totally depend on how much they decide to take out of the business themselves.

'Depending on what industry you choose to focus on (corporate, entertainment, etc.), you may have to start for free,' says one high-flying events organiser who began his own career in this way. 'I've worked on lots of events for free over the years to build my experience and to learn the ropes in as many areas as possible so that I can appeal to a range of potential clients. It's a way to learn co-ordination, planning, management and production.'

Skills-wise, organisation and attention to detail are key. 'What you can't learn, and which I think are imperative,' adds a hospitality guru, 'are personality traits such as caring enough about the event to put everything aside until you've achieved it. Depending on which side(s) of the industry you work on, it's also very helpful to be creative and think outside the box – I believe nothing is impossible; you just have to find a way of making it possible if it doesn't immediately appear to be.'

WORKING LIFE: Jade Fletcher runs Jade Green Events – the planner behind MOBO 18 awards and London 2012 Olympics parties

'The top three craziest events I've worked on are the London Olympics, a classical music concert and the MOBO awards. When you work on these types of events, you have to tread a line of meeting your client's expectations while ensuring the guests' and suppliers' experience is enjoyable and exciting.

There's nothing 9am to 5pm about the events industry, but especially not within entertainment, as creative clients tend to work different hours. There can be a lot of stress involved, too, which is why it's key to develop good relationships with people you trust.

As an events planner, every day is different – you plan your own diary. For example, this week I will be working on a PR launch in-house for one client, sourcing a suit for another for an award ceremony, attending a venue site visit, networking with some suppliers, working on a VIP members' club lunch event, and planning some of next year's events with another of my clients.

Event days are completely different. I try to get on site from as early as possible – usually between 7 and 9am. I can't normally sleep much the night before while I'm running through everything in my head, so I normally stay up late preparing my event box and all the checklists for the next day. Once I arrive, I run through my call sheet to check everyone is running to schedule.

I have a running order for the day, and am constantly assessing where we are on tasks, showing suppliers around as they arrive, and helping if anything is running behind. The last couple of hours before doors open are usually the most stressful, then once doors are open, I'm floating across all areas of the event to ensure the client, guests and staff are happy.

There's nothing better than being able to watch the event in full swing and see how much the guests are enjoying it. Watching a recent concert at the O2 that I organised was one of my favourite moments – it made all the stress of dealing with security, guest lists and VIPs pale into insignificance.

At the end of the night, I check the client and all the staff are happy then start packing down and tidying, checking everything is in its right place to go back to suppliers. For big events, it can be non-stop in the month before, grabbing a few hours' sleep in between in the run-up, and I'll be on my feet for anything between 15 and 20 hours at a time. Once the event is done I then take a couple of days to rest and review the next few projects as well as doing a de-brief for the team and client.

For me, the events and entertainment industries are a lifestyle; the money and working hours can fluctuate, so it's important that you're passionate about the industry and enjoy it.'

WORKING LIFE: hotel owner Philip Clift and his wife Annie built and run the Petite Anse Hotel in Grenada. They became hoteliers after sailing their yacht across the Atlantic, when they decided to buy coastal land and build a hotel on the Caribbean island.

'Around 6.45am, I unlock the office and open up, put the kettle on and have a general overlook of the pool, beach and grounds, before making a pot of tea and retrieving the takings from the bar safe from the previous day.

Then I start checking emails, have relevant meetings with ground staff and other staff as they arrive, and answer the phone. By 8am all the morning shift staff are in. At 9am I walk through to the dining room and chat to guests – we have 11 rooms and two cottages – as they breakfast, making sure there are no problems. I take a bowl of fruit and cereal back to the office and do accounts from the previous day.

Then it's on to a meeting to discuss new arrivals and any issues for the day. By 10am the kitchen will have decided what they need – tomatoes, lettuce, etc. – so I check in with maintenance staff if they need anything then head to [local town] Sauteurs to buy the supplies. I'm back by 11am, and return to the office where I spend the rest of the day dealing with paper-work, accounts, emails, staff meetings, office admin and any new issues.

I go home for a cup of tea and a break around 4.30pm, then I'm back at the hotel at around 6pm for the handover from the receptionist. I usually spend a further hour in the office, making arrangements for any late arrivals and ensuring the appropriate staff are aware of them, before chatting with guests, having dinner at the restaurant and then going home for around 9pm.

This job is definitely 24/7 – a guest rang at 10pm last Tuesday because he was on his way back from a trip to Victoria and got a puncture. What do you do? Get out of bed, dress, and go and pick them up . . . On average I work 60 to 70 hours per week.

The best part of the job is still meeting interesting people, and having positive feedback and seeing guests returning. The worst is being charming to people you really can't stand. You need patience, good communication and organisational skills, flexibility, a good sense of humour, sound DIY knowledge and an ability to multitask, a good smile, a passion for the job, and a supportive, understanding partner to run your own hotel. Oh, and to be able to cook if it's a small place – a hotel must provide good food, so a basic culinary knowledge is essential.

I'd advise anyone interested in hospitality to take a course in hotel management, and get some work experience with a large hotel group. You can also gain insight with magazines like *Environmental Management for Hotels*, *The Caterer* and an online magazine called BigHospitality.co.uk. Most of all, you need to be passionate – running a hotel isn't just a job.'

HUMAN RESOURCES AND RECRUITMENT

AVERAGE STARTING SALARY – £15,000–£19,000

ENTRY POSITION – Assistant administrator

TYPICAL WEEKLY HOURS – 30–40 hours

RECOMMENDED QUALIFICATIONS – Good general education and computer skills. Experience of office work/degree in HR

IF YOU LIKE THIS YOU MIGHT ALSO LIKE ... management consultant, PA, PR

Someone working in human resources (HR) is responsible for hiring and firing staff, developing and instigating workplace policies (such as holiday allowances, contracts, sick leave, etc.), ensuring a company complies with equality, diversity and other employment legislation, trying to keep both staff and management happy, and helping employees to be productive and to meet corporate targets.

In this industry, you'll need to be adept at talking to people, planning and being organised, have management skills, the courage to challenge the status quo, IT and numeracy expertise and commercial acumen, and be a good team-worker who is able to build strong relationships with people.

Big companies often run HR graduate training schemes, whilst smaller firms advertise entry-level and more senior HR roles like any other job. Some graduates and career-changers also move into HR after working in other parts of a company (having other employment experiences can make you better at the job), whilst some work their way up from admin positions. Most HR roles, however, are offered only to graduates; some also embark on a postgraduate qualification in HR or the qualification from the Chartered Institute of Personnel and Development (CIPD), which is often a requirement for senior roles. Some employers sponsor people through their CIPD studies, which can be full-time, part-time, or carried out via distance learning.

Salary-wise, junior HR roles tend to start at around £25,000, rising to about £40,000 with experience; senior HR directors in large firms can earn £80,000 or considerably more for those also working on companies' boards or involved with management, which is a possibility for HR execs since their job is so tied up with the business objectives of most firms.

To learn more about the profession, insiders commend the CIPD website, and the websites *Xpert HR, HR director, Personnel Today* and *HR Magazine*. 'Keep an eye on labour market trends – recruitment agencies and headhunters have useful insights,' adds one recruiter, 'and speak to your friends about their work experiences – what are they telling you about the HR practices in their jobs, good and bad, that you could introduce or learn from?'

Related roles are recruitment consultants and headhunters, whose jobs are to find the right people to work in particular roles. They mostly work for specialist companies where they network and build up pools of candidates, who they can then match with jobs when other firms get in touch wanting a position filled.

Recruiters also write up job ads on behalf of clients, advise on salary and training requirements, headhunt candidates (contacting those currently in a job to try to lure them to a new company), meet up with candidates, interview them, screen them with security and reference checks, and then introduce them to clients. These roles are available to both graduates and non-grads; career-changers with expertise in a particular industry can be much in demand: one top business journalist, for example, recently became a headhunter specialising in finding new bosses for major retailers – she already knew the head honchos from her previous role.

To work in recruitment, you'll need to be great at networking and negotiating, and be confident and self-motivating. The pay is usually heavily tied to commission or performance-related bonuses; starting salary might be £20,000, experienced consultants can earn around £40,000 plus commission, whilst team leaders with at least a decade's experience can be on £60,000 plus bonuses – which can be very generous.

WORKING LIFE: Sarah Hopkins is global HR director of the Financial Times (FT)

'As well as leading the HR team, my role is to ensure the *FT*'s employees contribute to the ongoing success of our business. Primarily I'm focused on talent – acquisition, retention and development – as well as organisational design. Alongside this I also ensure our HR initiatives and processes are simple, efficient and support our people.

My average day goes something like this:

8am: read the *FT* web app whilst on the train, check/respond to emails, check calendar for the day/week, read and check the @FTCareers Twitter feed where we promote our vacancies.

9am: prepare meetings for the week

9.30am: update call with Head of HR for Asia. Talk through projects, update on recruitment activity, talent retention, talk through exit data and any issues/concerns.

10am: year-end performance assessment review with an HR colleague. Discuss their progress against objectives, challenges and achievements and provide feedback on how they can develop.

11am: telephone call to discuss involvement in a panel for employers involved with vocational qualifications – BTEC Nationals in Creative Media Production.

11.30am: catch up with director – update on any issues/concerns, update on success of recent development initiatives and any concerns about people leaving.

1pm: attend board meeting.

2pm: telephone call with headhunter to update on shortlist progress for a senior board position.

2.30pm: work on HR strategy.

3pm: meeting to discuss new cross-company incentive [pay] target.

4pm: update with Managing Editor about progress on pay discussions.

4.30pm: review summary document from an HR colleague about a recent UK employment case which has implications for the calculation of holiday pay based on overtime payments. Consider potential cost impact.

5pm: meeting with union representatives.

5.30pm: home to pick up kids.

8pm: check/respond to emails, organise next day.

I started my HR career as a PA to an HR director. As part of my job, I was dealing with a lot of employee queries and HR administration, such as payroll processing, benefit administration and contracts. My manager then agreed to sponsor my CIPD professional qualification, and then I worked hard, built good relationships in the business and got promoted.

I didn't really know what HR was when I started. But now I really enjoy it: the people I work with are fun and helping the *FT* transition from a print business to a digital business, where two-thirds of our readers are online, has been a great achievement. I enjoy solving people-related problems within the business and meeting new people we might want to hire.

The administration and payroll can be boring, but it's essential we get it right. It's also difficult when we restructure [with redundancies] or make decisions that have an impact on someone's job and life, but we always treat people decently.'

Dream Job: Magician

Magic Circle member Marvin Berglas is a professional magician, the resident magic man at Arsenal Football Club, and also the creator of the Marvin's Magic trick brand.

'I have been lucky enough to combine my passion for magic with my entrepreneurial skills to build up Marvin's Magic, and our tricks and sets are now sold in around 64 countries worldwide. I've also performed magic all around the world for pop stars, politicians and royalty – like Michael Jackson, Tom Cruise and Sir Steve Redgrave.

For me, the variety and unpredictability of my profession make it exciting

– for others that may be daunting. You're waiting for the phone to ring for your next booking and potentially putting you in the limelight in front of an audience wanting to catch you out.

These days I start the day with a workout and then catch up on my emails, Twitter and urgent calls. On Mondays I chair a team meeting at our headquarters – often it's about planning our strategy for our trade shows in Hong Kong, Germany, the UK and the US. A fun part of my job is working with our designers and product development team to come up with our next innovative magic product. Evenings are often spent at a lecture at The Magic Circle.

A good way to start out in magic is by getting a quality box of tricks. Learning a few tricks really well will put you in good stead and you will start amazing people, and create an appetite to keep learning more and more.

There are around a few hundred 'gigging' magicians in Britain, but probably fewer than 100 are making a really decent living through magic. You start making serious money when your clients are asking for you by reputation and name rather than just any magician. Then you dictate your fees, whereas if you are competing on price, there is always someone prepared to do it cheaper.

So, my advice is practise, practise, practise and combine your magic skills with a great personality so that everyone enjoys being entertained rather than fooled.

Magic is a wonderful hobby but a difficult and competitive profession, but if you make it successful you will find it a rewarding, fun and innovative career choice that can take you around the world entertaining and meeting some very interesting people.'

JEWELLER

AVERAGE STARTING SALARY – £16,000

ENTRY POSITION – Trainee

TYPICAL WEEKLY HOURS – 37–40 hours

RECOMMENDED QUALIFICATIONS – GCSEs and experience in retail

IF YOU LIKE THIS YOU MIGHT ALSO LIKE ... fashion, graphic designer, photographer

Behind the glamour of diamond-sparkling jewellery shop windows, jewellers are the people designing necklaces, bracelets and rings and sometimes also running the shops that sell them. Some focus on sketching designs for others to make, whilst some jewellers are also involved in manufacturing their ideas – either in bulk, as for cheaper necklaces and other pieces, or small-scale or one-off (bespoke) designs that usually cost considerably more.

Jewellers working for large retailers – for example, Accessorize or Pandora – will usually have to come up with ideas for seasonal collections that might have to comply with the brand's identity or price-point, usually using computer-aided design or software; they might also have to determine and source materials like precious (or not-so-precious) metals, gems, clasps, etc., make up samples and visit trade shows and manufacturers (sometimes overseas).

Independent, self-employed jewellers who own their own shops or market stalls or sell direct to the public online will usually manage their entire production process – from the creative idea and making the jewellery through to marketing and selling it. Many take commissions from the public, say, a man with an idea for an engagement ring that he wants brought to life. Others create jewellery that is sold to wholesalers and other retailers who will stock the designer's products.

To be a jeweller, no particular formal qualifications are required, but most people take creative courses, HNDs or degrees in jewellery, silversmithing or 3D design; the production skills required will be expertise in mounting gems, casting detail, metal presswork, soldering, polishing, repair work, stone-setting, welding and engraving.

If you end up going down the self-employed route, you'll need business skills to deal with finances and bookkeeping (or to outsource this), whilst web skills can help you to sell online. Famous-name independent jewellers can earn six figures and beyond annually from celebrity clients and spin-off, branded ranges in high-street chains, whilst salaried jewellers at manufacturing firms can expect to start on around £17,000 and go up to £55,000 with experience.

'It completely depends on which facet of the business you go into, but the prospects for earnings, and more importantly job satisfaction and enjoyment, are great,' adds jeweller Theo Fennell (see below).

WORKING LIFE: Theo Fennell started as an apprentice at a family-run silversmiths in Hatton Garden, London, before setting up his own multi-million-pound eponymous jewellery business

'Every day is very different but I always spend some time drawing out ideas and designs and discussing them with the other jewellers in my studio and workshop which, unusually for our trade, are above the showroom in the Fulham Road [in west London]. I will see clients about commissions, and always face some inescapable admin and paperwork. I get a lot of emails all day long, asking me to do things, for help of various kinds, invitations and so on; I try to answer them all pretty quickly as human contact is really important in a business like this.

There are also spontaneous conversations with other members of staff here about projects, ranging from packaging to events and queries about suppliers or accounts. I'm pretty much involved in all areas – if your name is above the door, you always will be.

It's definitely not a 9-to-5 job: many evenings I am out spreading the word and meeting people at events and parties; I'd guess that is where the majority of our clients have come from over the years. I also do some public speaking and some mentoring work, plus there are charity events and shows that take up some evenings. And then weekends are the best time for me to catch up on admin that hasn't been done in normal time, organising mailing lists, etc. It's also often my best time for uninterrupted sketching.

How did I get to this point in my career? Mainly kismet: I left art school and got a job in a silversmiths, and it went from there. I learned as I went along. There were few people to ask then but now there is a wealth of information and the internet so no one has an excuse not to be savvy. Tenacity and belief in what you are making and designing are the key.

There really is no alternative to hard work and commitment. Beyond being artistic, you must really love the trade, the skills and the various mediums used in it. To do well you have to learn about the trade in depth – to love jewellery and/or silver, and its design and traditions. If you're keen to enter the industry, make trips to museums, to shops and, if possible, to workshops to become certain it really is for you. Learn everything you can about the techniques and the materials of the trade from books and websites and people in the trade. My favourite thing about my job remains getting to work with some truly extraordinary people and making things that will last and give pleasure for hundreds of years.'

JOURNALIST

Working in the media offers a seriously varied range of careers: that Welsh guy on the BBC's 10 o'clock news, the people behind the camera filming him, the author of your favourite newspaper column, the person who makes sure it's all spelt correctly, the creator of Buzzfeed's listicles – they're all journalists.

The job can mean making the news, presenting it (on TV, online, radio, or in the press), or commenting on it. A journalist's job is often about taking a complicated or little-known topic and turning it into something interesting. That can mean going undercover, sifting through stats to find an exclusive piece of news, or recording an insightful interview. You might be focused on politics, health, a partic-ular country, education, business, sport, ponies, accountancy . . . There are magazines, papers, websites and TV programmes on almost every topic you can imagine.

So that's the good news: a career in journalism means spending your days writing, speaking, editing or researching a huge range of issues which you'll often be passionate about (although the old-timer writing about rising A level results for the nineteenth year in a row may disagree). You could be flying to South Africa to report on a big trial, interviewing celebrities, or working in Parliament filing reports for TV news.

The bad news? The daily reality of journalism is sitting in your office, in front of a computer (only a handful of people are foreign correspon-dents in Iraq or national newspaper columnists or red carpet reporters). It's also competitive to get into, the pay isn't great and some say its glory days are over. 'You want to get into journalism? Your timing is worse than a booed-off comedian,' says one newspaper editor.

It's true, national and local newspapers plus magazine and TV budgets have been slashed, whilst most online upstarts are operating on a shoestring anyway. Work experience is absolutely key to securing a job – rarely do people find work in the media by replying to a job ad (when ads are even posted – most positions are filled via word of mouth). You need to be on the scene, often working for free, to find out about upcoming jobs and to be able to impress those who matter in the industry.

The working pattern has changed, too. RIP the long boozy lunches the industry was once famous for. ('I used to roll into my desk at 10am,' says one City scribe, 'read the papers until lunch, head down to the Savoy for aperitifs, then settle down for lunch with a chief executive, get enough stories for the week and drink enough for the month, then wobble back to my desk for a whiskey at 5pm to knock out a few words before it was time to go home.') So what's it like to work in journalism today?

There are two types of journalism jobs: editorial and production.

Editorial: In print journalism, editorial includes anyone who writes stories and decides how long or important they should be. In broadcast journalism, editorial workers make the same decisions but work on TV packages or programmes.

Production: In print media, production journalists (or sub-editors) take unedited text or footage, make sure it fits the page, reads well and has no errors, write headlines, and often also find accompanying photos. Traditionally, they faced set deadlines: on a daily newspaper, for example, stories would have to be filed (journo-lingo for written and submitted) by 6pm, before the papers went 'off stone' (it was sent to the printers).

Nowadays almost every part of the media is constantly famished: websites are hungry for content and rolling news means even those on monthly publications or one-off programmes will face constant deadlines. If news breaks, you'll have to write it up or edit it quickly and accurately to get it online fast. For news/reviews/feature websites, journalists are more likely to have to first write, then edit, then upload and find illustrations for their own work.

In broadcast journalism, the two main kinds of jobs are behind the camera or microphone, and in front of them. There are far fewer presenting jobs, and so there's much more competition for them than behind-the-scenes posts such as programme-maker, editor, sound engineer and researcher. But these too are tough to get. Most starting out in TV and radio secure posts as researchers, assistants or runners. (See the lowdown from one runner on page 317.)

A first job as a TV runner or editorial assistant for a paper will likely pay around £15,000, whilst a reporter can expect between £16,000 (for a first job) up to £80,000, depending on seniority. One primetime TV presenter tells me he started on about £18,000 as a researcher in the early 2000s, was on £48,000 as a senior producer and is now on £55,000 – a salary which is supplemented by making speeches and hosting awards. But money is not what motivates most journalists.

Freelance journalists expect to earn £250 to £1200 per newspaper or magazine story, although big glossy magazines will pay more. Senior journalists and editors can receive £100,000 plus, while some newspaper editors are on multi-million-pound packages – but they're the tiny minority.

For training, an accredited journalism course can open doors and be particularly useful for contacts and finding good work experience. The Broadcast Journalism Training Council specialises in radio, TV and online courses, whilst industry figures flag up specialist courses such as the MA in Science Journalism at City University London, or journalism MAs at the University of Lincoln.

As for hours: weekend work is usual, whilst reporters and senior editors often work late, until 10pm or 11pm. Many TV jobs involve shift work. News reporting tends to involve erratic hours but going freelance, working on features or for monthly magazines can mean more regular, and flexible, hours – although there's also the extra stress of an uneven income.

In those freelance and longer-term journalism spheres, the profession can be ideal for those with families, as working from home is a possibility and stories can be written at flexible times. Nowadays few journalists report suffering from gender discrimination either. 'I don't think being a woman has ever held me back,' says *BBC Breakfast* presenter Steph McGovern (see Working Life, below). 'In fact, I think it's helped. There aren't that many women doing business news and especially not ones with a regional accent. It's helped me stand out. '

Traditionally, journalists working in TV and radio were more outgoing and mouthy than those working in print, especially production work. But most of the media industry is currently cost-cutting and 'integrating' and many journalists now work across several platforms – newspaper reporters hosting radio shows, TV anchors writing columns, and production workers also writing or, more rarely, doing presenting work.

WORKING LIFE: Steph McGovern is a presenter on the flagship BBC1 morning show, *BBC Breakfast*.

'My alarm goes off at 3.30am. Before I get out of bed I check my two phones – one's for work, the other for friends and family – to see if anyone has been in touch, especially the *Breakfast* team working overnight who might have made changes to the programme or any breaking news.

I'm live on air from 6am until 9am, interviewing guests and reporting on the business news of the day. Sometimes I do some extra stuff for the BBC

News Channel and online. Then by 10am, I'm thinking about food and the next day's schedule.

From about 2pm until 4pm I try to squeeze in a power nap, unless I am doing extra work, such as making a speech somewhere or recording stuff for Radio 4. After about 5pm I'll check in with the programme to see if everything we have talked about for the following day is going to plan. Then I'll either set off to my next broadcast location (I always have a suitcase packed by the door) or I'll go to an evening business event, or relax at home. I'm in bed by 10pm. During the week I barely stop. But I love it.

The hours are crazy for everyone working in news. It's so unpredictable. You might start the week thinking 'it's going to be a quiet one', but by the end of the week you look back after however many breaking stories and think, 'Wow, where did that go?' You definitely need to get on with your team, because you spend a lot of time with them and it can be very high pressured.

Since the programme I work on is on air 365 days a year, in a sense I'm always at work, but I don't mind that because I love the job and the show so much. I don't work every weekend so my real downtime is normally on Saturdays when I head back up to the North East to my cottage in the middle of nowhere and relax. One of my favourite parts of the job is that, in the years that I've been working as a financial journalist, I have visited over 500 different businesses and seen things you couldn't pay to see. I've been out on an oil rig in the North Sea, watched people landing planes at air traffic control, helped a farmer sell his sheep at an auction, driven a steam train through a village, and met some of the most powerful people in the world – from bosses of the world's biggest companies to prime ministers and US presidents. Oh, and since I'm incredibly nosy, I also love getting to know the news before everyone else.

My advice for anyone keen on journalism is that there are so many routes into the media. Do as much media stuff as you can in your spare time or whilst you're studying. Write a blog, make videos for YouTube, whatever – just start being a journalist so you can prove to people you are genuinely interested in it. Be bold, too; email people you admire in the media and ask for advice. The worst that can happen is that they don't reply.

Also, focus: don't just say to people you want to 'work in the media', think about what it is you want to do within the industry. That will make you stand out from the hundreds of people who email places like the BBC every week and say they 'want to be in the media'.

Lastly, don't give up when you get knockbacks – we've all had them. Determination, ambition, taking risks and treating everyone with the same respect will get you far in journalism.'

WORKING LIFE: Lucy Tobin, newspaper business reporter and feature writer

'Working at the *Evening Standard*, my day starts earlier than at most other newspapers. The paper hits the streets of London in the afternoon, so most reporters are at their desks by 7.30am. Before I get into the office, I'm sniffing out possible stories. I have a scroll through Twitter (I'm addicted) to look for anything interesting on my "patch" – almost all journos have areas they specialise in, and mine include transport, business and personal finance. I read other newspapers on my commute, looking for stories to follow up or things I have missed, and catch up with industry contacts or moles to work on exclusive stories – those that no other newshound has got.

When I get into the office, I talk to my news editor about any stories I think are worth writing about for today's paper, and he tells me what he's spotted. He then makes a list of the top stories and takes them into conference – a meeting of the section editors (sport, news, pictures, business, features, online, comment) and the editor of the paper. They quickly read through the article ideas, discuss what is going to be the top news, and what will be on the front page, then head back to their departments – where we're all given a word length and story list to work through. I usually interview a chief executive: companies post their results, such as movie group Cineworld saying profits rose, but it's only by speaking to them that you get the "colour" – the interesting stuff on why a blockbuster about chocolate saw people spend more at the concession kiosk, for example. I'll often write four or five stories in a morning. Deadline is usually about 11am, when the production editors do their thing fixing mistakes, coming up with headlines and sending the actual pages to the printer (pressing some buttons on the computer).

By midday, the first edition of the paper has been sent and the pace calms down. I usually spend afternoons writing features (longer in-depth articles for the next day or even next week), phoning contacts or PRs to work on new stories, interviewing or writing up interviews. The office is a fun place: there are TVs blaring out news, stacks of cupcakes or free food lying around ("gifts" from PRs), and journalism seems to attract weird characters so someone, somewhere is often having a big argument worth watching.

My favourite thing about the job is that you get to learn about random subjects all the time. It can be hard to find great ideas or new stories, and sometimes the trend you think is amazingly interesting is deemed boring and dismissed by an editor. When pitching you need to be able to sum up your idea in one sentence.

In the office we have 'workies' – work experience people – in most departments. That's how I cracked journalism: I sent endless, often unanswered, emails to journos offering to work for free and eventually the *Sunday Telegraph* and *The Times* said yes. In my view, work experience can often be seriously boring – you might get left forgotten in a corner wishing you were instead enjoying your school/uni holiday – but be confident, go up to people and ask if there's any research you can help with or, and you'll hopefully start getting joint-bylines and start building your portfolio. That's still the best way to crack into this exciting career.'

ODD JOB: Professional mourner, worldwide

They're hired to look glum, cry, and make up the numbers at funerals – it's a big tradition in Asia, but one that's taking off here, too: for £45 an hour, fake mourners can be hired from Rent-a-Mourner, an Essex company which claims demand is soaring.

LAWYER

AVERAGE STARTING SALARY – £23,000–£42,000

ENTRY POSITION – Trainee

TYPICAL WEEKLY HOURS – 37–50 hours

RECOMMENDED QUALIFICATIONS – Qualifying law degree followed by a one-year Legal Practice Course or a non-law degree followed by a Graduate Diploma in Law followed by the LPC to be a solicitor

IF YOU LIKE THIS YOU MIGHT ALSO LIKE . . . banker, HR, surveyor

'How does a lawyer sleep? First he lies on one side, then he lies on the other . . .' Groan. There are a lot of lawyer jokes out there, yet they are the people laughing all the way to the bank once they've landed one of the UK's most popular, secure and lucrative careers.

There are two main types of lawyer:

Solicitors provide legal advice to their clients, on issues ranging from criminal litigation to buying and selling property, wills and estates, divorce and custody cases, mergers and acquisitions and compensation claims. Their responsibilities depend entirely on the nature of the case and the company they work for – major law firms mostly take on larger-scale cases, whilst high-street solicitors are more likely to focus on individual clients and small businesses. But either way, the job will usually involve drafting documents and contracts, negotiating with clients or other parties' lawyers to secure a particular resolution, attending meetings and negotiations, instructing barristers for court cases and preparing papers for court.

Barristers (in England and Wales – the law is different in Scotland where this kind of job is known as an advocate) are the ones who often wear the wigs and gowns. They argue the case of people or organisations in court and are usually hired by solicitors (see above) to represent a court case. Most specialise, for example in criminal or entertainment law, commercial law (on business deals and practices) and family, personal injury and housing law – known as common law. Most barristers work in offices known as 'chambers' alongside other barristers but are self-employed, although some work directly for organisations with a heavy workload for them, such as government departments or major corporations. Job responsibilities usually include managing legal briefs (cases), researching and understanding a wide range of the law, preparing court cases and representing clients there and quizzing witnesses.

To get to either of these roles, you'll need to graduate and then embark on further training. A law graduate has to take the one-year Legal Practice Course, or LPC, and on passing those exams, has to secure a two-year spell applying everything they've just learnt at a law firm, known as a training contract. Graduates who studied subjects other than law at university have to complete a one-year conversion course, followed by either the Graduate Diploma in Law (GDL) or the Common Professional Examination (CPE), then need to secure that same training contract. During these two training years, wannabe solicitors also need to complete the Professional Skills Course. Then, at the end of all that training, they can apply to be a member of the Law Society (as a solicitor).

Barristers, meanwhile, also need to pass the LPC or GDL, and then have to embark on the completion of the one-year (full-time) Bar Professional Training Course and what's called pupillage – a year of practical training with an approved training organisation or chambers, being supervised by an experienced barrister.

If all that training sounds expensive, it is: the average law student will have to pay about £15,000 for the LPC or £10,000 for the GDL, for example. But there are ways to get your studies paid for: barristers can apply for a funded pupillage before starting the BPTC (via the Bar Council's Pupillage Gateway – www.pupillagegateway.com) and look into research scholarships that are available from some Inns of Courts. Most would-be solicitors, meanwhile, try to secure a training contract from a law firm before beginning their studies. Major firms will then pay for the law tuition fees, whilst some also pay a salary to cover the cost of living during the year(s) of study.

To secure funding, though, you'll need top grades and an array of work experience – perhaps including doing pro bono work in student law societies. Competition is fierce, but can be boosted for those who get a place on a law 'vacation scheme'. These run during university holidays and are a good way to network with prospective employers.

Once you start working as a lawyer, the hours may be long: 'since everyone has a target of chargeable hours, there is a culture of working late,' says one City solicitor. 'I don't know any lawyer who leaves bang on 5.30pm and most lawyers don't leave until at least 7pm.' Trainee solicitors usually work in various legal departments to gain experience, so they don't have to specialise immediately.

There are good perks. Experienced barristers' annual earnings can be beyond £1 million, whilst even newly qualified barristers can earn up to £50,000 in their first year. For solicitors, those working in big City firms start on around £40,000; the salary can similarly hit six figures for a partner at a major company. The minimum starting salary recommended by the Law Society is £16,940 for solicitors outside London, and £19,040 for those in the capital. Pay is usually linked to performance and additional contributions such as client responsibilities or supervision and development of other lawyers.

Other perks in big firms may include private healthcare, a decent pension, cheap or free gym membership and plenty of social events both in departments and firm-wide, from sports societies, to drinks and opportunities to get involved with charity work.

There are a lot of women in law but in general, looking at private practice in particular, 'the more senior the role, the fewer women there are,' says one high-flying female. 'Managing the demands of a job in a major law firm with the demands of a family life – which society still mainly regards as the "woman's role" – is a major challenge. Law firms are starting to move towards more flexible working arrangements but they are far from ideal and you see a lot of women moving to in-house roles within a few years of qualifying.'

Skills-wise, precision, brevity and a first-rate understanding of the law are crucial for lawyers.

Other legal jobs include working as a barrister's clerk, which involves running the business activities of a barrister's chambers. The job demands knowledge about the workings of a court and the specialisms of that particular chambers, and legal know-how as well as excellent networking, organisational and teamwork skills.

Legal executives, meanwhile, face a similar level of training as solicitors in their particular area of focus (e.g. conveyancing – the legal side of buying and selling property, probate – dealing with wills and inheritance tax, family law, civil litigation – dealing with disputes between people, criminal law or corporate law), and access the job via one of the training routes offered by the Chartered Institute of Legal Executives.

Working for solicitors, **legal secretaries** provide admin support for lawyers and legal executives, such as preparing court forms and statements, dealing with fees and even attending court with lawyers. The salary range is about £16,000 to £40,000 for highly experienced legal secretaries in top firms. Another role is that of a **paralegal**, who takes on some of a solicitor's jobs, mostly the administrative and legal secretarial tasks and some research.

THE LOWDOWN: a new trainee solicitor at one of the big five London law firms, known as the Magic Circle

'My day is so unpredictable; as a trainee, you basically do what you're told, and when you arrive on a Monday morning it's impossible to know whether you'll still be at your desk at 2am or home by 7pm. Client deadlines are not always managed well by partners – they'll turn up at the office at 4pm after a day in court or meetings and demand you complete a task immediately, even though it can take hours and hours.

As for the actual work, before qualifying as a solicitor you do a range of what are called seats, or departments. In all of them, though, trainees get the dogsbody work – bundling (creating bundles of files for meetings or court), filling in tedious forms, drafting board minutes, photocopying and finding particular pages in books for more senior people.

The level of responsibility differs; in my first seat I was given a bunch of files and they were mine to work on: I checked absolutely every email with my superiors but I had ownership over the files. To begin with that feels scary, but as with every six-month seat, as you come to the end of it you really begin to feel comfortable and more on top of things.

Some departments and firms treat trainees with respect, spending time educating and mentoring you, but to others you are the "trainee" – basically code for doing all the crap that no one else wants to do. In my experience, though, enthusiasm goes a long way – a positive attitude and willingness to help will get you some good quality work.

Your working day is also impacted by the kind of work you do – often, transactional (mergers and acquisition) lawyers face extremely long hours when they're working on a deal, but that's counterbalanced by relative quiet when there is no deal in play. The US firms also have notoriously gruelling hours, many having 2,000-hours-a-year targets.

A few times I was still in the office at 4am, and then having to be in the office early the next day (just a few hours later), but it's more the weeks on end where you're leaving at 10pm, 11pm or 12am that wear you down.

My favourite parts of the job are attending court and the adrenaline rush that comes with being part of a case that might define the direction of the law in the future. I get a thrill from playing a part in a deal which you know may change the nature or shape of a big industry. There's also some intellectual satisfaction, whether from researching the law and coming up with a good argument for your client, or developing a litigation strategy. Working in law you are constantly learning.

Even after all the student law training and exams, a training contract is hard – it is basically a two-year-long interview. You can feel under pressure to impress everyone all the time, you can never turn down work, no matter how many hours you already spend in the office, just because you need to secure a job at the end of the two years of training. That is quite tough, and comes with a natural paranoia whereby you always feel watched and judged.'

WORKING LIFE: Richard West is a partner at international law firm Kennedys

'I have never had a boring day at the office. It can be very hard work – on an average week I put in 70 hours – but law is a rewarding career.

I arrive at the office between 7.30am and 8am. My days broadly fall into three parts – running my own cases, managing about 40 lawyers on a day-to-day basis and acting as a supervisor on some of their cases, and being a member of Kennedys Board, responsible for leading on the strategy for a large part of the firm. Plus I also have to stay well briefed on current legal developments, engage with clients and develop new lines of business.

Usually I devote the 9-to-5 part of any day to lawyering and managing the team – I specialise in "catastrophic injury" cases, defending such matters for insurers, so each case requires considerable thought and attention. I'll generally see clients after normal office hours but at least twice a week I try to get home in time to see my children before they go to bed. I'll usually then work for a couple for hours in the evening. I'm always in touch with the office, including during holidays.

Law today is really competitive; in my opinion there are too many law graduates going through law school and then competing for a relatively small number of training contracts. For those interested in applying, I'd recommend a thirst for current affairs and legal developments (there have been many in recent years), and reading a quality newspaper. When I interview candidates, I am looking to speak to a young person who has confidence – perhaps developed from working at weekends and during holiday periods – and who is able to express an opinion and speak fluently.'

ODD JOB: Witch, UK

The winning candidate for the £50,000-a-year job of witch at Wookey Hole Caves beat dozens of hopefuls by impressing employers with her cackle. The tourist attraction in Somerset has had a live-in witch for more than a decade; her job is mainly strolling around dressed as a hag so visitors can see what life was like in the Dark Ages.

LIFE COACH

AVERAGE STARTING SALARY – £18,000 (client numbers dependent)
ENTRY POSITION – life coach
TYPICAL WEEKLY HOURS – variable
RECOMMENDED QUALIFICATIONS – unregulated, so no set qualifications; most clients like to see a postgraduate award in coaching or neuro-linguistic programming
IF YOU LIKE THIS YOU MIGHT ALSO LIKE . . . hospitality and events management consultant, social worker

Britons have a new obsession with self-improvement, and the industry that's reaped the rewards of that drive is life coaching. Some coaches specialise in helping people to have a plan for their career, fitness, fashion, relationships or health, while others focus on corporate work, with a contract to help staff in an entire company, for example. The Life Coach Director says the job involves 'helping and empowering others to make, meet and exceed personal and professional goals – including excelling in the workplace, becoming happy and fulfilled in the home, exploring the self and the world, and achieving ambitions. By harnessing specialist techniques based on core psychological principles and natural intuition, life coaches provide clients with the tools to confidently face difficult situations, push past emotional barriers and eventually view life with fresh, hopeful and enlightened eyes'.

It's not a regulated industry, so whilst lots of colleges, institutions and some universities run training courses in both coaching and the related subject neuro-linguistic programming (NLP), which focuses on breaking people's behaviour patterns, you'll need to do some research to make sure yours is respectable. Look at testimonials, ask practising life coaches for recommendations, check the course includes some supervised work with a practising life coach, and offers advice, if you need it, on setting up a business as well as opportunities for continuing professional development.

Look at those courses accredited by organisations such as the International Coach Federation, and pick one that suits you – some are distance learning, online courses; some are face-to-face, some run for a term or more and others are intense, all-in-a-weekend sessions.

Perhaps even more important, though, are the personal skills you need to be a coach: empathy, great listening and analysis skills, patience and being a 'people person' – if you're the kind of person to whom random bods that you meet at the gym start pouring out their life stories, you might be on the right track. Some clients stay with their coaches from months, or even years, whilst others want a blitz of a few sessions.

Sessions generally involve talking to clients about their problems/situation/what they want a strategy for, talking about their background, aims and ambitions, setting goals for change and helping the client to work out how to achieve those changes, then helping them to stay motivated and on track.

Money-wise, it really depends on your level of experience, specialism and, most of all, number of clients. Life coaches are self-employed, and generally run sessions lasting between 30 minutes and one hour, charging between £30 and £60 a pop, although some top corporate coaches earn up to £400 for sessions. Others offer packages, such as a £300 deal including a set number of face-to-face sessions, and top-up emails and phone calls. Many coaches work from home, although others may rent space in a clinic or office building.

WORKING LIFE: Oliver Medill is a former actor-turned-life coach who has co-founded the Leadership and Change Consultancy, which works with some of the biggest companies across Europe

'A career in coaching is a serious undertaking. Many people believe that they can "do a bit of coaching" and blend it with other jobs as well. But if it's worth doing, you might as well do it properly. There are many different approaches and styles; I'd recommend consulting the life-coaching directory (www.lifecoach-directory.org.uk) for a comprehensive overview.

Because the coaching industry is a relatively new one, and guidelines have not been rigorously enforced to date, there are loads of charlatans out there without qualifications who have designed themselves a business card and call themselves life coaches, without any expertise at all. Again, the directory can help with some choices about qualifications. I gained an NLP (Neuro-Linguistic Programming) qualification, then spent a year gaining my coaching qualification on top. I chose to specialise in the business end of coaching, and so took a qualification in this area, too.

My clients are mainly senior executives, company owners and High Net Worth individuals, although I also do pro-bono work.

My average day is a combination of coaching sessions and new business development – aka telephoning old contacts, writing blogs and writing and giving speeches at networking events, plus travel to and from appointments and, in the case of foreign engagements, longer travel!

The best parts of a job are the "breakthrough" moments for a client, when they realise what they are capable of and discover "a way through" a situation. As for the bad parts – sorry to sound cheesy, but there aren't any! I suppose the endless air travel could be a challenge for some, but I use it to work, write and relax.

To be a great life coach involves endless practice, not just qualifications. Practise at any chance you get and look for opportunities to hone your skills. Once you've decided on a business model, you need to work on growing a client base – coaching is a business, and a good coach needs to be proactive about finding clients.

Word of mouth obviously is key, but a website is easy to build and provides a brilliant focal point for all marketing activity. The more testimonials you can get on there – from as impressive a client base as you can – the better.'

Dream Job: Celebrity

It's one of the most-wanted careers around – seems like everyone wants to hit the fame jackpot and score a career that involves flying around the world in private jets to swish parties. Only thing is, the very nature of fame is that it's pretty exclusive, so not many people can have the job – and those that do point out that all is not as it seems.

You can forget about incognito trips to Tesco and you should expect every single one of your exes to sell a story about you – true or not. Then there's the fact that thousands of Brit wannabes fail to find success every year . . . None of these 'career routes' are recommended, but if you're still desperate to be a celeb, how can you go about it?

Reality TV show

You'll have to leave your dignity at the door of a *Big Brother* house, *X Factor* audition or *Apprentice* office – and it won't be easy to get in there. But there are myriad reality shows on TV nowadays, so if you apply to enough of them, you might just scoop a place. Then you've got to be stupid/arrogant/annoying enough to capture the eyes of the media. And if all works out well, you too could be being paid to promote paint/biscuits/teapots in the not-too-distant future.

Date a famous person

If you're good at schmoozing your way into top parties or exclusive clubs, this might be the quickest route to fame. Simply track down a starlet and wait for them to declare their undying love . . . It worked for singer Rita Ora, who first grew famous for dating Kim Kardashian's little bro Rob, then was snapped 'stepping out', as the *Daily Mail* puts it, with a string of others including Calvin Harris and David Beckham's best mate Dave Gardner.

Make a sex tape

Controversial, this one, but for an overnight splash the sex tape helped make a millionaire of Kim Kardashian and Paris Hilton, the latter via her home video, uh, 'One Night In Paris'.

Release a single/hit YouTube video

Easier said than done, since there are approximately a gazillion videos languishing unwatched on YouTube and more singles trying to enter the charts than camels in the desert. But if you've got a simply amazing talent that will stand out from the crowd, or are so bad it hurts and don't mind becoming a national laughing stock, get yourself out there – then start spreading the word via social media.

WORKING LIFE: Stella English was thrust into the celebrity limelight when she won the BBC hit *The Apprentice*. English was given a £100,000 job with Lord Sugar's company then unsuccessfully sued Sugar for constructive dismissal, saying she was treated as 'an overpaid lackey'.

'Becoming a celebrity very fast was a surreal experience. I can't say that I enjoy or dislike "fame" one way or another. But generally people are very kind. Still, though, to kids who say they "want to be a celebrity" I say celebrity itself is pretty meaningless. You need to have something to back it up. Much better to be the best at something than be famous for fame's sake. I'm not really in a position to recommend qualifications as I left school without any and ended up working in banking. Just focus on a trade and set yourself a target in terms of what role you want. Work your socks off, listen and align yourselves with those who have already done it who can pass on wisdom and knowledge.

Sometimes I get invited to lovely events, which are fun, and other times

I'm knee deep in homework and the weekly food shop deliveries. That's the life of a working mum. Both before and after *The Apprentice*, I spent years and years working 12- or 14-hour days. I spent many years slogging away on trading floors working long hours, so by the time I entered *The Apprentice* I had been working hard for almost 15 years. A lot of blood, sweat and tears finally paid off.

I would follow the same career path again; I've had a varied and interesting career working with some of the best business minds in the world, from being a legal assistant to the Prime Minister's brother to head of business management of a trading floor and being a presenter on [Sky TV show] *CrowdBoxTV*. I wouldn't change it. I've had the time of my life and it's served me well.'

MANAGEMENT CONSULTANT

AVERAGE STARTING SALARY – £30,000–£40,000

ENTRY POSITION – graduate scheme

TYPICAL WEEKLY HOURS – 50

RECOMMENDED QUALIFICATIONS – 2:1 at degree level

IF YOU LIKE THIS YOU MIGHT ALSO LIKE . . . HR, life coach, actuary

It's another of those mind-boggling jobs; the kind where someone at a party tells you they're a management consultant and you secretly wonder, 'Okay, so what on earth do you do?'

Management consultants are usually hired by other companies to be the 'fresh pair of eyes' to sort out a problem or help a company grow. They might be brought in to organise a new corporate strategy, or implement major IT or HR changes, or help a company to turn around a struggling division.

There are generally two kinds of management consultant firms: major international ones (such as Accenture, BCG, McKinsey or Bain & Co) with thousands of staff, or smaller boutique firms with fewer than 100. The major ones generally tackle all kinds of work and are hired for specific projects – several were hired to work on the London 2012 Olympics and they'll always be running the behind-the-scenes of big music and live events too – whilst some focus on particular areas, such as HR, IT or finance.

In all kinds of consultancies, though, entry-level graduates will generally be very well paid and well worked. The hours are long, and many management consultants have to do lots of travel and even spend swathes of time living in hotels near client sites. On the flipside, many management consultants get to travel the world (in style) and have great in-work training opportunities.

At an entry level, grads might be involved in pulling together data (either via spreadsheets and models, or interviewing clients, staff, etc.), running focus groups, or making presentations. But some people enter the industry after gaining experience in other roles – career-changers who have proved their capability in industry are often welcomed by consulting firms.

Skills-wise, 'you'll need tenacity, creativity, amicability and wizardry in Microsoft Excel – and a really flexible mindset,' says one experienced management consultant. 'You're expected to know all of the answers, but you never will, and you will continuously face challenges that you've never seen before. Apply your experience and expand it to your current problem set and you will be successful.' Candidates generally also need at least a 2:1 in a good undergraduate degree, and will face a gruelling application process, usually including a written application, online aptitude tests, one or more interviews and even day-long assessment centre sessions.

For that, pay packages are generous: though they depend on the size and location of the consultancy firm, new starters can be on £40,000 in a large firm or £30,000 in a smaller one, rising to double that within five years. Senior partners in firms can pocket seven-figure salaries, although the brutal working hours mean many people use management consultancy as a stepping stone to launch their career and get a good grounding in business practices.

WORKING LIFE: Adam Rhino* is a management consultant at a major international firm

'There's a lot of travel involved in management consultancy – flying or training out on a Monday and returning home Thursday afternoon or evening. Most people who haven't yet been made a partner spend a month or two at a client site. If you have a good team, are single, or both, that's not so bad as you can get to know a city or town. But otherwise, it's difficult to be away so frequently.

Working up to 60 hours a week is a good week – during busy times you could hit 40 hours by Wednesday. So anyone thinking about pursuing this career should learn how to budget their personal time efficiently.

Since you spend a lot of time with your colleagues, it's lucky that in most MC firms there's not too much of a competitive environment in the office. Good teams know how to be competitive with other firms to win work, rather than with peers to get ahead. The best team rises to the top, of course, but it's a lot harder when you try to do everything on your own. Don't get me wrong, I run into my fair share of jerks. And it's an "up or out"

---

* *name changed for anonymity*

environment – if you're not doing well, you won't be kept on. But most people I know are team players and, more importantly, intellectually stimulating to be around.

Consulting firms also offer phenomenal benefits; some re-pay your university fees, there's great pay, gym membership, pension, etc. on top of working with incredibly smart people. Travelling internationally for work is sometimes pretty fun, too, in small doses. The worst parts of the job are being away from family, expense reports and logging your time. There's nothing more demotivating than having a great week solving your client's toughest problems, then realizing that you have to type out all of your travel expenses for the past two weeks.

My top tip for wannabe consultants is to be prepared to make the commitment, but don't sacrifice who you are. You can be successful in management consulting without selling yourself to the firm. They're hiring you for who you are, and the most successful consultants that I've met (and who have been made partner) have a certain factor to them that makes them stand out to clients and management. If you work hard, trust your abilities and instincts and bring that differentiator, you'll do well in the field.'

MILITARY CAREERS

AVERAGE STARTING SALARY – £16,000–£24,000

ENTRY POSITION – Officer Cadet

TYPICAL WEEKLY HOURS – Variable

RECOMMENDED QUALIFICATIONS – Nationality and residency requirements. Be between 18 and 26 years old. Full medical exam. Have at least 7 GCSEs including English, maths and a science or foreign language. 2 A levels or equivalent

IF YOU LIKE THIS YOU MIGHT ALSO LIKE . . . firefighter, police officer, hospitality and events

Camouflage, excitement, travel, injuries, risks and camaraderie: just some of the adjectives associated with working for a nation's armed forces. Every year, thousands of people sign up to the Army, Royal Air Force and Royal Navy. The Army alone hires young men and women for 200 different roles every year, from electronic warfare operator to bricklayer, aircraft technician to frontline soldier. The majority of recruits love their job: excitement, a feeling of national pride, plus great benefits and good pay were all cited as reasons why soldiers give their job a 64 per cent satisfaction rating compared to the 50 per cent provided by Britain's civilian workforce.

That's not to ignore the fact that military work can clearly be very dangerous, although the risks obviously depend on whether the country is involved in conflict and where you're deployed. The most dangerous job in the Army is currently that of infantry rifleman; according to the Ministry of Defence, the role has a risk of death or injury 12 times higher than that of any other army employee.

The jobs on offer can range from the high-profile combat role of the soldier to engineering, intelligence, IT, finance, human resources, pilot (Prince William served in the RAF with his final posting as a Search and Rescue Pilot) and medical posts: the Army points out that most of its roles aren't, for the majority of the time, about marching and living out in the field. Soldiers generally work normal hours in jobs that are similar to the ones found in civilian life. Except for a few frontline combat roles, women have access to the same jobs, pay, training and promotion as men in the military.

The key skills traditionally required include high morale, courage, fitness, intelligence, physical courage, determination, self-discipline, confidence, imagination, a sense of humour and an ability to relate to others. A senior army officer says, after three decades in the job, that the pros are the experiences of travelling the world, helping people, being part of a close-knit team, sharing extraordinary adventures with your friends, the challenges conquered and the unending variety. You're given free accommodation, too. 'The travel is good, and pay's not bad, and you'll have the best company car in the world if you drive a Challenger 2 Main Battle Tank or fly an Apache Attack Helicopter. Oh, and you don't have to choose what to wear every day . . .'

But, he warns, 'there are times when you're tired, wet and cold in a place you don't want to be, away from your family, but you still need to keep going. Now and again you may not agree with your superiors but you still have to get on with it. There are major challenges – like the 40°C-plus temperature in Iraq and Afghanistan whilst you're carrying heavy equipment with the possibility of being blown up or shot. It's no fun, although once it starts it's very exciting. You'll be wet through whilst training on the plains of Germany in autumn or trying to ski against a blizzard whilst towing a sled when it's -25°C. It may not seem enjoyable at the time, but with all these things you look back with a sense of satisfaction and achievement.'

You'll need have to have a background check to sign up: the Armed Forces, for example, say that 'no one should be employed who is, or has been, involved in, or associated with, any of the following activities: espionage, terrorism, sabotage or actions intended to overthrow or undermine parliamentary democracy by political, industrial or violent means.' But it does accept people who have criminal records. You'll also need to be physically fit, between the ages of 16 and 33 to join as a soldier or private (or 18 to enrol as an officer), meet some nationality requirements and pass a physical examination. The role of private does not require specific academic qualifications, but officers need five GCSEs grade A to C, including English, maths and a science or modern languages, plus two A levels (or their equivalent); there's a three-day selection test, and successful applicants then face a year-long course at Sandhurst, the Royal Military Academy. Across the services, many officers are already graduates. You can find out more about the requirements of each part of the military at your local Armed Forces Careers Office. Women can join the Army in 70 per cent of roles, including all of its parts bar frontline combat roles in the Infantry, Household Cavalry or Royal Armoured Corps.

Pay is influenced by the 'X factor' guarantee – the promise that military workers will earn more than a comparable civilian. The starting salary across the military disciplines is about £14,000 a year, rising to £17,000 for trained soldiers and £30,000 plus for a sergeant; those in the highest ranks can earn as much as £100,000.

Beyond the obvious risks of life in the military, the career progression is one of the steadiest around: the rise is clear from junior officer to middle manager (major), but it requires effort to get above that and into the senior ranking area. Most people spend one to two years as a 2nd Lieutenant or Lieutenant, three to five as a Captain, five to ten as a Major, between two and ten years as a Lieutenant Colonel or Colonel, and the same number as a Brigadier and then as a General.

If you're keen on the career, research which Regiment or Corps does what, and follow what you enjoy doing. Anyone aged 12 to 16 could join the nearly-50,000 members of the Army Cadets, or the Combined Cadet Force (CCF), the Sea Cadet Corps, and the Air Training Corps. Or find somebody you know who has been, or is still, serving and talk to them about their experiences.

WORKING LIFE: an Army operations soldier and her commander talk through their average day

- 0630 hours: alarm, dress in PT kit, check personal email whilst having light breakfast at home or in Officers' Mess.
- 0715 hours: personal training – normally held twice a week, lasting up to an hour. Anything from a basic run to an assault course, circuit session, combat PT.
- 0830 hours: formation parade. The squadron commander or another senior figure allocates individuals or teams to tasks – it could be vehicle or weapons maintenance, training lectures on the law of armed conflict or marksmanship, language courses or radio procedures for calling in aircraft or attack helicopters to prosecute a target.
- Commander: at this time I would normally go to my office to deal with work emails, perhaps covering representatives on parades, training exercises with other units, or lectures (giving and receiving). Twice a year, I have to write annual reports (about 500 words) on every soldier (up to 120 individuals).
- 1230 hours: lunch; normally one hour taken in either the all-ranks restaurant or the appropriate Mess, but increasingly some eat at their desks or use the break to do some personal physical training in the gym or go for a run.
- 1330 hours: back to work.
- Commander: I have meetings in Regimental Headquarters or another higher formation to discuss promotion boards, health and fitness boards, equipment boards, training boards, discipline boards, etc. – basically, discussing your soldiers and trying to ensure they are trained, fit, healthy, educated and motivated to carry out their roles. From

these meetings you will likely pick up some tasks that require your action.

- 1500 hours: NAAFI – tea or coffee break.
- Commander: at 1530 hours I would try to have a meeting with all my heads of department, and then they would be ready to pass on any messages to the soldiers before they finish work for the day, perhaps covering planning for whatever our next major event may be: parade, training exercise, overseas deployment, sports competition, adventure training opportunity, etc . . .
- 1700 hours: troops dismissed for the day, having read orders that are passed on verbally and printed on the unit notice board. Some troops may have duties, such as guarding the camp, extra training or revision for a forthcoming course. For a commander, there's more work to do – emails to answer, reports to write, plans to make.
- Commander: I get home between 1800 and 1900 hours. I'll then go for a run if I haven't had the chance to do any physical exercise that day.

There may be a function, dinner night or sports event in the evening, although there are a maximum number of 'nights out of bed' and you can't exceed that unless you are deployed on overseas operations. Most of the time your evenings and weekends are your own to do with as you wish. If you are single and live on barracks you spend the majority of this time with your friends and mates of the same unit and socialise with them.

Of course, when you are on operations or training exercises, the schedule is very different – it's 24 hours a day. But at regimental duty in barracks or as a staff officer in a headquarters, most work between 7 and 10 hours a day.

An example of a battery commander's career path

- 1 year at Royal Military Academy, Sandhurst, training to become an Army Officer.
- 3 months at the Royal School of Artillery to train as a specialist Royal Artillery officer.
- 2 years as 2nd Lieutenant based in Germany. Deploying to the first Gulf War.
- 4 years as a Lieutenant based in Germany, Canada and UK. Plus training in Canada, Poland, UK, Germany and France. Deploying to Northern Ireland on Operation BANNER.
- 1 year training to be a helicopter pilot in the UK.
- 6 years as a Captain based in Germany and UK. Training in Canada, America, Poland, UK, Turkey, Norway and Germany. Deploying to the Former Republic of Yugoslavia twice on Operation GRAPPLE as a United Nations observer.
- 1 year at the UK Defence Academy studying for my master's degree.
- 10 years as a Major based in UK, Germany and Australia. Training throughout the world. Deploying to Afghanistan on Operation HERRICK.

MUSICIAN

AVERAGE STARTING SALARY – Variable, £100–£150/day in an orchestra; £50–£100 for a set as a DJ

ENTRY POSITION – Orchestra extra, DJ, musician

TYPICAL WEEKLY HOURS – Variable

RECOMMENDED QUALIFICATIONS – Diploma in chosen instrument/Degree from conservatoire

IF YOU LIKE THIS YOU MIGHT ALSO LIKE … actor, hospitality and events, teacher

Be under no illusions: however talented you are, music is a tough industry to crack. Bar Justin Bieber and One Direction, you'll struggle to find many successful names in pop music who didn't have other jobs first. Kurt Cobain was a floor-sweeping caretaker before *Nevermind* took off; Ozzy Osbourne was a trainee plumber; Mick Jagger was a porter in a psychiatric hospital. Classical music requires more formal training, but it's no less impenetrable once you've qualified. Any artist you can think of, whether pop, classical, dance or DJ, almost certainly put in a (probably lengthy) spell in a dead-end job whilst sending off demos or spending nights in someone's dad's shed turning their friends-since-we-were-12 band into a real one. And many have put in years of training and study, too. Most classically trained musicians and singers will have spent years at university, college or a conservatoire before scoring a full-time role in an orchestra, band, back-up group, opera company, musical theatre, etc. But sadly the massively competitive nature of the music industry means that many wannabes can never support themselves financially with their instrument or talent and have to take on other jobs on the side. Trained musicians often branch out into teaching, either in schools or specialist colleges or individual tuition work, to boost their income; it's also a job that can fit alongside evening/weekend gigs or performances.

You'll definitely need to be dedicated, practising for hours each day, going to endless auditions, performing in concerts – sometimes for free, for a profile-boost or opportunity to catch an agent/producer/music bigwig's eye – and participating in recording sessions, doing lots of admin to arrange payment, perhaps filing tax returns, travelling around the country and even the world, organising social media and other self-promotion work, making recordings and getting them online and into stores, liaising with venues, and more. Musicians also face long, late and often unsociable working hours, and are often asked to spend time away from home.

Pay-wise, what a musician makes is utterly dependent on how successful they are and the nature of their job. The Incorporated Society of Musicians, which represents all kinds of musicians, says conductors and solo instrumentalists receive about £150 per engagement, orchestral players pocket about £115 for the same, solo singers can expect £250 and ensemble singers around £150 – although some pay extra for rehearsals. It also found organists receive £25 to £56 an hour and music teachers receive about £30 an hour. The Musicians' Union says that for casual engagements for groups performing in pubs and clubs lasting up to 3 hours, performers should be paid £111, and that freelancers playing for orchestras should receive between £92 and £161 per performance, depending on their experience and aptitude.

Other types of earnings include a normal salary – which is paid by some theatres and orchestras who employ musicians – and royalties for those who write or publish music. You can find out more from the group PRS for Music (prsformusic.com).

WORKING LIFE: David Lale is a cellist with the London Philharmonic Orchestra, has a chamber and solo career and has toured with Leona Lewis

'I've played the cello all my life, but it was only when I was at university doing an arts degree that I realised I wanted to make a full-time career out of music. I went on to do a postgraduate degree in music, which is an unusual route – most people go straight into an undergraduate degree at a music college or school (like Yehudi Menuhin, Purcell or Chetham's). Starting young is great, though there is an increased chance of burnout – practising 8 to 9 hours a day, you can get quite fed up.

Once you're qualified, the real dogfight starts as you all try to get experience. The main route to getting an orchestra job is to arrange to have a lesson or play with the principal of an orchestra or section (e.g. the principal cello of BBC Symphony Orchestra), and if they like how you play they'll put you on the extras' list, which is the mainstay of the freelance world – if you're on this list, when one of their regulars is ill or they need extra cellos for a concert, they call you. I did this for six years. Everything takes a long time in this industry. You can't be impatient.

Once you're more experienced you can begin to apply for vacancies in orchestras directly and do auditions. These opportunities are few and far between and hundreds of people will apply for a single position. Given you're auditioning for a seat for life, the process is taken very seriously and can take a long time. The audition for my current seat took me four years! Given these odds, you will spend a lot of time being unsuccessful but, while they are laborious and stressful, going to auditions is great experience; you make contacts and build up your CV. The more experience you have of playing live, in front of an audience and under pressure, the better you get.

My other advice would be to pay for a diary service like Morgensterns or MAS, as you can pick up short-notice work through them. And maybe don't learn the flute – the maths is against you. Remember an orchestra is made up of around 30 violinists, 12 violas, 10 cellos but just two flutes!

The worst part of being a classical musician is the terrible pay, especially given the training you have to go through and the costs you incur (my cello cost £60,000 and that's considered cheap!). On the other hand, it's still the best job in the world! The camaraderie of an orchestra is wonderful and I'm getting paid for doing something that I'd be doing anyway.'

WORKING LIFE: Laura Jean Marsh is a resident DJ at east London bar Steam and Rye, as well as being a model; she is signed with the Sauce DJs agency

'I got into DJing when I first moved to London from Bath, aged 18, and started a club night with a friend. We had lots of up-and-coming bands and a fancy dress theme every week, and used to play our own records in between the acts to save money, so I basically learnt to DJ by default. We were then featured in *Vogue*, *ID*, *NME* and *Time Out* magazines as London's finest party-starters! Modelling came later on when I was scouted in my early 20s.

The key skill in being a good DJ is being able to read a crowd – you're there to give them a good time, not preach what you like or what you think they should be partying to. You have to do lots of prep for each gig and bring more music than you need so you can switch it up if you need to.

Also, get a clear brief on what the organisers or club promoters want, and stay in touch with them, so you're all happy and on the same page. Technically, being good at mixing and running a smooth set just comes with lots of practice. I go onto autopilot for hours sometimes, knowing what tracks mix well together – my hands have a life of their own.

Sometimes when I'm tired and I've had a long day, I just want to crawl into bed and watch a movie, rather than leave the house in some crazy dress at 9pm to go to work. But there's no better feeling than watching a crowd go crazy jumping around to your set.

There are perks, too – some events are kind enough to give you cool stuff as a "thank you". I was given a pair of sunglasses from Miu Miu and an outfit from Chloé when I played at their store recently. It's also really fun to play abroad – my favourite places to play out of the UK are Milan and Rome.

When I started out I was happy to take any fee for a set; £20 for a few hours was quite common, plus free drinks. In those days I was more interested in partying anyway. Experience will get you everywhere, so it's better to take any gigs you can in the early stages. Now I'm lucky to earn a lot more than that for a set but I do "mates' rates" as well – being flexible to people's budgets is a good business skill as you can get more work from them in the future.

Anyone wanting to get into DJing should shadow a DJ for a while, go to their gigs and watch what they do, then jump on to practise a bit, if they let you. Bring a few mixes of your favourite party music, but obviously think of the crowd. Practising in your bedroom is all very well but decks are expensive and DJing in the real world is completely different. Just get yourself out there! You'll make tonnes of mistakes at first; don't freak out if you have any skips or gaps or do a bad mix: as soon as you drop another big tune the crowd will immediately forgive you.'

Dream Job: Cake tester

Will Torrent, 28, is pastry chef consultant at Waitrose

'I always knew I wanted to be a chef, and securing work experience at Heston Blumenthal's The Fat Duck when I was 15 certainly cemented that desire. However, it was only when I was training at the University of West London that I really discovered my passion for all things sweet and decided to specialise in pastry. I went from my training into a global skills competition called WorldSkills, competing in Japan as the UK representative in pastry against the rest of the world. From there, I started work at a small, Swiss-style patisserie to knuckle down and learn the trade. Then the opportunity arose to meet the then Executive Chef of Waitrose to work on one specific project. Nearly four years later, I am still here, working on many different aspects of Waitrose's sweet range, from chilled and frozen desserts to confectionery and bakery.

My day normally starts with a team meeting and then on to tastings with product developers or suppliers, and then some development on recipes and new ideas. As a team of chefs, we get to play with a lot of recipes. We always do this with a goal in mind: thinking about how we can convert one kitchen dish or recipe into a product that will appear on hundreds of shop shelves.

I eat a lot of cake! Anything sweet that is being developed has to be tried and tested by my team. We often visit our cake suppliers where we taste cake all day, including many different variants of each recipe, to ensure we find the best. But I don't get fat because we don't eat everything we try; quite often, we taste a product and then spit it out into a cup, just like you would with wine. Otherwise, our sugar and cholesterol levels would go through the roof – as would my waistline!

I would definitely recommend my job as a career; the hospitality industry itself has so many different avenues to pursue and is never boring. Having had the chance to work in restaurants and hotels, I love the continual changing face of retail and product development. You work with so many different people and suppliers, which means you're always on your toes.'

NURSE

AVERAGE STARTING SALARY – £21,000–£28,000

ENTRY POSITION – Nurse

TYPICAL WEEKLY HOURS – 37 hours and overtime

RECOMMENDED QUALIFICATIONS – Nursing degree and 2 years' post-qualifying experience

IF YOU LIKE THIS YOU MIGHT ALSO LIKE . . . paramedic, physio, social worker

Nurses form the largest group of staff in the NHS, which itself is Britain's biggest employer, and the fourth-biggest in the world (only the Chinese People's Liberation Army, the Walmart supermarket chain and Indian Railways directly employ more people). So it's safe to say that there is both a serious demand for nurses in the UK and a huge variety of roles.

Those doing the job warn it's a tough, low-paid industry with long hours. But they also flag up high job satisfaction – when you do a good job at caring for a sick patient, you can save or change that person's life.

The key skills are being caring, compassionate and having a commitment to help people. You'll also need great communication skills, to help patients understand about potentially difficult health issues and to work as part of a larger healthcare team.

To work as a nurse in the NHS, you need a degree in order to register with the Nursing and Midwifery Council. During training, student nurses choose which branch they want to specialise in – adult, children, learning difficulties or mental health. After qualifying, there is further opportunity to specialise. For example, Katy Murphy, the qualified children's nurse who discusses her job below, has worked on a paediatric surgery ward, for a home respite care team, in a children's mental health unit, in the emergency department and also on a neonatal intensive care unit.

But it's not all hospital jobs: as well as working in the local community or in GP surgeries, nurses can work in prisons, the armed forces, research labs, for overseas medical charities, in schools, theatres (surgery, not the stage: theatre nurses complete extra training and work in operating theatres and anaesthetic/recovery areas), oil rigs and even cruise liners. British-trained nurses are highly sought after and have the opportunity to work anywhere in the world.

Nurses don't usually have to battle for promotions, either, as it's a very tiered progression, structured in 'bands'. It tends to be that people move up the bands in order rather than jumping ahead – a newly qualified staff nurse will start at a band 5, a team leader or nurse specialist will usually be a band 6, a nurse manager or advanced nurse specialist will be a band 7, a senior manager or nurse consultant will usually be a band 8, and a nurse chief executive will be a band 9. It's possible to move from a band 5 to a band 6 within a few years, but beyond that takes longer. A nurse advancing to a band 7 and beyond would be expected to have extensive experience and have undertaken further specialist training.

Those bands have a close link with pay, too: nursing in the NHS is set via structured salary levels, with a newly qualified nurse currently starting on £21,500 a year. Even without applying for a promotion, most would expect to increase their salary every year for eight years until they reached the top of the band, where they would receive £27,900 per year. A top band 6 (nurse team leader) will earn £34,500, a top band 7 (nurse advanced) will earn £40,600 and a top band 8 (nurse consultant) will earn £81,600. In the private sector, a newly qualified nurse working for an agency could earn up to £35 per hour. Nurses usually earn more than their basic salary because they get paid bonuses for working unsocial hours at nights, weekends and bank holidays.

To crack the profession, first you'll need that nursing degree. The qualifications you'll need depend on the university, but most demand three A levels; all nurses have to have at least a grade C in GSCE maths and English, too. At least one science A level will help you understand medical conditions and treatments. On top of academic qualifications, work experience is vital. 'Taking time out to work as a healthcare auxiliary or healthcare assistant or for a charity can give you a real sense of what a career in the nursing profession would be like, and will help you to work out whether you're cut out for it,' says Katy Murphy. Alternatively, the nurse apprenticeship course is clinically based and designed to give would-be nurses insight into the profession.

The degree training itself involves a mixture of academic lectures and courses, and clinical work. Once you've graduated, you have to apply for entry onto the Nursing and Midwifery Council registry.

WORKING LIFE: Katy Murphy, sister at a neonatal unit in a major UK hospital

'Work as a nurse definitely slips out of the "Monday to Friday" – if you work on a hospital ward you will almost always be expected to work on weekends, bank holidays, evenings and overnight. Hospital nurses do shift work, typically starting very early in the morning (about 7am) and finishing late in the evening (about 8.30pm) and then the night shift take over. But an increasing number of nurses opt to do a "Long Day", where they work the early and late shift together. As a result, they may only have to work three days a week.

This may all sound hideous, but remember that many of your friends are likely to be nurses, too, so you quickly get used to switching your social life away from weekends and bank holidays. Alternatively, working in the community you are likely to work less unsocial hours or even "normal" office hours. Also, the unsocial hours are rewarded with generous holiday entitlement – when you first start working for the NHS you will be entitled to 35 days' annual leave and this increases depending on how long you have worked for the NHS. After 10 years, a nurse will be entitled to 41 days. There's also a generous sickness absence policy on the NHS: you receive full pay for a significant period of time when off sick.

There are good opportunities for people to move up the ranks and become a sister, nurse specialist, nurse practitioner, nurse consultant or nurse manager. Nursing is also a profession that consists mainly of women, and because of this, it's a great profession for women to work in. After having a baby, NHS nurses are entitled to a year's maternity leave, and then when you return to work the provisions for flexible working hours are pretty good. Some nurses who are mothers on my ward have chosen to reduce their working week to 15 hours and/or also only work early shifts because that is what fits in with their childcare arrangements.

Nursing can be stressful and some people simply aren't prepared for all of the pressures that the job can entail. But from my experience, not many nurses leave the sector, instead, they tend to stick with it and eventually develop coping strategies to deal with the stress. It can be a very rewarding job and there will be plenty of times when you feel very privileged to be part of this unique profession. There is no better reward than seeing someone you've cared for be well enough to go home – and to know that you were part of making that possible.'

Other nursing roles

Healthcare assistants (HCA) work alongside nurses in hospitals, GP surgeries and anywhere else nurses are found, carrying out duties such as washing and dressing patients, helping with meals, toileting, bed-making and monitoring patients' temperatures, pulse or weight. Work patterns follow those of nurses. Some healthcare assistants may work alongside specialists such as physiotherapists or occupational therapists to help with patients and organise equipment. Pay tends to start at £13,000, rising for more experienced and qualified individuals to £19,000. Some employers demand that healthcare assistants have a Level 2 or 3 qualification (e.g. in Healthcare Support Services or Clinical Healthcare Support), while others will help HCAs to gain these qualifications on the job. It is also possible to become an HCA via an apprenticeship.

Midwives help women during all stages of pregnancy, labour and with their newborn babies. Some midwives now work in the community, in women's homes, clinics, children's centres and GP surgeries, but many are still working in hospitals, on antenatal, labour and postnatal wards and neonatal units. Some midwives are qualified nurses who have continued to study in order to register as a midwife, others study directly for a registered midwifery degree. Newly qualified midwives earn from £21,000 whilst senior ones could earn double that.

ONLINE ENTREPRENEUR

AVERAGE STARTING SALARY – Variable

ENTRY POSITION – Blogger, vlogger, social media expert, etc.

TYPICAL WEEKLY HOURS – Variable

RECOMMENDED QUALIFICATIONS – Good writing skills, organised, knack for business

IF YOU LIKE THIS YOU MIGHT ALSO LIKE ... entrepreneur, management consultant, tech industry

A decade ago, the idea that you could sit at home and earn a fortune from a business or website set up from your laptop was laughable. Now, thousands of people around the world are doing just that – for every mega-famous internet entrepreneur like Facebook's Mark Zuckerberg there are many more uni- and school-leavers and career-changers who are successfully shunning top jobs to start a blog or online entrepreneurial idea for themselves.

And for most there was no 'lightbulb moment', but hours of brainstorming, researching and honing – like charity site JustGiving (one of the founders was running the UK branch of charity Médecins Sans Frontières and looking for a low-cost system to accept donations online. It didn't exist, so after months of musing, she began working on it) and card-maker Moonpig (its founder received a pay-off from his old employer and studied for an MBA whilst considering ideas). The current culture of online entrepreneurship – much of it backed by the government – means there are a huge number of funding and advice initiatives and networks to help start-ups achieve success, and since Britons spend more time online than most other countries' citizens, there's a large pool of consumers waiting for your idea.

Starting your own online business

If you're considering a career as part of a web start-up, you could think big (set up the new Google) or small (establish a food blog, see if it takes off, network to get advertising, maybe a cookbook deal, etc.). The best thing you can do is close a gap in the market – like Zoopla founder Alex Chesterman, who set up his property website because his own search for a new home saw him toiling over spreadsheets to work out house values in his potential new street, and he thought a website could do it for others.

Most online businesses stem from one of four routes: an idea which evolves organically from a hobby (for example, Martin Lewis set up Money Saving Expert as a forum to share financial ideas with his friends . . . it grew until he sold the website for £87 million), a business idea springing out of lifestyle (like a new mother launching a baby app), an idea based on your own skill set (such as a translator setting up a foreign proofreading business online), or ideas which improve an existing online product or service. The maestros of the latter field are

Germany's Samwer brothers, who have built up a huge business copying sites such as Pinterest, Groupon and Airbnb, giving them a new name and launching them in new territories.

It's tough to pin down a potential salary or training/qualification requirements for these kinds of entrepreneurial online jobs – the former could be huge or might be non-existent. And as for training, some web wizards are IT experts who code in their sleep, but others have a big idea and bring on board a team to do the tech work. But if it's your career plan, you should work out how your online business is going to make any money from its launch. Funded by advertising? Then you should be aiming to draw in as many surfers as possible through entertainment or information. Focused on sales and e-commerce? Then work out how to keep users on-board from homepage to receipt page.

For some ideas, you may need to think about funding – some online start-ups stick to 'bootstrapping' – creating a site whilst working in another job or consulting at the same time, or using savings. Others seek out funding from friends or family or business angels, often swapping cash for a stake in the business, or borrowing from the bank. Government prodding means banks are trying to fund more small businesses, but an increasingly popular alternative option is crowd-funding, using websites like Kickstarter to raise cash from online investors, and/or making the most of government-backed investment incentive schemes, like the Seed Enterprise Investment Scheme tax break. For some web ideas, such as starting a YouTube channel or blog, there are very low or no costs, but be aware that while setting up an internet business is more accessible than a 'bricks and mortar' business, it requires exactly the same level of planning. Coming up with the idea is the easiest part, then you'll need to be seriously self-motivated to get it off the ground.

Be sure to do lots of market research before ploughing your life savings into an idea you think is amazing: is there a large enough market out there to be successful? Talk to as many of your potential consumers as possible. Find out what sites they use now, whether they'd use what you're proposing, how often they would visit, how much they would spend, if appropriate; plus designs, marketing and other features that they like.

It's easy to quiz people via online questionnaires that you can make on sites like SurveyMonkey, but a face-to-face interview could yield better results. You'll also need to research competition in the market and write a business plan.

Blogger

It's the job that seems to tick every box: you can do it from bed and dump the suit, transform your hobby into your career, and even get rich . . . We hear stand-out success stories like Zuckerberg, who started Facebook as a university pastime and a way to meet girls, before it transmogrified into one of the world's most popular websites.

Some reckon it was easier to make money from blogs back in the early days of the internet when bloggers were a rare species; now there are thousands of cooking, beauty, travel and parenting blogs out there – and brands considering advertising or sponsoring a post will only go for the really popular and unique ones. Still, research by marketing agency Optimus found that the average 'lifestyle' blogger could earn more than £900 a year from affiliate marketing – where you earn a fee if someone buys a particular product after clicking through from your site. So a beauty blogger recommending a particular lipstick would earn a cut – usually between 5 and 15 per cent – of total sales made by readers clicking from their link.

As a blogger, like all freelance work, the earnings are unpredictable. My own food blog, finchleykitchen.com, has been around a year and so far earned me . . . £2.84 in ad revenues, despite having several hundred hits per month. I do it mainly to keep all my favourite recipes in the same place!

For many, blogging is a nice top-up income, but while setting up a blog is easy and speedy on free sites such as Wordpress or Blogger, keeping them updated and looking good takes a long time and a lot of effort. As well as regular posts, you'll need to build up a following by directing people to your blog through social media such as Facebook, Instagram, Pinterest and Twitter; you might want to start making video blogs, too.

Write at least five posts before you even start thinking about domain names and design and you'll have something to work with when you do. 'This will also give you an idea of what you like writing about and whether you feel you have the dedication to keep it up,' adds one expert blogger.

The top skills you'll need are efficiency, writing, communication, PR, technical know-how, creativity, organisation, willingness to learn, commercial awareness and an eye for design. According to one top blogger: 'Sorting out receipts for my accounts and going through emails from people trying to get me to promote their products for free are the most boring parts of the job.

'But if you're keen to jump in, start to read blogs – all kinds. See what your favourite bloggers are doing to make money. This will usually be obvious on their homepage sidebar, or some even have a post about it. There are some really good websites about blogging, including problogger.net, copyblogger.com and moz.com. Study those sites and then see if you still want to do it.

'You need to be really passionate, totally dedicated and willing to invest time and money before you can expect to make any cash back. Working as a travel blogger, for example, is definitely not just a case of setting up a Wordpress and then bringing in advertising and getting invited on amazing trips. It takes hours and hours of graft, learning on the job, and constantly evolving to set up a good blog. And then keeping at it is even harder.'

WORKING LIFE: Jamal Edwards, 23, is a self-made millionaire who grew up on a London council estate, gained six GCSEs, then launched online youth broadcasting company SBTV, where he interviews stars like Sir Richard Branson, Bruno Mars, Nicki Minaj and Jessie J., and has nearly half a million YouTube subscribers. He is now estimated to be worth £8 million.

'My average day is 7am to 10pm and I'm connected to work all the time – this is my life. If you want to be an entrepreneur there is an element of work becoming lifestyle. But I don't see what I do as work if I'm being honest, so I guess that makes it easier.'

Edwards' career was launched when he received a video camera for Christmas at 15, and started filming foxes in his garden. 'I thought I was

Steve Irwin. I uploaded it to YouTube and got 1,000 views and was like, rah! I could do something here, so I went on my estate and filmed local rappers.' From there, chutzpah and dedication saw his one-man operation secure bigger and bigger stars – and more hits. 'Perseverance and consistency is key in my world, but that doesn't guarantee success. I think it's still about networking and making sure the right people know about what you do even if they are not the biggest fans of it to start with,' he says. 'I am a part of a generation that feels like there is no hope for us, so to be able to inspire my peers and get them thinking about innovating as entrepreneurs means the world to me.'

Edwards' favourite parts of his online job are 'meeting new people, meeting some of the greatest minds on our planet today, and seeing the world through travel.' He admits it's tough to be a young person in the established media industry: 'The corporate culture is scared of change, elitist in nature and very dismissive. But I don't think it will be this way forever – change is here, it just takes a little time to feel its effects.'

To students leaving school now who want to crack into the online world, Edwards says: 'take training in anything that allows you to work with people and understand the world – department stores, old people's homes, etc. – learning to deal with different types of personalities is one of the greatest skills anybody can have. And make sure you have English and maths qualifications at least, as they are fundamental to surviving in our society. Do your research and look into the personal testimonials of people that have done the same job you want to do. A great place to start is LinkedIn; you can learn about the desired career path by looking at the people you admire and seeing how they've got there.'

WORKING LIFE: Victoria Philpott is the travel blogger behind vickyflipfloptravels.com, through which she has visited 25 countries in two years

'There's definitely no average day as a travel blogger, it depends where you are, who you meet, who you're with and the Wi-Fi connection . . . If I'm away, I'll be seeking out fresh and exciting adventures; otherwise, I write for my blog, develop my e-books, write for various clients, interact on social media channels, answer emails and pitch ideas to people and companies I'd like to work with.

There's no such thing as regular working hours. I might not do any work all day and then keep going well into the night. This suits me perfectly as I can roll with the inspiration and creativity when it arrives.

I arrived at this career after always enjoying writing. I studied a communications degree, then an NCTJ postgraduate diploma in magazine journalism at Harlow College in London. I managed to find freelance work on LinkedIn with a train travel company and that led to my boyfriend and I travelling round Europe until the money ran out. My lightbulb moment was when I got a job as a content editor at hostelbookers.com – part of my job was to work on blogger outreach; I got to know all the travel bloggers of the time, and set up vickyflipfloptravels.com as a way to practise what I was doing at work.

I started to go to networking events in London and met a lot of great travel bloggers. I then got a job as content manager at gapyear.com, and during the 18 months I worked there my blog grew, and so did the freelance and travel opportunities. I decided to take the plunge and go for the freelance way of life. Now I love my job. My favourite thing is the freebies – I recently went to St Lucia for an incredible week.

When I'm looking at new trips, PRs and travel boards have very different approaches – if they're switched on, they'll want to work with bloggers and if they don't, they will in time. You can measure all your statistics using tools like Google Analytics – I have about 20,000 readers a month, but have said no to about 90 per cent of the trips I'm offered. Press trips are actually quite a lot of work; they're not just a free holiday. You need to make sure you provide value to the host and work with their goals as well. Some companies can expect quite a lot in return so you can't just go saying yes to anything.

Money-wise, some travel bloggers I know earn zero and others bring in six-figure salaries. It's incredibly hard to get that, though, and it's good to have a reality check. Two years ago bloggers were making thousands selling links, but Google banned that. Now most bloggers take part in sponsorship deals, speaking engagements, run courses, charge to go on press trips, write e-books or even bring out product ranges. I only went freelance and full-time on my blog this year, and am set to earn about £27,000 a year. It's less than in my previous job, but the freedom that travel blogging brings is well worth it. If you're really passionate, the sky is the limit. But no one should ever go into travel blogging for the love of money or the freebies; you'd be better off getting a regular job. Working as a travel blogger is definitely for the love of travel and writing and photographing it.'

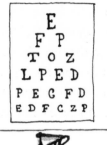

OPTICIAN

AVERAGE STARTING SALARY – £18,000
ENTRY POSITION – Dispensing optician
TYPICAL WEEKLY HOURS – Variable
RECOMMENDED QUALIFICATIONS – General Optical Council approved course and an exam
IF YOU LIKE THIS YOU MIGHT ALSO LIKE . . . beautician, dentist, doctor

I confess I learnt something whilst interviewing eye specialists for this chapter – it turns out an optician is probably not the person who ushers you into a darkened room and asks you to read the letters on the chart: that's an optometrist. An optician – the full name is a dispensing optician – is the person usually based in the waiting area, who is trained to fit glasses and contact lenses, based on the prescriptions written by optometrists or ophthalmologists (medically trained doctors who specialise in eye problems).

That's a lot of o-professions. So, tackling optometry first, what does the job involve apart from that eye chart? It's all about examining and testing people's eyes and diagnosing any problems. It's not just short- and long-sightedness that they can spot, but also eye diseases, such as glaucoma, and other health problems like diabetes, high cholesterol and high blood pressure.

In Britain, most optometrists are based in high-street practices – aka opticians – with a growing number now owned by big chains like Specsavers, but thousands still independently run. General daily tasks for optometrists include examining patients' eyes, finding the correct prescription, looking out for health problems, offering advice on any problems like dry eye, liaising with doctors like ophthalmologists, GPs and other healthcare professionals, talking to glasses and contact lens manufacturers (many have specific sales targets), continuing their professional training and staying up to date with new developments and potentially managing staff and the admin of a practice.

Some optometrists work in other settings, like hospitals, schools, prisons or the military, or carry out academic research, or work for pharmaceutical firms. Wherever you're based, though, as an optometrist you'll need good people and communication skills and that famous desire to help people, as well as a scientific educational background.

You might also need to be willing to move for a job: The College of Optometrists has just embarked on a survey of the optical workforce, as some pockets of the UK are desperately short of optometrists whilst others are saturated. 'From a career perspective, optometrists who are willing to move to a new area to work will have more choice and may achieve higher salaries than in areas where demand is higher than supply,' says Sarah Farrant, optometrist and council member of the College of Optometrists (see below for her working life).

Before that, though, you'll face some training – at least four years of it. To qualify as an optometrist, you have to be registered with the General Optical Council, and to do that, you have to graduate in a degree in optometry approved by them, then tackle a year of (paid) pre-registration training under the guidance of a GOC-registered optometrist, before taking, and passing, GOC final exams. There are currently nine unis running courses approved by the GOC: Anglia Ruskin, Aston, Bradford, Cardiff, City, Glasgow Caledonian, Manchester, Plymouth and Ulster. Most demand at least AAB at A level, or equivalent qualifications, with at least two science subjects.

Dispensing opticians, meanwhile, need a minimum of five GCSEs at grade C or above, including a science subject, English and maths, or equivalent – although career-changers with some serious optical experience behind them can succeed in getting onto some courses in dispensing optics. Again, these need to be at a GOC-approved institution; these include ABDO College, Canterbury, Anglia Ruskin University, Bradford College, City and Islington College, City University and Glasgow Caledonian University. Full-time, the course lasts two years followed by one year's supervised work under supervision.

Pay-wise, most optometrists are paid between £20,000 and £25,000 for their pre-registration year in practice, then around £30,000 for a newly qualified role, rising to double that with experience and more for practice owners. Dispensing opticians earn about £18,000, rising to between £26,000 and £40,000 with experience and depending on the size and location of the practice.

WORKING LIFE: Sarah Farrant is an optometrist working in Somerset

'I normally arrive at my opticians' practice at around 8.30am to get everything ready for patients to arrive, check my emails, meet up with my team and catch up on any admin work.

At the moment I work in the practice for three days a week, and spend about one day a week working from home or at meetings. I have an 11-month-old baby, so I make sure I have time for her too.

My first patient arrives at 9am and I see a wide variety of interesting people each with different problems and requirements for me to solve – usually eye exams, contact lens appointments and specialist clinics, like dry eye management.

I see one patient every half-hour until I finish work at 5.30pm, but also have space in my clinic to see emergency cases with acute eye problems for me to diagnose, treat and manage.

I do work in the evenings, but by choice! I enjoy reading interesting articles and working on my business. I also chair the local optical committee which requires occasional evening meetings to work towards developing local services to best serve the eye care needs of the people in Somerset.

I reached this point in my career after studying for a degree in Optometry and Vision Science at Cardiff University. Then I had a 'pre-reg' year in practice and a series of professional exams, before spending six months working in New Zealand after qualifying. I did locum work for a while when back in the UK, and was then employed by an independent practice. I took further exams in glaucoma and independent prescribing to up my skills, and developed an interest in managing patients with dry eye. I also met lots of industry leaders and through developing relationships began lecturing both nationally and internationally.

The best part of the job is seeing a wide variety of patients, choosing and developing my own specialist skills and the variety – I also enjoy writing articles and lectures to present to the profession. As it's a specialist field, the work can get repetitive, but the people are all individual. And with an ageing population, the need for good eye care and eyewear is ever increasing.'

Dream Job: Wimbledon umpire

Mike Pitcher, 31, works at tennis events around the UK

'Back in 2009, I was talking to my former boss when he suggested that I should think about taking up tennis umpiring, given that I was an avid spectator of the sport. I went and looked at the LTA's website (lta.org.uk/volunteers-officials/Becoming-an-Umpire) and managed to secure my place on an initial training course. After passing, I was invited to become a member of the Association of British Tennis Officials and began line umpiring at local club and junior events across the country. Gradually I moved up to umpiring professional events such as the Aegon International in Eastbourne and eventually on to umpiring at Wimbledon for the first time in 2012.

There are two types of umpire in tennis: a line umpire, calling the lines on a tennis court, and a chair umpire, who is responsible for calling the score and ensuring that the rules of tennis are adhered to. You need to work your way up to becoming a chair umpire by starting as a line umpire and progressing from there.

All line umpires start with a grade of L4. Positive assessments and work rate will lead to promotion; once you reach L2, you become eligible to work on one of Wimbledon's show courts (Centre Court, Courts 1, 2 and 3), and once you reach L1, there is the possibility of being selected to umpire a Wimbledon Final.

Every day is different in umpiring – as a chair umpire, I collect the items needed for the match (e.g. balls, scoring PDA computer, tape measure, coin). As a line umpire at Wimbledon, the day consists of working one hour on court and having one hour off court until all matches on that court are completed (or the weather intervenes!). Most people umpire as a hobby – my day job is media relations manager at Nationwide building society – and there is no salary involved. Instead, umpires (there are about 400 of us around the UK) are given expenses at each event that they attend.

My favourite part of the job is definitely umpiring during the UK's summer grass court season, culminating in being able to take an active part in the world's most prestigious tennis tournament at Wimbledon, one of the world's most iconic venues. Last year I worked on Centre Court for the first time – it was an experience that I will never forget.

As for the worst part of the job? That would probably be being shouted out by a player when you are a chair umpire or, as line umpire, it's a ball coming at you at 130mph and having to duck or swerve out of the way in time before it hits you – something that I have been unsuccessful at on a number of occasions.'

PARAMEDIC

AVERAGE STARTING SALARY – £21,388

ENTRY POSITION – Paramedic

TYPICAL WEEKLY HOURS – 37.5 hours

RECOMMENDED QUALIFICATIONS – Health and Care Professionals Council (HCPC) approved qualification. Driving licence. Good physical fitness

IF YOU LIKE THIS YOU MIGHT ALSO LIKE . . . doctor, firefighter, nurse

Surprisingly, none of the paramedics I interviewed about their jobs for this book named slamming on the 'nee naw' siren as a key thrill of their job: the novelty must wear off pretty fast. They did, however, say that working as the person providing immediate response to emergency medical 999 calls is rewarding, stressful, and involves a huge amount of teamwork.

At the beginning of a shift, paramedics don't know if they'll be having a relatively easy day treating minor injuries or dealing with the aftermath of a massive terrorist attack such as the 7/7 bombings; helping to deliver a baby at home or having to tell relatives that their family member has died.

The main tasks of the job are medical ones, such as assessing patients, resuscitating and stabilising them, liaising with the police or other emergency services, administering treatment to injured or sick people, applying spinal and traction splints, dealing with casualties from crashes, disasters or violence. But there's also admin work, writing up case notes and updating hospital or other medical staff. Most paramedics work in teams of two, based in an ambulance, but some also work on bikes, motorbikes or medical helicopters (although air ambulance crew have extra training). Emergency rescuers can even be found on skis in winter sports resorts.

To secure a job as a paramedic, there are two routes in: some local ambulance trusts ask applicants to have only GCSEs or an NVQ or equivalent, starting as a student paramedic and training up on the job – this could be the best option for career-changers. Others demand a diploma, foundation degree or honours degree. Either way, to be a qualified paramedic you'll need to be registered with the Health and Care Professions Council, so you'll need to opt for one of the approved courses it lists at hpc-uk.org (these include university courses, diplomas and workplace learning). To apply for a job or find out more about them, all ambulance service trusts advertise on the NHS Jobs website (www.jobs.nhs.uk). It advises applicants to also visit ambulance service trust websites directly, and Jobcentre Plus, where some roles might be advertised.

To drive an ambulance, you will also need a full manual driving licence and, if you passed your test after 1996, you may need to take an extra driving qualification to drive bigger vehicles and carry passengers. In terms of experience, one man in the green paramedics' outfit advises: 'If you think you're interested in this as a career, St John Ambulance is a great way to get an insight into First Aid, and you can volunteer from a young age as a cadet.'

Perks-wise, you'll be paid on the NHS sliding scale, starting at just over £21,000, although working unsocial hours including bank holidays triggers a 25 per cent increase in pay. Experienced paramedics will earn about £35,000, and other benefits include an NHS pension, relocation package and access to courses of counselling, physio and stress management.

WORKING LIFE: a paramedic working for the NHS in the south of England

'My shift starts either at 6.30am or 6.30pm, and there's an unspoken rule of arriving 15 minutes earlier to relieve the crew before you – otherwise they could get stuck on a call that would take them well past their finishing time. Once you're out on a call, you are committed to it until the patient is treated at home or in hospital or the control room tells you to step down.

Once I have a vehicle at the start of my shift, I need to check it from top to bottom. Are the monitor and defibrillator working? Are the correct amount of drugs on board, and are they in date? Are the oxygen masks, bandages, cannulation kit, airway management tools, diagnostic tools, intubation kit, cardiac arrest drugs, intra-osseous needle (into the bone), burns kit, maternity pack and spinal immobilisation kit all there? And spare parts, too, to be able to refill the items when used. The second crew mate will check the vehicle, whether it's roadworthy, and that the lights and tyres are working.

Shifts last 12 hours with a half-hour unpaid break. During the 12 hours, calls are categorised to the type of emergency and graded accordingly, and you're sent out by the control room. I mostly work three days on, three days off, then three night shifts.

I find the toughest situations to be any involving a child who is seriously unwell, either due to illness or a trauma. It's also never easy to deal with a patient who is unconscious, or when you're in a public place, and you have the eyes of the public staring at you. Sometimes I face groups of drunk friends, and they can be threatening. But the absolute worst part of the job is having to tell family that their loved ones are deceased.

There might not be many "fun" parts of the job, but there's a huge sense of satisfaction when you go to a call and it brings out all the skills that you've been trained for – and if you're called out to a birth at home, there is a special feeling when that happens. There's also a great work culture – my colleagues are like a second family, we all care for each other, laugh, joke and hurl friendly insults about, but we are all there for each other if one of us gets a bad call.'

PERSONAL ASSISTANT (PA) AND ADMINISTRATION WORK

AVERAGE STARTING SALARY – £18,000–£25,000

ENTRY POSITION – Personal assistant

TYPICAL WEEKLY HOURS – 30–40 hours

RECOMMENDED QUALIFICATIONS – Good educational background. Office skills qualification. Work experience

IF YOU LIKE THIS YOU MIGHT ALSO LIKE . . . hospitality, HR, civil service

They're the cool-as-a-cucumber office stalwart who can track down an 18-piece brass band with a performing elephant at 10 minutes' notice, or the amazingly efficient bod who can get their boss home from an overseas trip even when the whole of European airspace is shut . . . That's the new breed of super PA, or personal assistant. Not so long ago, the average British office would have banks of secretaries providing administrative and typing help to workers; the rise of computers consigned many of those roles to history, but administrators and PAs are more prevalent than ever.

An Office Administrator usually has responsibility for running the workplace – answering the phone, dealing with email enquiries, running filing systems and people's diaries, perhaps also word processing and typing up dictations, managing the office budget and running the stationery cupboard and office post. Normally, the role means being at your desk from 9 to 5, or longer depending on the office hours, working about 35 hours a week, and expecting a starter salary of around £14,000 which can rise as high as £40,000 for someone running administration in a big London office (but the average is much lower).

A PA's role tends to involve a bit more variety. You might be organising the emails, diary management, travel, budgets and social media for a busy individual, but if you were working in a small firm or for a frantic entrepreneur, for example, you could also be managing global projects and helping out with HR and marketing and more, or be flying around the world with your boss.

Money-wise, someone in a first PA role in London could earn between £18,000 and £28,000, but the pay might be as much as a third lower in the regions. Second jobbers can expect £25,000 to £35,000, more senior roles tend to start from £40,000. A top PA in London can earn over £100,000, but there are only a few who do so.

Top skills you'll need include discretion, reliability, calmness, patience, commercial and business acumen, and having a flair for entrepreneurial or independent thinking. There are boring parts, though: 'I am sorry to say that after 16 years of taking minutes of meetings, I would pass on doing these any day,' says one PA. 'Similarly with filing, when we have electronic versions of everything.' She adds that the worst part of the job can be 'the way you are treated as a PA – especially from those colleagues that don't see it as a profession. They think that you have fallen into the "you are not too clever, so be a PA" bracket. I would love for more of my colleagues to walk a mile in my shoes so they understand the competing demands of the job.'

But on the flipside, for those with stellar organisational skills and problem-solving abilities, this is a reliable, fulfilling career which is much in demand at all times and often gives you a role close to the heart of power in a company. It's also one industry where women dominate: the gender ratio for PAs in the UK is 97 per cent female to 3 per cent male. But those in the sector say they're working on 'getting more men in'. Another option is being a Virtual Assistant. These are usually self-employed PAs who run their own businesses from home, working for several individuals and billing on an hourly rate. They pick how many hours and clients they want to take on, and generally work for entrepreneurs or small businesses who might not be able to afford (or require) a full-time PA.

The PA role traditionally hasn't demanded higher education – personal qualities are usually seen as more important. But those in the role recommend doing a college or Pitman (office training firm) diploma to secure secretarial-related qualifications. There are over 800 related courses out there, viewable on Executive Secretary Magazine (www.executivesecretary.com). Other useful resources include *PA Life Magazine*, PA-Assist.com – a free resource website for PAs, and The Office Show – the biggest exhibition for personal assistants in the UK. Try to secure work experience (see Victoria Darragh's experience below) and try to find an experienced PA willing to act as a mentor to help you out at the start. 'Network, network and network some more,' advises Darragh. 'It is often a case of not what you know but who you know when it comes to looking for a PA role. Oh, and if you can, try to learn a language.'

WORKING LIFE: Victoria Darragh, executive assistant to HR director of recruitment firm Hays

'My average day starts at 5am, which isn't typical for PAs – I just find I get a lot more work done before 9am! The first thing I do is to check our Hays LinkedIn accounts, and respond to tweets on the two work Twitter accounts that I run. I also check my boss's Twitter account to see what he has been talking about overnight, and visit LinkedIn as my other director quite often publishes articles too. I also have Google Alerts for my company and my bosses so I check these in the morning just to make sure all is okay and to see what the press is talking about. With a previous boss I also used to check football scores during the season so I could tell what kind of mood he might be in when I got in the office!

I arrive at the office at 7am, make tea or coffee and get cracking with emails. My first job of the day will be to clear what is still outstanding from the days/weeks before and also see what is on the list for the current day. I worked my way up via the old-fashioned route, Office Junior to Secretary to Personal Assistant to Executive Assistant, so I know this role is about lists, lists and more lists!

You can't predict what you are going to be doing on any given day – you're reliant on your boss asking for something or giving you a task list and your work stems very much from their objectives and meetings. I don't take a lunch break every day but I do grab something to eat.

If there are no events I have to manage or board meetings that I have to be around for, then I always try to leave on time at 5.30pm. But I'm on my phone all evening – I work for an international company and British nine-to-five hours do not seem to meet the growing needs of today's business world. Sometimes I'll need to be on a conference or Skype call with Australia late at night, for example, or speak on a Sunday evening with the States. But there are many PA roles that are standard nine-to-five if that is what you are looking for. On average I work around 10 hours per day at least, so maybe 50 to 60 hours a week, but it can be more if I've any events to attend.'

PERSONAL TRAINER

AVERAGE STARTING SALARY – £50 an hour

ENTRY POSITION – Personal trainer

TYPICAL WEEKLY HOURS – Variable (by the hour)

RECOMMENDED QUALIFICATIONS – Qualified fitness instructor/apprentice-ship. First aid trained

IF YOU LIKE THIS YOU MIGHT ALSO LIKE . . . military careers, teacher, physio

If hitting the gym or doing PE lessons is (or was) your favourite part of the day, a career based around sport might be right up your street. Anyone excelling in a particular area might be considering competing or playing it as a career (see page 258 where Michael Owen describes life as a professional footballer), but for those who aren't one of the nation's best but still love sport, it might be worth thinking about a career inspiring others, as a sports coach, PE teacher or personal trainer. It's also a popular option for career-changers: many personal trainers have previously worked in another industry, and changed because they've been inspired by their own training, want a non-office career, or want an active job that fits around their family or other commitments.

'I'm getting paid to do something I love, and that I would do for free anyway,' say many personal trainers (PTs). They're passionate about exercising and helping people who are struggling or risking injury whilst training or working out. Many PTs work outdoors – in parks, leading running groups or aerobics sessions – as well as in gyms; most are self-employed, either paying gyms (or giving them a cut of earnings) for hosting them, or going into clients' homes with equipment.

Others, who are employed by gyms, might find their days are a mixture of one-to-one and group personal training sessions, demonstrations of gym equipment and exercises and gym inductions, as well as general gym duties, such as keeping the machines clean and tidy, working behind reception and answering questions. Sports coaches usually work in schools or in sports centres, sometimes part-time in evenings or at weekends for those who specialise in set sports or games such as badminton or tennis.

The downsides of working in sport? You might have to stop eating junk food in public – it wouldn't be good if you were caught by a client – and you'll have to keep in shape yourself: you're the best advertisement for your skills. But for most sports-loving trainers, that's not particularly onerous. The hours can be long, as you'll often need to fit around clients' nine-to-five day jobs, but you can usually schedule your own time to fit PT work alongside other jobs, or family commitments.

Skills-wise, you'll need empathy and compassion as well as know-how about the top training techniques, healthy living and anatomy. 'You have to have the ability to communicate with people and motivate without patronising but you also need to be patient, calm and tactful – even when you know you're not being told the truth by clients,' says PT Alison Wheatley (see below). 'And you have to be creative and imaginative to keep training interesting as well as have amazing organ-isational skills.'

There's a wide range of training courses to become a qualified personal trainer; the recognised ones include Level 2 Certificate in Fitness Instructing – Gym; Level 2 Diploma in Health, Fitness and Exercise Instruction; Level 2 Diploma in Instructing Exercise and Fitness, and Level 3 Diplomas in Fitness Instructing and Personal Training or in Personal Training. Professional organisations the Register of Exercise Professionals (REPs) and the National Register of Personal Trainers (NRPT) have more info on reputable courses.

Often, the broader your training and experience, the better: for many clients, their PT is also their therapist, health advisor, dietician and even part-physio, so it's worth knowing a lot about muscle care, injury recovery, diets and more. But training courses all come at a cost, and there are other fees involved in the industry, too. The vast majority of PTs are self-employed: the earning potential comes down to how many hours you are willing to work and how good you are at securing, and retaining, new clients, while the costs could include personal liability insurance and council or gym fees, as some parks and all gyms make you pay to use their property for work. You also have to be wary of getting injured yourself, which could see you lose your income.

Starting out, earnings might be £15,000 to £25,000 a year. Experienced PTs can receive between £40,000 and £55,000 a year, or perhaps £30 to £40 for a one-to-one session. In London, fees are usually higher, and some high-profile trainers receive as much as £100 an hour and do high-profile media work alongside exercising with clients.

WORKING LIFE: Alison Wheatley, personal trainer based in Sheffield

'I've always taken an interest in health and fitness and trained for a number of years. In my previous career I was working for a debt collection company, but after having children I was looking for a career that could fit around my family as well as something I was passionate about, and training as a PT was the natural next step. I took my professional training courses back-to-back in five months to qualify more quickly than usual.

Now my average day goes something like this:

5.30am: arrive at gym. Switch on systems and check gym diaries. Ensure equipment ready for opening at 6.30am.

6.00am: first client: one hour personal training.

7.00am: run 30-minute class, usually kettlebells or boxing.

7.30am: second client: one hour personal training.

8.30–9.15am: first break. Check personal diaries, update client training and food programmes.

9.15am: second class: usually 45 minutes cross fit.

10.00am: third client: one hour personal training.

11.00am: fourth client: one hour personal training.

12.00pm: fifth client: one hour personal training.

1.00–1.30pm: lunch.

1.30-3.30pm: do my own training, generally weights followed by cardio.

3.30pm: collect my kids from school and take them to my mum's. Eat dinner.

5.00pm: back to the gym – evening personal training work, with one client every hour.

9.00pm: finish.

9.30pm: get home, update diaries, check Facebook and emails. Eat supper and sleep.

Between that schedule, though, as a personal trainer you're always connected to work – you need to be available at the best times to suit your client. I'm often on social media, email, phone or WhatsApp providing clients with support, even at "unsociable" hours. Generally, people are looking to you to help them to make changes in their life – mostly weight loss, an emotional subject which often involves frustration and tears.

My advice to anyone interested in PT is, if you're still studying, to do well in science and biology and become familiar with human physiology as well as get a good grounding in different types of food and nutrition. Beyond that, there are so many books and online resources available for career-changers; I'd recommend getting started with a strength and conditioning book like *The National Strength and Conditioning Association*

(NSCA) Basics of Strength and Conditioning Manual, which can be down-loaded for free.

I love every aspect of my work – I couldn't put in the hours that I do if I didn't – seeing people transform and become happier and confident is what drives me. But there are boring parts, mainly sitting at the computer, writing clients' training and eating plans.

I've found it harder to change people's habits than I expected when I started PT training. I thought everyone was as passionate as me, but with time I have come to realise that the majority of people actually dislike exercise – my job is more about habit changing than just delivering training sessions.'

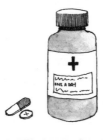

PHARMACIST

AVERAGE STARTING SALARY – £21,388

ENTRY POSITION – Pharmacist

TYPICAL WEEKLY HOURS – 37.5 hours

RECOMMENDED QUALIFICATIONS –MPharm. Pre-registration training course.
Registration exam

IF YOU LIKE THIS YOU MIGHT ALSO LIKE . . . academic, doctor, dentist

Working as a pharmacist, aka the UK's only kind of legal drug dealer, there are two main routes to take: either providing expert advice on the most appropriate medicines and dosages for patients in hospitals, or working in the community in pharmacies such as Boots, supermarkets and GP surgeries.

Either way, your main roles will include checking prescriptions, dispensing medicines and providing advice on the correct dosage and best form (such as tablet, injection or inhaler).

Hospital pharmacists might also be involved in the buying and testing of medicines, as well as working closely with doctors and other healthcare professionals, going on ward rounds, taking patients' drug histories and even setting up and supervising clinical trials.

Community pharmacists, meanwhile, also advise patients on the use of their medicines, and may offer specialist health screenings, such as blood pressure monitoring or diabetes checks, as well as selling over-the-counter products, advising about minor wounds or illnesses and managing a sterile needle exchange.

Both kinds of pharmacists face the same initial training and must keep up to date with current legislation throughout their careers. Pharmacists have to complete at least five years of training, including a four-year Master of Pharmacy (MPharm) degree and a one-year pre-registration training course, and are strongly encouraged to continue (see working life, below) for another four years of training.

'I would advise anyone going into pharmacy to be really careful about their university choice,' says one new graduate. 'Unlike with medicine and dentistry, the government have not put a cap on the number of pharmacy students, which has led to new pharmacy schools popping up all over the place. In the not-so-far-off future, we will have a large excess of pharmacists, and pre-registration places and junior positions will be very competitive. I'd advise students to carefully research the credibility of the newer pharmacy schools before applying as this could greatly affect your future employability.'

Being a pharmacist can be a great job for anyone who enjoys science and meeting people, but it has a cocktail of skill requirements, including: attention to detail (no part can be missed from a prescription) and good analytical skills (for the clinical assessment of drug charts and of patients' symptoms). You have to be able to consider a lot of information from other healthcare professionals, from patients, and from their medical notes, and analyse it in minute detail. Communication skills are also vital: 'I think a really valuable skill to have is the ability to alter your verbal and written style depending on your audience,' says one hospital pharmacist, 'be they patients, relatives, other pharmacists, consultants, nurses, occupational therapists, etc. This will help you develop a rapport with everyone involved.'

Perks-wise, the starting salary for a pharmacist largely depends on what sector you go into. Hospital pharmacists begin on about £26,000 and salaries rise with length of employment, further qualifications and increased managerial responsibility; a senior pharmacist earns between £40,000 and £55,000, while a chief pharmacist can earn somewhere in the region of £80,000, although these jobs are fairly restricted. Within NHS roles, the holidays are generous (27 days per year, plus days in lieu and bank holidays), rising to 33 days per year after ten years' service.

For community pharmacists, the starting salary is somewhere around the £30,000 mark. 'There isn't so much a ceiling within community pharmacy as you can go into a management role of a large corporation, or start your own business,' says one insider.

Just like in dentistry, it's now tough to set up a new pharmacy business from scratch. There are opportunities to buy out existing high-street drug outlets, but prices are really high because demand exceeds supply. And like optometrists, pharmacists who are willing to move to a new area to work will have more choice and may achieve higher salaries than in areas where demand is higher than supply.

Other job options beyond the white coats behind the Boots

counter and in hospitals include working in industry (on, for example, clinical drug trials), in academia and in public health. 'I would urge students to gain as much experience in a number of different environments as possible before making any lasting career decisions,' says the graduate pharmacist.

WORKING LIFE: Lily Sitwell* is a newly qualified hospital pharmacist

'My working day begins at 9.00am, when I start accessing an updated list of patients on my assigned ward(s) and compare it to yesterday's list, highlighting the new patients. I then check the hospital computer and annotate the list with recent test results (e.g. bloods, microbiological reports). The next two to four hours are spent on the ward. I try to see all patients every day but on a very busy day I'll prioritise the new patients, followed by the patients being discharged. For each patient, I read their medical notes, assess their drugs chart and plan what to do next – it might be writing notes about possible medicines for the doctors to see later, or bleeping the consultant for serious or urgent matters.

How I spend my afternoon depends on my rotation – as a junior pharmacist in a hospital, I switch departments every two months to develop my overall competency. Currently my afternoons are based in the dispensary, where I'll be doing the clinical checking of outpatient prescriptions and discharge paperwork, and check all the medicines dispensed by our technicians for accuracy.

----

* *name changed for anonymity*

We tend to have a ten-minute break in the afternoon – breaks are really important when you are carrying out a repetitive task like checking, as it prevents mistakes being made. Other rotations include working in Medicines Information, where we receive enquiries, mainly from healthcare professionals but also from patients, about drugs, and within the oncology department. The complexity and potential risk of chemotherapeutic agents mean it's a specialist department.

I normally leave work at 5.30pm, but all pharmacists are on a late rota, working late one night every two weeks in the dispensary – when you leave whenever all outpatient scripts and discharge prescriptions are dealt with, which can be around 6.30pm. We also have to work nine-to-two on some weekends, but you do receive time off in lieu the following week.

I studied pharmacy at university, and pretty much thought that when I was qualified that would be it, in terms of formal study. But that's far from the case – after university and the pre-registration year, hospital pharmacists have to embark on a three-year clinical diploma whilst working full-time, then a year-long prescribing course is strongly encouraged. So that's roughly nine years of formal training and study before you can take a breath. It is fulfilling and worthwhile, but there's no getting away from the fact that it's a hard slog.

The worst part of the job is the checking – it's definitely necessary but it can get very monotonous after a while. And it can be emotional when patients – especially those you've known for a while – deteriorate. Still, my favourite part of the work is meeting the patients. You come across so many different characters all the time and it's rewarding to see them improve as a result of your contribution.'

PHOTOGRAPHER

AVERAGE STARTING SALARY – £12,000

ENTRY POSITION – Assistant photographer

TYPICAL WEEKLY HOURS – Variable

RECOMMENDED QUALIFICATIONS – Courses and knowledge of relevant software

IF YOU LIKE THIS YOU MIGHT ALSO LIKE . . . fashion careers, graphic designer, teacher

Images you capture could end up on newspaper front pages, or immortalising a couple's wedding, or illustrating articles in magazines, websites, or corporate reports – or providing evidence of the darker side of humanity in war zones or riots. A career in photography certainly provides a huge range of outlets.

But a career in photography has also changed enormously as

technology has developed: where once newspapers, for example, would have a roster of staff snappers who would supply the majority of their images, now many come from agencies or from 'citizen photographers' – people with cameras or just a smartphone who happened to be in the right time, at the right place, to photograph an exceptional image.

Professional photographers usually work to a brief set by the person they work for – someone taking pictures for BP's annual report, for example, might be sent off to an oil rig to get a particular image; a war zone photographer usually travels with a journalist to work on a report together, whilst a wedding, family or baby photographer usually has set images to take, too: those requested by their client. Photographers (who usually are either self-employed or work for a specific company or photo/news agency) can specialise in one area, such as:

- social photography – weddings, babies, families, parties and portraits.
- advertising – for magazines, billboards, bus stops, photo libraries, etc.
- press – for newspapers, magazines, online, news agencies.
- Corporate – company PR material.
- fashion – photographing models and clothing for magazines, catalogues and websites such as Asos and Net-A-Porter.

Pay and conditions are enormously varied across these specialities – wedding photographers can be in work during all 52 weeks of the year, but arguably they have less creative freedom than fashion photographers, who may have less reliable work demands. Many freelance photographers now wear all kinds of 'hats' and take commissions from some or all of these areas in order to secure enough varied work.

As a professional photographer, you'd be talking to clients to seek new commissions and find out more about their requirements, researching and preparing shoots, setting up lighting and checking test shots, taking photos using the latest cameras, lenses, lighting, etc., digitally retouching or doing edits using software like Photoshop, providing proofs for clients, perhaps liaising with others involved in the job, such as journalists, picture editors, book commissioners, graphic designers or art galleries, organising finished products (usually framed prints, albums or computerised images) as well as running the business side of the job – invoicing clients, promoting the business and carrying out the admin of organising shoots and studios.

All of which mean the average photographer's hours can be erratic; most work at least some evenings and weekends to cover events; a paparazzi-style photographer might work more nights than days, following celebrities around town. Some, particularly wedding photographers who find most of their jobs on the weekend, may be part-time snappers and have another job in the week. That possibility means career-changers can test the water of the career on weekends at first before quitting their current job.

Salary-wise, assistant photographers (often the first rung on the ladder and a useful way to make contacts) start earning between £12,000 and £17,000 a year; a busy full-time photographer would expect to be making between £25,000 and £50,000 a year, although it depends how many hours are put in, as most freelance snappers are paid per job or on an hourly/daily rate.

Famous photographers who clients ask for by name, particularly in fashion and magazine photography, earn a six- or even seven-figure salary. And some get lucky: one student photographer I know happened to be at a university event where Kate Moss unexpectedly turned up, and made more than the average annual salary just by selling that one snap in the UK and overseas. Be aware, though, that most sell their photos via agencies, such as Alamy, who will take a cut.

Training-wise, you'll need a good eye for a great photo, and a dash of creativity, as well as technical camera skills. You'll need to be good at putting people at ease, organised and able to run the business side of the job, as well as tenacious – there's a lot of competition out there. For formal training, many professional photographers take a college, evening or university course to develop their technical skills. There's a huge range on offer, so ask for recommendations whilst on work experience or from another pro, to find out which are most respected for particular areas; they include the Certificate in Photography and Photo Imaging at Levels 2 and 3, and courses in digital retouching software, such as Adobe Photoshop.

WORKING LIFE: Nigel Howard is a freelance photographer and night picture editor of the *London Evening Standard* newspaper

'As a busy photojournalist I am always on the hunt for a story – checking emails, IM messages, Twitter, Facebook, Photographer's Forum, and listening and watching for whatever I can pick up on that will give me a steer faster than others. My day officially starts at 4.30pm and finishes between half midnight and 5am, as I work nights to get photos into the next day's newspaper, but I'm checking for news stories long before that – I need to be ahead of the competition.

I got my break by submitting a picture to a paper that was taken when a siege broke in Clerkenwell – I got the picture that someone else missed. Since then, I'm always proud of my exclusive photos – from gritty news stories to cycle incidents, Millennium Bridge fireworks to Mayoral and general elections, police stories and lighter snaps too.

The worst part of the job is taking images for "vox pops" [getting quotes from people on the street about topics] and door steps [approaching news subjects at their home or office address to quiz them]. We all have to do them but they can take ages – they're only speedy if you are working with a smart, tenacious, hungry reporter who is switched on. Oh, and I don't relish covering riots when I am in physical danger, or dealing with PRs who have no understanding of what I do.

It was a hard slog to get to this point in my career. I just kept pushing, searching, and looking for a news picture and submitting them all the time to newspaper and magazine picture desks. I kept on phoning in – you can't be shy in this job, you have to submit pictures "on spec" and build up contacts along the way.

Some people claim you have to be born a photographer, but I believe that you can learn how to do anything. You can learn how to use the tools that you have: camera, lenses, lights, etc. It is true, though, that you need that natural eye and the ability to frame and make a picture. You need to be able to look for something different, and have the ability to best illustrate what is in the written story. Technical knowledge and skill are important but if you cannot put them to use and make a picture work, then you'll struggle.

To someone thinking of getting into photography, either as a first job or a career change, I would say look at all the photo magazines, take a keen interest in news agencies, news on TV and radio channels and, of course, newspapers, who still predominantly lead the way in news coverage, breaking news and features. Also look at photography groups on Facebook and viral snaps on

Twitter. There are a number of personal skills you need for the job, too: a friendly, personable manner; you have to be inquisitive and probing and unafraid to ask questions, but still respectful. You have to dress as smart as you can for the occasion you are covering – and smile where appropriate.

The best thing about my job is being able to meet extraordinary people that I wouldn't normally meet, and going to see places that the public don't get access to – sometimes at the forefront of a breaking news story before no one else knows about it. And not forgetting seeing one's work in print or online, then discussed on radio phone-ins or TV – I'm always proud of seeing my bylines on photos. It's still as exciting today as it was the very first time.'

PHYSIOTHERAPIST

AVERAGE STARTING SALARY – £21,300

ENTRY POSITION – Physiotherapist

TYPICAL WEEKLY HOURS – 37.5 hours

RECOMMENDED QUALIFICATIONS – Physiotherapy degree

IF YOU LIKE THIS YOU MIGHT ALSO LIKE . . . doctor, nurse, personal trainer

You could be called upon to dole out treatment during the FA Cup Final, or help a child to learn how to walk again after a car crash: physiotherapy is a seriously varied profession, involving treating people with movement problems caused by accidents, injuries, illness or ageing. Some physios work in hospitals, ranging from helping unconscious patients keep breathing in intensive care, to helping people get back on their feet with rehab after operations, strokes or other difficulties. Others work in high-street treatment centres or inside GP surgeries, with specialist equipment to help patients.

Most physios gain general clinical experience then go on to specialise, for example on a particular part of the body, or working with older people or children; with stroke victims or those in recovery from brain surgery in neurology; in oncology with cancer patients; in cardiology with heart patients; in women's health; with outpatients with musculo-skeletal problems or amputees; or working with mental health patients.

Skills-wise, you'll need to be strong and good with your hands, patient, good with people and empathetic, flexible and hard-working, with excellent communication skills and happy working as part of a team.

Then you'll need a physiotherapy degree or postgraduate award approved by the Health and Care Professions Council in order to register and join the Chartered Society of Physiotherapy. To secure an undergraduate place on a physio degree, you'll normally need three A levels, including biology and often another science too, plus five GCSEs at grades A–C. Different unis may have different demands; some accept Level 3 diplomas.

NHS pay for fully qualified physios is between £21,000 and £28,000 a year, rising to about £34,000 for a specialist and as much as £50,000 for a manager or highly qualified physio. Insiders say it takes about ten years to become manager of a small department, but it varies from hospital to hospital.

As with most NHS jobs, the work is in shifts, with most hospitals now moving towards seven-day working patterns, so you will be expected to work a weekend shift every three or four weeks. Some hospitals will pay you extra for doing so, whilst other hospitals will give you a day off in the week after working at the weekend. There are also plenty of opportunities for private work as a physiotherapist, or even to open your own practice. Most physios do so only after training and securing at least three years' experience in the NHS. Running your own private practice is potentially lucrative, but means taking on the responsibilities of running a business, such as grappling with employment law, taxes and property maintenance.

'There is a high turnover of staff so there are always NHS jobs available,' says one senior physio. 'You might have to wait a little while for your "dream job" in your "dream hospital", but the job market for newly qualified physios is improving – a few years ago, it could take up to a year to get a post, but more recently most physios have been able to get a job soon after graduation.'

All NHS posts are listed on the NHS Jobs website. After applying online with a personal statement and application (which might remind you of UCAS), shortlisted candidates have an interview, which might also involve a group task, presentation or written exam.

WORKING LIFE: Corey Brown is an NHS hospital physio*

'I start work at 8.30 in the morning, when I am in my tunic and ready to go. What's on my treatment list can vary massively by the day – some patients may be elderly, some young. My main job is to maintain our patients' function and mobility. First thing, we have a team meeting to discuss the day ahead.

At 9am, there's a ward meeting – it's catchily called a "multi-disciplinary team meeting" – with doctors, a nurse, speech and language therapist, occupational therapist and me, to discuss the daily plan for all the patients. From 9.30am until 12.30pm I treat patients on the ward. Some days, I also help with nursing roles, such as taking patients to the toilet or helping to clean them – you have to be willing to get stuck in.

At lunch I might tackle some of the most boring parts of the job: note-writing and admin, then from 1.30 to 4.45pm it's more patient

---

* *name changed for anonymity*

treatments on the ward, before home time at 5pm. The best parts of the job are treating patients, especially when someone has been unwell for a long period of time, stuck in bed and very weak. It's you who gets them walking, sitting in a chair, able to go to the toilet on their own, and ultimately gets them home. It really is amazing.

Usually there's at least one meeting each week where every patient is discussed in detail with lots of different health care professionals, including occupational therapists, speech and language therapists, doctors, nurses, social workers, psychologists and others. There's also scheduled weekly teaching time for the team.

Once I'm home, I can usually switch off unless I'm on call: about once every six weeks I'm on call from 5pm until 9am. We cover the entire hospital, so if someone becomes very sick and has difficulty breathing or coughing and clearing sputum from their chest, then we might get called to help the medical team to treat the patient.'

ODD JOB: Oshiya (people-pushers), Japan

You thought the 7.49 into Paddington was busy, but in Japan, the bullet train operators hire pros to shove the maximum possible number of people into each carriage. Personality required for the job: you've got to be pushy . . .

PILOT

AVERAGE STARTING SALARY – £21,000

ENTRY POSITION – Co-pilot

TYPICAL WEEKLY HOURS – Variable

RECOMMENDED QUALIFICATIONS – Airline Transport Pilot's licence. Good physical fitness and eyesight/hearing

IF YOU LIKE THIS YOU MIGHT ALSO LIKE . . . engineer, military careers, police officer

What was once considered one of the most glamorous jobs around might be a bit more automated nowadays – Ryanair's boss Michael O'Leary once told me 'we have two pilots on board, one to not touch the computer, and the other one to make sure he doesn't touch the computer' – but a career as a pilot is still pretty exciting.

You jet around the world flying passengers (and/or cargo) and the range of jobs stretches from captain of a passenger jet for an airline like British Airways to the pilot of a private jet. Your hours are tightly regulated (for European airlines, the maximum number of flying hours in 12 consecutive months is 1,000), but also usually subject to awkward shifts. The pay, however, can be high: Office for National Statistics figures ranked being an aircraft pilot as the second-best-paid job in the UK, with an average salary of £78,300.

Co-pilots (first officers) tend to earn between £22,000 and £50,000 a year, depending on experience, while experienced captains of jumbo jets earn between £60,000 and £100,000 a year. There is also the big perk of free or seriously discounted staff travel rights, which are often also offered to friends and family.

On short-haul passenger airlines like easyJet, Ryanair and Thomson, most pilots and their cabin crew return to their UK base each day, but stopovers are common for pilots on long-haul routes flying for the likes of British Airways, Emirates or Virgin Atlantic.

On-board, it's not just flying a plane: pilots have to make lots of calculations, such as how much fuel is required, and the implications of changing weather patterns or air traffic control instructions. There are two people in the cockpit: usually a captain and first officer (or pilot and co-pilot) – the captain has completed more flying hours, while a first officer has the same level of qualifications but fewer flying hours. A pilot's jobs usually include pre-flight checks of the plane, engines and fuel, calculating the best route, communicating with on-board cabin crew and the air traffic controls of various airports, as well as constantly checking flight data, updating passengers on the progress of their journey and writing flight reports.

To become an airline pilot you will need to have good teamwork skills, strong concentration and hand-to-eye coordination and maths skills, and you'll also need to be able to remain calm and take charge in an emergency. The famed rule that you have to have 20:20 vision is not the case, but you do need healthy, well-performing eyes. (You can find out more about the rules at www.caa.co.uk.)

There are lots of tests and training in a pilot's career – most airlines demand they take a simulator training flight every six months, with a pass or fail result. It's a popular career for job-changers, too, and a large number of civil aircraft pilots used to fly planes for the military.

For new pilots, though, there are hefty amounts of exams and expensive training before they are allowed in a cockpit. The first hurdle is to get an Airline Transport Pilot Licence (ATPL), for which there are 14 written exams, covering a broad spectrum of aviation-related subjects such as navigation, meteorology, aviation law and flight rules and workings, as well as numerous flying tests. If you pass, you're awarded a 'frozen ATPL', which allows you to fly as a first officer. Then once you have completed enough flying hours (normally 1,500, with at least 500 as co-pilot) you can apply for a full ATPL (you must be over 21) and qualify as an airline captain.

You can choose to do all that studying in a classroom setting by going on a full-time residential course, or you can complete a distance learning course. 'If you study hard, and study full-time, you can probably complete the ATPL exams in six months,' says Captain Mark Wood (for more on his working life, see below). Every commercial pilot is also required to pass a full health check, including heart checks such as an ECG and EEG, blood test, urine test, eye test and audio test. This is repeated each year.

'It's forecast that there won't be enough pilots in the future due to the rising costs of training,' adds Wood. Training at a Civil Aviation Authority (CAA) approved school generally costs about £100,000 in the UK, although some find less expensive courses overseas. Very few airlines offer sponsorship programmes, so most people have to self-fund, although some airlines do offer 'conversion courses' for those who qualified as a pilot in the armed forces. But, again, there is strong competition.

WORKING LIFE: Captain Mark Wood flies for easyJet

His first job was as an electrical engineer, but Mark Wood loved aeroplanes and so he self-funded himself through flying exams when he had the time and the funding available. He worked as a First Officer for British Airways, then in the same role for easyJet for five years before becoming a pilot on its Airbus 320. He has now been with the airline for 14 years.

'My alarm goes off at 4.20am, giving me 1 hour and 10 minutes to get up, washed and dressed and make a coffee before my drive to the airport. I check in at the crew room at 5.30am to report for my flight from Luton to Lisbon. I log onto our intranet and print off my crew check-in sheet, which tells me about my crew for the day.

The first officer (FO) will also be checking in and printing all the necessary flight plans and paperwork for the day. We then have 15 minutes to go through our flight plans, the weather reports and NOTAMs (notes about each airport and the facilities provided) for the airports we're operating from and to. The cabin manager informs us that the crew have all checked in and then we head out to the aircraft. Once there, I check our Technical Log and then we fire up the aeroplane using a GPU [Ground Power Unit, this provides electrical power to all the aircraft systems], then we have a quick brief with the whole crew discussing the weather and flight times and any other pertinent points for the day. The dispatcher usually turns up to the aircraft 35 minutes before departure, handing us a load sheet, which informs us of the number of passengers and bags on board the aeroplane. Next, I set up the aircraft for the first flight of the day, whilst the FO does a 'walk around', checking the aircraft externally, and the cabin manager will tell me when it's OK to start boarding the passengers. The FO will then get our air traffic control clearance; this tells us which runway and departure procedures we can expect.

Once the passengers are all on board I will say a quick hello and introduce the rest of the crew. The doors of the aircraft are then shut and the FO requests push and start with air traffic control. We then taxi out to the runway, carrying out a few checks en route. After departure we climb to our cruising altitude. Once established in the cruise, we check our progress and complete some paperwork. We carry out fuel checks to ensure that we're using the amount of fuel we expect to and get updated weather reports. The next task is to set up the aircraft for our arrival – organising the instruments for the approach and briefing the FO about how I'm going to configure the aircraft and what speeds I'm going to fly at which points. We then inform the cabin crew that there's 10 minutes to landing so they can tidy away the trollies, collect rubbish and ensure all the passengers are seated. Once we've landed we are designated a stand, where we then have approximately 25 minutes to turn the aircraft around – disembarking passengers, tidying the aircraft, completing any paperwork, setting up the aircraft for the departure and the return route, then boarding all the passengers for the return flight, closing the doors and pushing back to make our return journey.

We can do up to four flights a day. Our working hours are linked to flight destinations and could include nights, weekends and public holidays, but the hours you can work as a pilot are strictly regulated for safety reasons. One of the best times in the job is on a really early morning when it's dark, wet and miserable – and then you break through the clouds and see the sunset. It's fantastic. By contrast, cruising at 39,000 feet on a five-hour flight can be boring.

At easyJet we don't work a 'normal' Monday-to-Friday week: we work a fixed pattern of five early duties followed by three days off, then five late duties followed by four days off. We may get one weekend off every 4–6 weeks, depending on when our days off fall. Once we leave work, we generally aren't connected to work at all, but we have to keep up to date with any changes in our operating manuals. Every six months we have a simulator check, so we have to study emergency procedures and keep abreast of the aircraft's technical systems. Being a pilot is one of the most tested professions in the world.'

POLICE OFFICER

AVERAGE STARTING SALARY – £19,000

ENTRY POSITION – Student Officer (probationer)

TYPICAL WEEKLY HOURS – 40 hours

RECOMMENDED QUALIFICATIONS – Citizenship or the right to work in the UK indefinitely. Three years' residency. At least 18 years old. Pass background checks

IF YOU LIKE THIS YOU MIGHT ALSO LIKE ... fireman, military careers, teacher

Being a member of Britain's police force is one the most visible professions around, especially since successive governments have started pushing for more 'bobbies on the beat' patrolling the UK's streets. Police are supposed to be a part of the community that they serve, but work as a police officer is very varied – jobs range from desk work to being a uniformed officer on foot or in a patrol car, undercover work to carrying out international investigations into issues such as suspected terrorist plots. Most police careers start, however, in the emergency response team – responding to calls for help from the public, making arrests, investigating crimes, taking witness statements, searching for missing people, covering custody suites and policing large public events and demonstrations.

After starting out as a general police officer, there's then a chance to specialise in specific branches of the force, such as SOCA, the Serious Organised Crime Agency, drugs squad, the economic crime unit, traffic police, royal and diplomacy branch, mounted (horseback) police or Criminal Investigation Department (CID).

'Problem solving, patience, the ability to stay calm in stressful situations, strong character, an ability to remain impartial, being a quick decision maker and resilience are the key skills,' says one experienced bobby. The police recruiters themselves say it's a 'tough and unpredictable job, but it is also an extremely rewarding position. Every day when you put on your uniform and go to work, you will be making life safer and more secure for your friends and neighbours.' You could face harrowing scenes and frightening situations, but you will receive support and the police provide full training for new recruits.

To get a place you'll need to apply to a specific local police force (they handle recruitment separately; find a list of each here: police.uk/contact/force-websites); the general requirements are that you will need to have lived in the UK for three years (although there are some allowances for those who have been overseas serving in the armed forces, for example), be over 18 and pass security checks and assessment tests in aspects such as numeracy, reading and writing skills, data handling and decision making, as well as fitness and health checks.

New rules also mean some police forces have a pre-entry requirement, with candidates having to complete the Certificate in Knowledge of Policing before attempting to become a new police constable.

One way around completing the Certificate, which involves paid-for training, is to become a special constable. These are volunteer police officers who work alongside regular officers, wearing the same uniform and equipped with the same powers and responsibilities. You have to give up at least 16 hours of your spare time each month, with duties including foot and vehicle patrols, anti-robbery initiatives, working in schools to talk about safety and crime and helping in the event of accidents, fights and fires. Special constables who have completed 200 hours of operational service and gained their Independent Patrol Status can apply to become a new police constable, without requiring the Certificate in Knowledge of Policing, so for career-changers this is a good way to test out your enjoyment of the career before you commit to it.

Two new fast-track schemes have also recently been introduced to allow career-changers and graduates to apply direct to senior policing roles. For 180 years the normal way to enter the police was to join as a constable and rise up the ranks, but the new programmes are aimed at allowing 'experienced leaders' from the private, public and charity sectors to join as superintendents, as well as a separate scheme for graduate recruits which sees them rise from constable to inspector in three years.

Pay-wise, the average starting salary for police constables is between £19,000 and £23,000, depending on location, rising to almost £26,000 after initial training. There's also a London weighting for those in the capital, and extra money for overtime. Police receive automatic pay rises every few years, until they have completed ten years' service. Promotions are also rewarded in the salary: a sergeant can earn around £37,000, an inspector earns roughly £50,000, whilst a commissioner can earn as much as £250,000. For constables, the normal rota is 40 hours a week on a shift system, which may include nights, weekends and public holidays, plus overtime.

WORKING LIFE: policewoman Kate Smith* worked in an emergency response team in London before leaving the Met to retrain in another career

'I filled out an application form for the police force during a recruitment drive, before being invited for an assessment day and then a fitness day, and was eventually offered a job. The job was shift work, so we were expected to work days and nights and weekends. Knowing what I know about the job now, I wouldn't work on the response team again – it involves covering 24/7 emergency policing, working round the clock to patrol the streets and responding to emergency calls – but other jobs in the police would attract me back to the Force.

On an average day, I'd wake up at 5.30am to get to work for 6.30am. I would then change into uniform and be ready for briefing (information and intelligence about your borough). By 7am we would be officially on duty and answering any calls. The rest of the day would differ according to what calls came up. We would be due to finish at 4pm but that rarely happened due to paperwork from arrests, etc. I'd be working about 55 hours in six shifts, plus

---

* name changed for anonymity

a lot of overtime, then have four days off. There were definitely enjoyable parts of the job, like driving on blue lights, car chases and working as part of a team with lots of camaraderie and helping each other and members of the public. But there were also really boring parts, such as standing around on crime scenes and having to watch people in custody who had mental health issues for entire shifts.

Winter was the worst time – shift work when it's dark seemed to last longer, and standing around in the cold, especially during the night, is tough.

There were a lot of times when I felt in danger from a criminal, but when you work on a response team you know that your colleagues will look out for you; everyone made sure everyone else was safe. The culture in the police is quite difficult to explain – when dealing with difficult situations it is sometimes easier to make a joke, so there is a lot of banter. You need to be able to take a joke and also have thick skin so that you don't get upset when being abused by members of the public. You do get some good perks working in the police, though, such as free travel on London's Underground, and various discounts in restaurants or shops, such as Nando's!

I left the police, as others do, because I wanted a job with more regular hours and to know what time I was going to finish work, as well as looking for a better work/life balance – and more respect in a private sector job.'

POLITICIAN AND CIVIL SERVANT

AVERAGE STARTING SALARY – £21,000–£24,000

ENTRY POSITION – MP or Civil Servant

TYPICAL WEEKLY HOURS – 37 hours

RECOMMENDED QUALIFICATIONS – General, Local or European Election, or Civil Service Exam. High literacy and numeracy. If you have a second-class degree or above, you can apply for fast stream.

IF YOU LIKE THIS YOU MIGHT ALSO LIKE . . . academic, PR, teacher

Working in politics might be one of the most derided careers around: like estate agents and journalists, the profession's reputation is lower than a snake's belly. But shove aside a few scandals, and politics can offer a chance to shape policy on a national level. There are a huge range of jobs and unique opportunities: the childcare minister Sam Gyimah, for example, explains below how he has access to the boss of the nation's biggest companies and can create policies and vote on issues that will change Britain, or even the world.

While Members of Parliament work long hours, they also earn

healthy incomes (the basic annual salary is currently £67,000, plus expenses to cover the costs of running an office, employing staff, having somewhere to live in London and in their constituency and travelling between Parliament and their constituency; Ministers receive a higher salary) and can work towards lofty positions. The job interview – getting thousands of people to believe you'll do a good job and vote for you – is harder than average, though.

Being an MP is far from the only job in politics. Others include:

- Being an elected politician in other institutions, like the Scottish Parliament, Welsh Assembly, European Parliament, local council, etc. The nature and volume of the work depends on the level of involvement, but largely entails representing constituents, resolving their problems, debating, holding bosses of major private and public institutions to account and voting on both new laws and international affairs. Many elected politicians begin down this road via 'grass roots'– joining a party, campaigning and networking – but it's also a popular second or third career for changers, who may start in law, consulting or another profession and network to become selected in a particular area.

- Working as a political researcher for an elected official, political party, trade union, PR firm, charity, industry trade body or non-government organisation. The job mostly involves digging through facts, legislation, research and media sources to find stories, angles and campaign ideas, as well as finding the answers to questions on behalf of a boss or employer.

- A role as a politician's assistant means being their right-hand (wo)man – providing admin support, helping with research, publicity, dealing with constituents, diary management, social media and online updates, helping with speech-writing, reports and briefing documents. Many wangle their way into this role, and that of political researcher, via work experience, as politics is a very networking-driven industry; check out the website w4mp.org to find out more.

- Civil service: there are two main ways to enter the civil service – the half a million staff who help the government of the day to develop and deliver its policies. The first is 'direct entry', which means applying for a permanent or fixed-term contract in a full-time or part-time role, something that would appeal to career-changers. The second is the fast-stream programme for graduates. The latter is an accelerated programme where graduates tackle a range of postings in different government departments and agencies (including opportunities to be seconded into charities, the private sector, other public sector bodies and even roles abroad). You could work in education, the economy, foreign affairs, defence policy, health, the environment and many more areas. Responsibility comes very quickly; you'll get a wide range of experience in a very short space of time as well as public sector perks such as flexitime and a good pension. The official entry demands are certain nationality and immigration requirements, and at least a second-class degree in any subject, but its places are much in-demand and you'll need a great application and interview process. Find out more at gov.uk/fast-stream. Pay starts at £25,000 and goes up to around £45,000 with four to five years' experience, but it's often not so good in the more glamorous departments, such as the Treasury and Foreign Office.

Despite the usual stereotypes, people enter politics from a wide range of backgrounds and at different stages in life – there's no 'one size fits all' route into most jobs in the industry. 'Some people enter after a career in another industry, but young people should not be put off – if you are old enough to vote, you are old enough to have a point of view,' says Minister Sam Gyimah (see below). 'To be an MP you have to have something to contribute, so the best preparation is to be involved in the things you are passionate about.'

Some politicians are whizzes at policy work and scrutinising the detail of legislation, others bring real expertise on particular issues, or are highly effective debaters, media maestros or simply excellent constituency workers.

'But there are some personal qualities that are essential for any MP to be effective,' Gyimah adds. 'Politics is about having the empathy – to put yourself in someone else's position, to understand their needs and their aspirations. You have to enjoy helping others solve problems, and to be fearless in your desire to challenge wrongs, whether in your local community or the country. You also need to have good stamina and resilience to keep going when you get knocked back.'

WORKING LIFE: Sam Gyimah was first elected to Parliament in 2010 and is now Childcare and Education Minister as well as MP for East Surrey. He says he took 'the scenic route', studying politics at university then working in investment banking and founding his own small businesses before standing.

'An MP's day varies enormously – I'm often reminded of an episode of [the BBC satire] *The Thick of It* – the idea that you go from a high-level policy meeting in the morning to looking at the cracks in a garden wall in the afternoon is not too far-fetched!

Working as an MP is unlike any other job. There's no formal contract, no clocking in or out time, and your performance review comes once every five years – at an election.

But you're also under far greater public scrutiny than in almost any other job, whether it's someone taking a curious glance into your shopping basket at the supermarket, or the activist who once asked where I had been on the grounds that he hadn't seen my curtains drawn in a few days!

It's competitive, too: unlike doctors, lawyers or scientists, there is a very strict limit on the number of people who can do the job – 650, to be exact. So you can only enter when someone else chooses to retire, or if you oust them in an election. Every party has its own process to become a candidate, but the final interview is always the same – you have to win the support of a majority of the 70,000 or so people you wish to represent.

As a rookie backbench MP, my day was very different to my next job, as Parliamentary Private Secretary to the Prime Minister – then my timetable had to reflect the day's events at Number 10. As a Government Whip [issuing voting instructions to other MPs] I then spent far more time in the House of Commons; now that I am a Minister, my time is split between two departments, Parliament and my constituency.

This is my average Friday:

7am: wake up to the sound of the *Today* programme, the backdrop to almost every politician's life. A quick glance at the newspapers and a scan of Twitter.

8.30am: arrive at the Department for meetings with civil servants.

10am: respond to a debate in the House of Commons.

11am: arrive in my office to catch up with Parliamentary team on constituent correspondence, casework and local media stories.

2pm: arrive in the constituency to meet with local residents on a campaign issue.

3pm: speak at a local school or open a new community facility.

4pm: hold an advice surgery at constituency office, to work through individual issues in 15-minute pre-booked slots.

7pm: public meeting or Q&A session at a local community hall.

10pm: arrive home.

The job definitely spills out of the normal 9-to-5: the House of Commons can sit until 10pm, and even when you do make it home, as a Minister you often have a red box with papers to review for the following morning.

One of the best things about being an MP is that you have a fantastic platform to engage with people at a very high level on whatever issue you care about. When a constituent comes to you with a financial problem you can write to the chief executives of the major banks and the banking industry's trade body – not only resolving the constituent's issue but driving wider changes to the industry, too. You can arrange meetings with whoever can drive an issue forward – whether it is another minister or the chief executive of Gatwick Airport, and hold public bodies to account, be it the taxman, NHS, or the passport office.

It's also a real perk to have a seat in the "mother of all parliaments", and a vote on the major questions that shape the future of the country, whether it's the economy at home or intervention in Syria.'

THE LOWDOWN: fast-stream civil servant Kamal Shah*

'I normally get into the office at around 9am and leave at around 7pm, with about a half-hour for lunch at 1pm. I'm currently working in a department linked to environmental work, and my key tasks are developing a specific piece of policy, meeting industry stakeholders to explain the government's position and to understand their concerns, and writing submissions to ministers explaining the intricacies of a particular issue, or asking them to make decisions.

What is the job actually like? You're working with lots of bright, committed people, often pushing policies through on really tight timescales, reacting to newspaper headlines and struggling to get all the different bits of government (from the various policy teams, to ministers, other departments, and the Treasury or the Prime Minister) to line up behind a vaguely coherent strategy.

The best parts of the job are seeing a policy you've worked on finally being approved and published – particularly if it's a good policy! There's often also a strong sense of camaraderie in teams. The boring bit is how long it can take for government to make a decision – it can feel like you're actually in a political TV satire sometimes – and dealing with angry or frustrated industry representatives.

When I started on the fast stream a few years back, there was more

---

* *name changed for anonymity*

money for training and lunchtime seminars – you could go on professional development courses to develop your employability – but now that's been cut right back. There's definitely no longer such a thing as a free lunch – and certainly not a boozy one!'

Dream Job: Professional footballer

Former England footballer Michael Owen helped Liverpool FC win the cup treble of the UEFA Cup, FA Cup and Football League Cup. Since retiring from the game, he's been involved in businesses including working as ambassador for football jackpot Colossus Bets.

'When you say you're a professional footballer, people expect that you go out and play once or twice a week – in front of 50,000 people in the Premiership – scoring goals, having great fun, and then go home. But there's a lot more to it: the training, the thinking about everything that goes past your lips – is it going to help or hinder my performance? – the going to bed at certain times. It's not just training for a few hours in the morning then the odd game. Every minute of every day, you're assessing how everything you do will affect your performance.

As a footballer, I was training for about 15 hours a week on the pitch, and about the same in the gym or around the club doing fitness work. On an average day, I'd get up at 7am, get ready and get my kids ready, then do the school run and drive straight to training, arriving at 9am and heading for the gym. Most people think when a footballer's on the pitch, they're 100 per cent fit, but actually – especially from Christmas towards the end of the season – most of us were being patched up every time. Normally about half of the team will be in the gym, doing core work to make them quicker and stronger, and the other half will be in the treatment room getting strapped up under their socks, or having painkilling injections. It's a lot harder than people think – your body isn't always at its peak.

Then we'd be on the pitch for about an hour and a half, followed by a shower, maybe another gym trip or more treatment, then lunch and home, or other tasks like talking to the media, doing interviews, attending club supporters' events, making hospital visits, work for sponsors, replying to fan mail, or doing photoshoots for sportwear companies. You're never allowed to do that kind of work on the day before a game, though.

Sometimes there'd be a double training session but I'd usually be home by 2pm to go and pick the kids up, then have dinner and normal life – well, normal-ish: you're not allowed to do anything risky, like ride a horse or a motorbike, or go skiing. You've got to be very careful. Even when the kids wanted to play football with me in the garden, I had to say no if I had a match the next day.

Still, all the sacrifices are worth it when you score a goal. You put in so much work throughout your life, starting as a youngster aged three, four or five – honing skills, practising, making sacrifices, a lifetime of dedication – then when you score a great goal and feel the adrenalin . . . It's unparalleled.

Being a footballer isn't something you can learn – you can't go to university and work your nuts off for three years and then say "I'm a footballer". You need the natural ability, plus the right physical attributes, balance and co-ordination, but even if you have them, it's still unlikely that most people will make it. Amongst kids at school, probably 0.01 per cent of people are going to be able to make a living as a professional football player, in any of the leagues; even amongst those picked for an under-15 football academy, the chances of success are probably about 5 per cent.

Having said that, a lot is made of how to reach the top, but if you're a good player I don't think the facilities or equipment make too much difference – if you've got it, you will make it in this country everyone's on the lookout for talented players. Lack of opportunity isn't an excuse.

If you do make it, obviously the rewards are great. But I don't begrudge any footballer their wage – they're drawing the crowds, making people turn on the TV, and it's a very short career. I retired at 33 and, since I started at 17, I had an above-average length of career.

It's wise to start planning for a career after football in your mid- to late 20s. The last thing I wanted to do in retirement was wake up and think, "Which golf course shall I go to today?" It would get pretty boring after a month or two. I wanted to keep busy for my mental state. Now I really enjoy doing TV commentary work for BT and running Michael Owen Management, looking after a group of young players and advising them on how to make it. It's something to get up for – I haven't woken up once since retirement and thought, "What shall I do today?" and I think that's important – there are plenty of horror stories of ex-footballers ending up in trouble.'

PUBLIC RELATIONS (PR)

AVERAGE STARTING SALARY – £18,000–£20,000

ENTRY POSITION – Publicity Assistant

TYPICAL WEEKLY HOURS – 30–40 hours

RECOMMENDED QUALIFICATIONS – Relevant degree in journalism or advertising, marketing and communications, business, management, English or politics. Work experience

IF YOU LIKE THIS YOU MIGHT ALSO LIKE . . . advertising, journalist, teacher

As a PR, your role is to manage someone – or something's – reputation. It could be a government campaign, a chocolate bar, or a drug-taking, non-stop-partying celebrity who wants to be known only as a clean-living daytime TV presenter. Whoever or whatever it is, you'll be tasked with talking to the media – the traditional stuff, as in TV and the press – as well as monitoring and influencing what PRs dub the 'online conversation' to boost (or hush-up) your client's name.

It's a fast-paced, often fun job, depending on who you're working for, and it's an industry where a lot of people enter after a career change (often from journalism to almost-always-better-paid PR work, but also from other jobs). Boozy parties and jaunts abroad are often part of the job. Some PRs work in-house within companies, others for agencies or consultancies that brands or individuals hire for advice.

Daily jobs might include sending out press releases (with story or news ideas); 'crisis management' if a client's public profile needs, uh, some help; answering questions from the media; seeking out surveys or data that could make interesting stories about your clients; collating and analysing media coverage; writing or organising in-house magazines, speeches, case studies or annual reports; running press conferences or helping executives be 'media trained' and ready for a public grilling.

Skills-wise, 'you need to be able to look someone in the eye, marshal a conversation or bring a dead one to life,' says one veteran PR. 'You also need to be able to step back very quickly and think of the ramifications of a certain course of action or client response. PR is rather like a game of chess – you need to see as many moves ahead as you can.'

You'll need to be a bit of a news hound, too, watching and understanding it constantly, at the very least the sector you're working in. 'Oh, and it also helps if you can handle your drink. PR and journalism are two of the hardest-drinking sectors out there,' the insider adds. You'd better have a thick skin, too: the journalists that you need to get on-side often snarl down the phone or hang up; the clients whose business you need to win moan you're not getting enough results and want you available 24/7.

Most PRs, though not all, are graduates – but of almost any degree. The pay starts at about £22,000, rising to £33,000 with a few years' experience. Top managers, such as PR agency founders or heads of corporate affairs within a big company, often earn more than £100,000. It's a competitive industry to crack, but once you're in, PR jobs are very broad and offer a safe career with a clear route to promotion.

WORKING LIFE: Dominic Hiatt is founder of Rhizome PR and Just In Time PR – a 'no coverage, no fee' agency.

'As sad as it sounds, if I wake up in the middle of the night, I check my emails. PR is one of those lines of work where you can't really be doing your job correctly if you're not always available. I tend to start working at around 7am, as most of the news tends to break in the morning. The first thing I do is go on the BBC website or check Twitter. If anything's happening, those two will usually cover it.

I work about 60 hours a week – if a client has an urgent problem to deal with, or a journalist wants some comment on a Sunday morning at 9am, you have to respond. I've always got my phone on. Clearly, I don't expect my staff to "always be on", but it's essential that if they're not, then there's someone else that can deal with anything that crops up.

I used to be a journalist and got fed up with the crap money, so I sold my soul to the PR devil and set up a firm. At first, I had just a couple of clients and it grew from there. PR can really get the adrenalin pumping when you're on a breaking news story or a big announcement. I do enjoy it, at times, and I get to meet lots of very singular individuals, from billionaires to gnarly news hacks. I enjoy reactive PR – responding very quickly to breaking news stories with clients' comments. Because I was a journalist before, I like to think that I know how to present a client's views in a way that will get them picked up by the media. I've had clients on the front page of many newspapers as a result of reacting quickly to the news.

Perks-wise, PR offers up a lot of lunches and corporate jollies. If you're starting out, eating in London's top restaurants and taking journalists on ski trips can be great fun. After a while you get bored of that, though.

Lots of people have gravitated towards jobs in social media and SEO [search engine optimisation, aka making web pages more prominent in internet searches] in recent years, rather than PR, thinking that's where the money and growth potential is. The reality is that PR equips you with a media expertise, both social and traditional, that would be impossible to get through any other channels.

You don't need any specific qualifications to work in PR. You'll need to be confident with people, know how to look someone in the eye, and generally have a bit of energy. You also need a sense of humour in this line of work. Most journalists are pretty bleak.

If you want to become a PR, personally, I'd avoid rags and websites like *PR Week* like the plague. I couldn't think of anything more dull. Focus on having a good time and, when you've left university skint, try to get your first job in PR and have a crack at it. We just hired a maths grad who was going to be a teacher. Zero experience but he's bright, and slightly warped, and that was enough for us.'

PUBLISHING

AVERAGE STARTING SALARY – £14,000–£18,000

ENTRY POSITION – Editorial, rights or publicity assistant, junior agent

TYPICAL WEEKLY HOURS – 45 hours

RECOMMENDED QUALIFICATIONS – A degree or work experience

IF YOU LIKE THIS YOU MIGHT ALSO LIKE ... author, journalist, TV producer/ director

If you've not been put off by the doom-mongers' tales of a dying industry and you want to work in the book-making industry, you might think it sounds like cups of tea and reading books all day long, looking for the next *Fifty Shades of Grey/One Day/Book of Jobs*. But it's a lot more complicated than that. Selecting manuscripts is just a small part of the industry, which includes people working in design, production, rights, sales, PR and marketing, plus the usual business roles such as finance, contracts and law, and the editorial jobs too have much to pack into their days beyond next-big-thing-hunting.

The industry is fast changing: it went from being 90 per cent print to 30 per cent digital in just 12 months, according to the Publishers Association, and e-books require a whole new range of experts. It's also seriously competitive: one literary agent tells me she had 590 applications for an entry-level job in her small firm. That imbalance of supply and demand of people also means pay can be lower than candidates expect.

But it's an exciting industry where you can help turn a whole bunch of words on a computer document into a physical book – perhaps even one that's the must-read gripped in everyone's hands on the train. So what are the major roles?

Editorial: responsible for acquiring and publishing the books. Staffed by editorial assistants (the most common first job into the industry), who liaise with authors, agents and all the other departments in a publishing house to keep on top of a manuscript's progress, copy editors (who carefully read the manuscript to check for mistakes, repetition, factual errors, etc.) and commissioning editors, who pick new authors and titles that will, hopefully, sell well and help the publisher to be profitable.

Contracts: work closely with editorial to negotiate book deals with authors, checking rights and royalties. Most contract specialists work their way up from an assistant role.

Design: work on a book's cover, size, typeface, text, commission any illustrations, photoshoots, etc. Often have a graphic design background (see page 114).

Production: work on turning a computer document into a physical book – from picking the paper to organising the binding and keeping the project running on time. A few formal courses exist, like the one at the London College of Communication, but many employees work their way up from an entry-level job as a production assistant.

Publicity and marketing: make the loudest possible noise about new books and authors when they're published. Publicity is a PR role (see page 261), while those in marketing work on ads, promotions and events linked to the book to create a 'buzz'.

Sales: liaise to get books from the warehouse to third parties like bookshops, Amazon, supermarkets, gift stores, etc.

Rights: responsible for maximising a book's money-spinning potential, by selling the 'rights' to translate it into foreign languages, getting it into other countries such as the US, or in other forms such as selling merchandising, TV or film rights. The job revolves around key international book fairs. Most enter this department by working their way up from a rights assistant.

Literary agent: has a list of author clients who he/she acts on behalf of, striking book deals with publishers. The job is about finding and championing new writers, spotting trends and gaps in the market, networking to meet writers and publishers and negotiating for more money and better terms. Another work-your-way-up-from-assistant kind of job.

Proofreader: now mostly carried out by freelancers, this role is for those who are experts on spelling and grammar, and adroit at checking for continuity.

Don't get too keen on one of these specific roles, however. Most positions in publishing are still secured the old-fashioned way: work experience and networking, then working your way up from being an assistant. So don't narrow your options before you begin, as you'll need to get a foot in the door and then you can try to transfer. Even if you want to ultimately be, say, an editor (and the editorial department is by far the most popular) you'll need a working knowledge of the other departments, too, so starting as a rights assistant, for example, can be invaluable.

It's not just English graduates who are wanted by the publishing industry. Most, though not all, entrants are graduates, but the nature of the degree usually isn't relevant unless you're going for a job with a specific science, medical, legal or art publisher, for example, when subject knowledge may be required. Master's degrees in book publishing are becoming more popular as candidates try to stand out from the crowd. Good networking opportunities might crop up at events run by The Society of Young Publishers and Women in Publishing (the latter, obviously, just for women) and The London Book Fair (register as a visitor and research exhibitors before you go, armed with multiple copies of your CV).

As is clear, publishing is an industry where networking is key, both to get in and succeed, so being confident helps; other key skills are loving books and reading and knowing what will sell well; organisation and ability to stick to deadlines; teamwork, attention to detail and good negotiation skills. It is possible to change careers to enter into publishing, and especially to become an agent, but this is usually from within another media discipline rather than a totally different industry.

You'll be rewarded with a starting salary of between £14,000 and £18,000 for assistant-level editorial roles, rising to about £30,000 to £40,000 with experience; senior commissioning editors may be on £50,000-plus; in-house copy editors can expect to earn between £20,000 and £38,000, while freelance copy editors earn a fee per hour or per book, which usually works out at around £25–£35 an hour. Literary agents' earnings are usually tied to a commission of their writers' income – usually about 15 per cent.

WORKING LIFE: Susan Watt, Publisher

'No two days are the same. Generally, I'll start the day by reading global and industry news (*The Bookseller* and some publishing blogs), then there will often be some morning meetings – usually discussing editorial, publicity, scheduling or art. The shape of the day after that depends on what stages my books are at – it could be editing a manuscript, meeting an agent or author, negotiating a contract, discussing issues with colleagues, giving a jacket brief or writing cover copy. Publishing is a team effort so you will always be working alongside colleagues in other departments. Many editors or publishers will be responsible for overseeing 10–20 titles at any one time, so the role requires plenty of juggling of priorities and skills. This also means that the job can easily expand to fill as much time as you are willing to give it. There is always something more you could be doing on a title or in researching new authors and reading the competition, and much of this takes place on evenings and weekends. Having said that, it's a career that is often a labour of love and so reading five books a week doesn't feel like work.

I started out working in bookshops and then got a job working as a publicist at a US publisher. I knew I wanted to be in editorial eventually, but it's often much easier to move across into editorial once you're in a company than to apply from the outside. It's also a good idea to get training across other departments where possible. It takes about twenty years to climb to the top of the ladder in publishing, depending on your department, but as with most industries, the higher you rise, the less contact you have with individual books and authors.

The best aspect of being a publisher is developing an author and a talent, meeting a fascinating variety of people and learning about a diverse range of subjects. The worst part is seeing a book in which you've invested time and emotion fail to sell and not understanding why.

For those looking to enter publishing, it's a wonderful career full of dedicated and stimulating people. There is no one way of publishing a successful book and so it's an industry where new ideas and creative approaches are welcomed – and that's rarely boring. Read books – plenty of them and a diverse range – and read industry blogs and publications. Most people begin with work experience, but with declining staffing levels in print publishing, it's worth also looking at non-traditional publishing areas, like digital-only publishers, bookshops and book-focused PR companies. It's not easy to get a foot in the door but once you do, it's an enormously rewarding and enriching (of spirit, if not of your bank account) career.'

THE LOWDOWN: Joel Richardson works at Twenty7 Books

'I knew I'd need some work experience to break into publishing, so started applying for internships whilst I was still at university. For my first one, I was lucky: a literary agent who had attended my university set up an internship scheme for which only current students could apply. That was great as it reduced the volume of competition; I got it and spent three weeks producing a Rights Guide. It's definitely worth paying attention to opportunities from your university or your local area.

My second internship took more hard work – having already applied, unsuccessfully, to all the major publishers, I found a list of small publishers from the Independent Publishers Guild, and wrote to them individually offering to help. Seventeen didn't respond, two said they had no space, and one said yes. I spent a fortnight editing the audio for an app they were making, and was allowed to attend meetings, which were probably the most helpful part of the whole experience.

There was a significant amount of drudgery in both roles: reorganising bookshelves, taking mail to the post office and sending out rejection letters. But I also learned how to use InDesign software and an audio editing programme, and I was also trusted with evaluating submissions. The best part, though, was the support I was given when I learned that I'd been called for an interview at another publisher.

The worst moment was when I attended a meeting where they were talking about the need for more app testers. The managing director pointed to me as evidence that there were endless young people willing to work for publishers for free, which was rather demeaning.

Indirectly, the internships also led to my first job. When I got back in touch with the literary agency they were downsizing so couldn't help, but they had a connection to a publishing recruitment firm and wrote me a glowing reference, which led to me being placed as a temp in the publishing company where I ended up finding a permanent job.'

SOCIAL WORKER

AVERAGE STARTING SALARY – £19,500
ENTRY POSITION – Social worker
TYPICAL WEEKLY HOURS – 30–40 hours
RECOMMENDED QUALIFICATIONS – Degree in social work
IF YOU LIKE THIS YOU MIGHT ALSO LIKE . . . lawyer, life coach, nurse

Social work is for people who care about others and want to make a difference; some say it's a calling, like medicine, in part because the pay isn't brilliant, so a desire to help the vulnerable will be what gets you out of bed in the morning. The role is about working with kids, adults who need assistance, the elderly and others to support them through tough times and ensure they're safe from harm. But it's a role that sadly hits the news only for negative reasons: 'Where was the social worker?' scream headlines above stories about children suffering from abuse or neglect.

'Too much paperwork' claim other reports, suggesting that social workers have to spend far too much of their time stuck behind a desk form-filling, rather than with the people who need their help. All of which means that we rarely hear of the thousands of social workers working every day with families or adults in need, with great success. So what's it really like to do the job?

Social workers usually specialise, working in either adult or children's services. The former tends to involve helping individuals with mental health problems or learning difficulties, ex-offenders as they return to the community, homeless people or drug addicts or alcoholics, and older people who may need help with their medical needs or with organising benefits. Working in children's services could include supporting kids who aren't attending school, or who may be living in children's homes or who have been adopted or fostered.

Whatever the age of clients, for most social workers the average day consists of a mixture of visiting people to assess or review their care needs, and being in the office writing up visits and organising follow-up appointments. One senior Birmingham social worker says: 'You need a BA or an MA in social work these days, and to get onto a decent course you need to do some volunteering and have quite a bit of experience of working with people under your belt.

'Once you qualify, you have to do what's called a "newly qualified year", produce a post-qualifying portfolio and attend various learning sessions. Then for the rest of your career you have to demonstrate your continuous professional development to the regulator – plus all of that's on top of an already demanding and paperwork-driven job. If you can't stomach this, social work may not be for you.'

But lots of social workers regard their job as amongst the most rewarding around. Most are employed by the NHS or local authorities, whilst a small number work directly for charities. Salary-wise, graduates entering the profession post-qualification receive £22,000 to £32,000, with the higher figures usually reserved for those working in London. Pay approaches about £40,000 for a senior worker with direct contact with clients, depending on the local authority. 'Any more than that and you need to be in management or policy,' says one Cambridge social worker. 'Directors of social services can make over £100,000 a year in some places, but obviously those are incredibly responsible and demanding jobs and there are only a handful of them in any area.'

WORKING LIFE: adult social worker Bernard Ali*

'I decided I wanted to be a social worker a couple of years after finishing my university degree in politics. I'd had experience working with adults with complex needs from a charity job, so I was accepted onto a decent social work MA course, then got a job after graduation.

For my average day, I get in at 9am, check email, check voicemail (I get a lot of them), and spend the first hour chasing people up. Often I need to call doctors or district nurses; I try to call them at the beginning of the day to give them as large a window as possible for getting back to me. If I don't have a visit planned, I will start writing up one of my previous visits, or begin writing a care plan – that's an incredibly convoluted process. It usually involves the council spending money, so it needs to be costed, checked and signed off by five different people in different teams, including a panel of senior managers.

An afternoon visit usually takes two hours or more, and I like to have

---

* *name changed for anonymity*

enough time to write up the visit and still leave by 5pm. I often don't manage to leave by then, though, and end up going home at 5.30 or 6.

As a support worker, you get to know people in social services very well. But that's not the case as a social worker – you generally get allocated a case, go out and do an assessment, make whatever changes are necessary and get out.

Progression can be difficult if you want to carry on working with people. In nursing or teaching, for example, you can become more senior (as a matron, or head of department, etc.) and still work with the patients or pupils. With social work, most senior jobs are managerial roles, which not everyone wants.

So much of the job is form filling, but most of the forms are badly designed and you find yourself copying and pasting from one section to another. Then you have to chase people on the phone and deal with calls from other parts of the council about incredibly mundane things.

But having said that, actually working with people is enormously interesting and I don't think the other jobs where you work with the same groups of people – such as a doctor, psychologist or lawyer – provide the same scope for intervention. If there are allegations of a vulnerable adult being abused, for example, they raise concerns to social services. We are the ones who deal with it.'

Dream Job: Comedian

Matt Lacey is the funny man behind the hit 'Gap Yah' sketch on YouTube; he's performed from Tokyo to New York, via Edinburgh and Glastonbury, and on the BBC, Channel 4 and Comedy Central channels.

'One thing you quickly learn is that most people in acting or comedy have another job when they're starting out that they do for money. Jimmy Carr's quip sadly rings true: "I always say the same thing to any aspiring actor or actress I meet. I always say, 'I'll have a coffee, please.'" Although we're not all part-time baristas: I run a business supplying lasers to the construction industry. It pays the bills and takes away the terror of living from one acting job to the next. The key is to get a job that's flexible enough to work around your other commitments.

Expect your starting salary to be in the minus figures. You'll have to start out doing unpaid gigs that cost you more to get to than you'll get paid for. In the end, TV actors and comedians can earn crazy money, but they're at the top end of a pyramid. At its base is some very low pay indeed.

My day might include auditions, evening gigs, or days filming with Hollywood stars, then I'm back selling lasers. As a comic, you've got to be ready to abrogate your social life for evenings spent in sweaty dives making strangers laugh. But that's only if you gig regularly. Most aspiring comics start out gigging in pubs, at student unions and local shows – if you can survive stand-up there, your jokes must be pretty good. My agent picked me up from a play I was doing at university, then I started writing and performing comedy and have just lurched from one opportunity to another. In order to succeed, you've got to be self-assured enough to stick to the path in the face of any barrier. You also need intelligence and obtuseness for comedy, openness and intuition for acting. And practice and belligerence for both.

I love the variety, and the utter silliness, of my job. Recently I was shooting a short film that essentially had me dressed up as a British colonial officer and sword fighting with Kulvinder Ghir (from *Goodness Gracious Me*).

Other tips? If you've hit a comedy wall, try partnering with someone to write as a team – one of you will say a joke, and you bounce off each other. You need to get in front of audiences as much and as frequently as possible. Don't expect it to happen overnight – it even took Michael McIntyre a decade to be noticed.

And know that you'll have to do another job for money, and that can be dull. That, and self-employment tax returns. You'll want to stuff a P60 form down the gullet of anyone who says "tax doesn't have to be taxing". Oh, and if you want to see the worst end of the acting spectrum have a look at the @castingcallwoe Twitter feed – it's full of creepy student directors who seem to have written casting calls when they actually just want an escort agency.'

SPY

AVERAGE STARTING SALARY – £18,000

ENTRY POSITION – Intelligence analyst

TYPICAL WEEKLY HOURS – Variable (shifts)

RECOMMENDED QUALIFICATIONS – Nationality and residency requirements. Over 18 years old. 2:1 in a relevant degree (history, languages, politics, economics, maths, law) and fluency in languages

IF YOU LIKE THIS YOU MIGHT ALSO LIKE . . . civil servant, military careers, translator

Recruitment into Britain's secret service is no longer a tap on the shoulder of the 'right chaps' strutting around Oxbridge (not least because they frequently turned out to be the 'wrong chaps' who were actually spies for the Soviets). These days you can gain entry from any university or background, and there is no single 'spy type' that recruiters look for – apart from intelligent, independent individuals who are patient, fit, good at observation and who can, uh, keep a secret. Thoughts about working in the intelligence industry are, for most job-hunters, pretty tied up with the lifestyle of Bond.

But while you could well own every crazy gadget under the sun tackling a glamorous, evil global enemy, a lot of the time intelligence workers are huddled over a computer at the office. It can be a lonely job, too – you can't discuss your work down at the pub with friends, and you might be aware of global events or working on operations that you can't talk about.

The jobs on offer are seriously diverse: the UK intelligence agencies include the Security Service (MI5), the Secret Intelligence Service (MI6) and the Government Communications Headquarters (GCHQ), which work to counter threats such as terrorism, drug smuggling and the proliferation of weapons of mass destruction. The three agencies collect, investigate and analyse intelligence, have agents in the UK and around the world, use languages and are experts on technology.

MI5 is the UK's national security intelligence agency, protecting the country and its citizens against threats like terrorism and espionage; staff are mostly based in headquarters near Lambeth Bridge in London; though they are posted at one of the regional offices for a spell, but rarely abroad. The jobs range from translators, technologists, researchers, mathematicians, librarians, through to intelligence analysts. The other UK agency, GCHQ, is based in Cheltenham and focuses on national security threats; it uses advanced technology to inform national security, military work and law enforcement, as well as safeguarding the Government's own IT networks.

MI6 is the intelligence agency which supplies the government with foreign intelligence. Staff operate worldwide and are stationed across the globe. Most officers undertake at least one foreign posting, usually lasting for two to three years, and they can generally be accompanied by their partners and children.

Many of the UK's intelligence workers are graduates who speak more than one language; they all face a very tough vetting process, but there are no specific requirements for degrees or qualifications. The application process is long and hard, often including test weekends, several assessment days and interviews, and months of security vetting. The starting salary across the three agencies is about £26,000, plus benefits such as a public-sector pension and training. The base salary levels for the next two grades are £31,000, then £39,000 after five to ten years' service; there are steady pay rises with experience and bonus opportunities. It's not just a career for grads, either: a lot of the specialist technology and linguistic roles attract those with work experience in other industries; there's no formal 'accelerated entry' scheme but it's worth contacting the services to find out more. There's also the Higher Apprenticeship programme in the MI5, MI6 and GCHQ: 'You'll be earning a salary and gaining a unique insight into the world that you won't find on any university course,' they promise. The two-year programme includes classroom learning, technical training and work-based placements and projects, and applicants must have or be expecting to achieve three A levels at grade C or above, and two of these must be in Science, Technology, Engineering or Mathematical (STEM) subjects, or equivalent qualifications in a STEM-related subject.

WORKING LIFE: Fatima, Intelligence Officer, Digital Intelligence Unit

'Before joining the Service I was studying for my A levels. I then took a temporary job working in retail before joining the Service as an Administrative Assistant. I was promoted to the role of Intelligence Officer and worked in Northern Ireland investigating Northern Irish Related Terrorism. I also spent several years working in the International Counter Terrorism branch. I now work in the Digital Intelligence Unit. I begin my day by checking my emails, and will transfer any digital intelligence that I deem to be of interest to the investigations on which I am working into a report that I will then forward to the relevant Intelligence Officer or team. In my job, good written and communication skills are important. You need to be able to organise your workload according to priorities and these can change on a daily basis due to the nature of our work. It helps to have an interest in IT and the internet in my current role. Discretion is also really important for any member of the Security Service, and surprisingly it is not as difficult to deploy 'cover' as you might expect. Cover briefings are given during the recruitment process and when you join.

Generally I arrive in the office about 09:30 and leave around 18:00. There are times when I'm required to work longer hours or at weekends but in general the work/life balance is pretty good. Management really encourage people to recharge their batteries when they can. If you're thinking of joining, I'd say don't expect every job you do to be exciting – it's not like *Spooks*. However, the work here is rewarding, varied, and you have the opportunity to move sections and acquire new skills.'

WORKING LIFE: MI6 intelligence officer, Louise

'I joined MI6 in 2007 after six years working for a global investment bank, based in London and Hong Kong. I had briefly considered MI6 whilst studying at Oxford University but had decided that, because I had not been "tapped on the shoulder", I did not have what it took to work for the Service.

But I'd become increasingly disillusioned by my City job. I had never been solely motivated by money and wanted to do something that made more of a difference. I stumbled across the MI6 website and applied on something of a whim. As the application process went on and I discovered more about the Service and the role of Intelligence Officer I became more and more convinced that this was somewhere I wanted to work. The role offered every-thing that I enjoyed about my previous work – interesting subject matter, engagement with people – but critically also offered a chance to play a role at the heart of global events and do something of real importance for the United Kingdom.

After a tough but exciting three-month induction course which covered the basics of the different roles of being an Intelligence Officer, I moved straight to a further three-month advanced course that taught tradecraft (the techniques we use to be able to operate safely and securely) and agent running and recruitment. Identifying potential new agents, recruiting them to work with us and then running them securely is very challenging but relies on the same interpersonal skills I had used during client-facing roles at the bank. There's nothing superhuman about this work, and the training taught me a lot, but it does require a genuine understanding of people and emotional intelligence. My male colleagues would disagree but I have always felt that women have a head start in this regard.

My first role after this was as a case officer in the East African counter terrorist team; running and recruiting agents to provide intelligence on the Al-Qaida-affiliated terrorist groups in the region. I loved working with the agents themselves. This involved travel across the region and some meetings in strange locations. The importance of this work was never in doubt but was emphasised during an operation to free a group of Westerners kidnapped in the region. This was literally a life and death situation and I was at the heart of the planning and delivery of the operation. The greatest thrill of my working life was when this went to plan and the kidnap situation was resolved successfully.

After three years in this role I did a further course of training, this time in the skills required of a targeting and requirements officer. Following this I went on a posting to South Asia. Here I worked closely with the local security service as well as GCHQ/MI5 and other international partners, to identify threats to the UK and identify potential agents who we could recruit to pass us intelligence on these threats.

South Asia was a fantastic place to live for both me and my husband, who worked in finance and had transferred to a role based locally, and we took full opportunity to travel around the region. The allowances were also pretty generous and, on top of being able to rent out our flat in London, we lived a very comfortable life.

On return I became lead case officer in one of our counter intelligence teams and managed a team of case officers and targeters. I took a year's maternity leave for the birth of our daughter and have returned to the role working three days a week. This has offered me the necessary work/life balance to do the two things I love: work and spend time with my little girl.'

SURVEYOR

Train as a chartered surveyor and you'll find yourself very popular around the time that your friends and family want to buy a house. Most people think of chartered surveyors as the people who look for hidden defects and problems in properties up for sale, but while some of the country's 82,000 chartered surveyors do indeed do just that, the job title covers a huge breadth of areas. Some might be involved in advising developers about the value of their land, others might have a role in roads and town planning, some might be advising miners about the potential value of mineral resources, others estimating and running the costs on big infrastructure projects.

Surveying involves measuring, valuing, protecting and reporting on property, be it a City skyscraper or a rural forest. The job generally involves checking that buildings are built according to regulations, valuing homes and commercial sites and identifying any risks that could affect them, or managing properties or wealthy estates. In addition, surveyors are often also involved in co-ordinating big projects, such as building the London 2012 Olympic Park.

There are a few main types of surveyors:

Building surveyors: carry out structural surveys of properties, with reports detailing their condition and how much they're worth.

Commercial or residential property surveyors: cover estate agency, working out the values of offices or houses, organising their sale or leasing and managing buildings on behalf of their owners.

Land surveyors: focus on natural resources, environmental management and protection, planning rules and land use.

Planning/construction surveyors: oversee development and regeneration projects, from multi-million-pound sites to historic properties, including considering planning regulations.

Quantity surveyors: work with architects to draw up designs for clients' homes, offices or projects, including working out the materials, work and funds required.

To become a chartered surveyor takes a while. You'll need to be a member of the Royal Institution of Chartered Surveyors, or RICS, which normally requires three A levels and then a RICS-approved degree, such as Land Economy, Construction Management and Property Finance. The final year of university means it's time to apply for a training position at a firm: graduates have to gain at least two years' practical experience in a relevant job as part of the RICS's Assessment of Professional Competence. After that came APC exams, and an RICS assessment interview; pass these and you can join the RICS to become a qualified chartered surveyor. There are alternative routes to qualification for those who have worked in the industry for around 10 years.

And the reward for all that effort? Figures show chartered surveyors are amongst the highest-paid graduates in the UK, while most also report a good work/life balance, rarely being in the office late at night or at the weekends.

The key skills for wannabe surveyors are technical and practical ability, attention to detail, and being able to interpret and apply information to a particular set of circumstances. You also need to be a good communicator so that you can deal with client relationships as well as negotiate against other surveyors. Jobs-wise, chartered surveyor Nicholas Fell (see working life, below) warns that most graduate opportunities are tightly bound to the property market. 'As an example, surveyors were quite badly hit during the recession between 2008 and 2011,' he says, 'with a lot of people made redundant, especially at the large global firms, and graduate training programmes scaled back. For a number of years it was difficult for university leavers to get training places. Now, the trend has started to reverse and there really seems to be confidence back in the market and a drive for new surveyors to expand growing teams.'

Graduate salaries during APC training are usually in the region of £25,000–£28,000 in London, slightly less outside the capital. After qualifying, most surveyors' salaries move to around £40,000, although this depends on the company, an individual's own competency and area of specialism. About 7–10 years after qualification, surveyors working in London earn on average £60,000 to £80,000. Partners at good firms will earn hundreds of thousands per year, but it usually takes 20 or more years' work to get there.

To find out more, check out the RICS's careers website – rics.org/uk/the-profession – and browse professional journals, such as the *Estates Gazette* and *Property Week*. If they're too expensive to buy regularly, you might want to ask a local firm if you can have their old copies to read.

WORKING LIFE: Nicholas Fell is a chartered surveyor at Strettons in London

'My job is to advise clients on the value of their development sites, and provide them with strategic advice to help to extract the best price. So I usually spend about three days a week in the office working on reports and the other two out and about at meetings or at sites.

For an office day, I usually get into our City HQ for about 8am and check emails and have my first coffee of the day. I catch up with my team and discuss any issues or respond to fee quotes for new work, then start writing reports and work through until about 6pm, before catching up with my team again and dealing with any issues from the day. I work around 50 hours a week, and although I check my emails most evenings, I try to have a break from work at weekends.

We are certainly expected to work hard and there is an expectation that you will bring in fees. Everyone is set a target at the start of the year and you need to monitor your progress throughout the year to ensure you stay on track. One of the perks is spending time securing new business for the firm – this usually involves quite nice lunches, and dinners, and often a round or two of golf! The most boring part of the job is probably when you're having to read five 100-plus-page leases in a day.

I got into surveying after a law degree at university – I decided that being a lawyer wasn't a career path I wanted to follow, and ended up getting a placement at the BBC, working as a junior project manager on the redevelopment of Broadcasting House and their new Media Village at White City. I really enjoyed it and decided to look into making this my career. So I did a one-year Master's in Property Development and Planning, then worked for a private developer in the West End on a major regeneration scheme in north London, before joining my current firm as an APC [the scheme that leads to professional qualification and membership of the Royal Institute of Chartered Surveyors] graduate and spent around two and a half years training. I've now been qualified for seven years and am an associate director in our City office.'

TEACHING

AVERAGE STARTING SALARY – £21,000–£22,000

ENTRY POSITION – Teacher or Teaching Assistant

TYPICAL WEEKLY HOURS – 37–40 hours

RECOMMENDED QUALIFICATIONS – Achieve Qualified Teacher Status (QTS) through Initial Teacher Training (ITT)/ BA resulting in QTS. If you already have an unrelated degree, you can take the Postgraduate Certificate in Education (PGCE)

IF YOU LIKE THIS YOU MIGHT ALSO LIKE . . . academic, author, civil servant

If you fancy a job working 8am until 4pm and really long holidays with no work demands whatsoever, then teaching . . . isn't it. We've all looked at the people at the whiteboard in schools and thought, 'What cushy hours,' but the planning, testing and marking that goes on behind the scenes means it's one of the most demanding jobs around.

And, as one with a well-used red marking pen puts it, 'You're not just a teacher. You're a role model, a counsellor, a diplomat, a manager, a life coach, a sexual health advisor, a dietician, a careers advisor, a motivational speaker, etc. Oh, and at secondary school, you're also a subject specialist . . . You're basically mum. You need to be caring and supportive but occasionally you have to show some tough love. As an educator, interacting with different students, you have to be organised, quick-thinking and creative.'

That's a lot of skills on top of a heavy workload, but ask a teacher about their top perks and it won't be foreign jaunts (although someone has to lead the Year 8 French trip), but, as one tells me, 'things like seeing the students who have worked hard achieve success. You can't beat it. After a good day of teaching or marking an excellent essay, there is no better job in the world.'

To get into the industry, there are two routes: school-led training, where you take on a job as a trainee teacher and generally embark on a year-long course that leads to qualified teacher status (a postgraduate certificate in education, also known as a PGCE, where master's-level credits are often included), or university-led training, where graduates spend another year at university or college completing a year-long PGCE, which usually includes at least two school experience placements. The fairly short training time makes teaching ideal for career-changers. Many teachers come to the role later in life after getting sick of corporate life or because they want to give something back. Once you're in the classroom, the nature of your work will obviously depend on whether you're teaching at a primary school, with children aged 4 to 11 years, or secondary, teaching students aged 11 to 18. At the latter you'll need to be a subject specialist, with the job involving planning and delivering lessons, marking work, giving feedback and recording pupils' progress via reports and parents' events, staying up to date with subject knowledge, pastoral duties, such as being a form tutor or careers advisor, helping students through exams, organising extracurricular activities like sports and trips, departmental meetings and training, and liaising with other professionals, like teaching assistants and special educational needs experts.

Many of these roles are also involved in teaching primary-aged pupils, but here you'll be covering a much broader range of subjects – from maths to English, science, art and IT. You're helping to shape young children's lives; Government research shows that children who perform well in literacy and numeracy at age seven go on to achieve well at GCSE level.

Beyond the classroom teacher, other jobs in education include teaching English as a foreign language (which can often lead to a lot of travel), a higher education lecturer, private tutor, or a special educational needs teacher.

So, is teaching for you? You'll need to be passionate and enthusiastic, and really want to work with children. The work is creative – there's a National Curriculum to follow in state schools, and many private schools stick to it fairly closely, too; there are also often exams to tackle, but you decide how you teach the children in your care.

There are lots of opportunities for career-changers: schools often appreciate the diverse experience brought to them by those who come to teaching later in their career. And although teachers always point out that their days don't finish at 4pm, the working day can be more family friendly than other professions, especially as you'll be off for the summer holidays, Easter and Christmas and half-term, too – which can offer amazing opportunities to travel, volunteer, or do something from completely different from your day job.

You can be promoted fairly speedily, too. 'A lot of young people are taking up head of department posts,' says one twenty-something who has done just that. 'It only took me three years to run a department. Then a headship might follow – although to be an effective head, you have to have considerable management skills and knowledge of education policy and initiatives, which can take years to achieve, rising from head of department to other senior positions.'

Why do people leave teaching? 'Many leave to reclaim their lives because they have grown to resent the personal time they have sacrificed for seemingly ungrateful students or, worse, ungrateful managers,' says one teacher. 'People rarely hear the words "thank you" in this profession. Or they may, as I do, find most of the meetings utterly intolerable and pointless, or get frustrated when time set aside to prepare lesson materials gets consumed by admin tasks. And some long for a job that they can shut the door on at 5pm.'

Pay-wise, a qualified teacher's starting salary is about £22,000 a year (or £27,000 in inner London) in a state school. Experienced teachers can earn up to £64,000 in London and £56,000 outside the capital, while heads of department, deputy heads and head teachers' salaries are higher – heads can receive six figures, while a few private school head teachers are paid more than £300,000. You can also join the teachers' pension scheme, and some teachers take on extra work as private tutors or exam markers, or writing study guides and teaching packs, to boost their salary.

To boost your CV for a potential teaching post, try to secure a work experience placement in a school. 'The more experience you have at different schools in different sectors, the more likely it is that you will get onto a teacher training course,' says one who's doing just that. She adds: '*The Times Educational Supplement* is worth the subscription. With many articles written by teachers, senior-ranking managers and knowledgeable practitioners, it boasts considerable insight. And it's where most teaching jobs are advertised, so it's essential reading for getting a job.'

WORKING LIFE: Shaun Passey, 29, teaches English and drama at a secondary school in Birmingham

'Every day is different but on my busiest day, I arrive at school sometime before 8am. I will usually grab a coffee and check my emails for important announcements, then my first lesson commences at 8.45am – AS level Drama. It's over by 10am, when I'll rush over to the English block to teach AS Literature. At 11.15am it's back to the drama studio to teach another AS class. I get a short break before the lesson starts, and if I'm lucky, time to gnaw on something to keep myself going until lunch.

At 12.45, I run either a lunchtime workshop or a one-to-one session for a student for half an hour, so any absentee students can go over topics or ask me for help. After a working lunch, I teach another AS Literature class before teaching AS Drama. Lessons finish at 4. I'm technically free to go, unless a meeting has been scheduled, but I invariably stay until 6, spending those two hours planning lessons for the next day. At certain times in the year I run play rehearsals until around 5.30, too.

Once I'm back at home, that's not it – I don't know a single teacher who doesn't work in the evenings or at the weekend. Teaching is only a part of the job. To cope with the planning, you have to work in the evenings.

Teaching has changed. We have to find memorable ways of transferring knowledge to students and then of testing their understanding. The old blackboard rote-learning is over – you have to make the lesson engaging, and to test understanding you have to devise creative tasks that encourage students to apply what they have learned. Google can fulfil the old idea of a fact-filled education – it knows more than I do and it never gets tired! But Google can't provide engaging, interactive environments in which to apply knowledge. It can't help students to solve creative problems. I spend most of my time thinking about interesting and exciting ways of engaging students in the learning process and developing their conceptual understanding.

As a result, I easily work in excess of 70 hours a week during spring, my busiest term. In a 'normal week', I probably work around 60 hours.

I got my job after applying for a temporary teaching post and striking up a rapport with my colleagues. When a member of the drama department retired, I took up the post in September 2009 – a year after graduating. Since then, other colleagues have retired and I now run the department full-time.

I love teaching students – they make the less pleasant aspects of the job bearable. But when I'm staring at a large pile of marking at midnight or I'm moaning that there really aren't enough hours in the day, I imagine myself switching careers. Teaching is a perfectionist's worst nightmare. You will never produce the perfect lesson but you can have lots of fun trying. Stay positive and remember that you're there for the students. Everyone else can wait.'

ODD JOB: Odour tester, worldwide

You're hired by a deodorant company to sniff people's armpits to see if their products work. F'real. Since that might not be a full-time position, mouthwash manufacturers similarly have staff to sniff people's breath, to test out their mouth-cleaning products' efficiency.

TECH INDUSTRY

AVERAGE STARTING SALARY – £20,000–£30,000

ENTRY POSITION – Consultant

TYPICAL WEEKLY HOURS – 40 hours

RECOMMENDED QUALIFICATIONS – A degree in information systems, computer science, electronic/software/electrical engineering, business or maths. Work experience

IF YOU LIKE THIS YOU MIGHT ALSO LIKE... Online entrepreneur, graphic designer, spy

Want to work in an industry where your office will almost certainly have more beanbags than printers and the stroll to your desk involves treading on AstroTurf, not carpet? Then tech could be your answer. The UK's youngest, fast-growing industry likes to think it's a bit quirky – so Google's offices have free corner shops inside with unlimited chocolate and sweets (and that's on top of the free lunches), whilst start-up SwiftKey gives its new joiners £100 to spend on whatever they want for the office (there are lots of drum kits and foot-balls lying around).

But you can't pick a job just based on its perks. The tech industry spans a huge number and type of jobs, from app developers making the likes of Candy Crush to forensic computer analysts tackling IT crime for the police, and from software developers and engineers to IT support staff and web designers.

Unsurprisingly, given that practically every man and his dog now has a laptop, smartphone, tablet, work computer and more, giving an insatiable appetite for IT support, flashier websites and new apps, the UK's tech sector is booming. The rate of job creation at British tech firms has outpaced the private sector as a whole for the past four years, according to research by management consultant KPMG. So there is lots of work out there – but what do all those computer-huggers actu-ally do?

App developer – someone who writes computer programs to meet specific requirements. You'll be the one dreaming of coming up with the next Angry Birds. Most specialise in a particular area – games or education, for example, and for a particular system such as Windows or Android, or platform such as mobile or tablet. The job involves conceiving, designing, building, testing and re-building apps. You might work solo – Apple says the UK has the biggest community of iOS app developers in Europe, and claims those on its system have earned $6.5 billion since 2008 – or have a salaried job at an app firm. Graduate salaries usually start at £20,000.

IT consultant – this job involves advising companies how to best use computers and IT to help their business flourish. Work covers a huge range – it could be helping a small architecture firm pick and use the best computer-aided design software, or it could involve working for a huge multi-national firm to help them have the best hardware, software and networking. Many IT consultants work as a one-man band, hiring themselves out to companies for between £200 and £500 a day, depending on the work involved, whilst others take a salary working for a large consultancy firm or in-house. Pay starts at £20,000.

IT technical support officer – you're the miracle-maker, the one that Coby in accounts calls because his computer won't do ANYTHING and his biggest meeting of the year starts in half an hour and he needs his documents. And you come down, show him the screen is not turned on, and all is well. That's on a good day. Working in tech support means being Mr or Miss Fix-It; you'll maintain and repair the computer systems and networks of an organisation, either over the phone or in person. You'll be blamed for everything that goes wrong and get little praise when it all runs smoothly, but it's well-paid and secure employment. In big companies, you may specialise; in smaller ones, you'll have to know how to do everything, including potentially organising staff IT training. Starting salaries are usually £17,000 up.

Systems analyst – this job involves designing new IT systems for a company, or improving existing ones, to make the firm's work more productive. You'll be talking to the client non-stop about what they want, and building or tweaking the office computer network and related technology in response; you'll need to know all about the latest hardware and software and its average lifespan, as well as be able to train new users in anything you're installing. The starting salary is usually around £22,000.

Web designer – you design and improve websites, with lots of coding. Similar to web developer, but that's usually a more specialist job, focusing on the back-end of a site, whereas a designer may have more interaction with the client about the overall site. Pay usually starts at about £19,000, a little more for a graduate. A senior designer makes about £60,000 per year, while someone at the top of the industry at a major company would be on something more like £100,000.

To anyone wanting to break into any part of tech, studying maths and science is useful, as most jobs require logic and problem solving. A computer science degree often helps, but there are lots of bedroom coders and computing experts who've succeeded by teaching themselves how to be excellent at IT. Coding-wise, there are lots of resources on the web that can help you learn to code for free, such as Code Academy and Team Treehouse. Also keep an eye on the tech news – lots of new things coming out will require developers with those skills, such as Google Glass and Oculus Rift.

Or you could work as a home developer: there are also opportunities for self-employment – Apple's App Store, for example, makes it a lot easier to release your own games to the public, which some fit around another full-time job. It's rare, but not impossible, for an independent game with little to no marketing to make a good amount of money.

THE LOWDOWN: a 20-year-old working on a big corporate's IT support desk

'Tech isn't a stuffy industry that demands loads of experience: in fact, people expect me to be even more computer savvy because I look like I just left school. My role can be stressful – on my second day at work I was called down to fix the laptop of the boss of a massive retailer, and he was really moody about the fact that it was broken – but it's not like other industries where you have to make tea and coffee for months before you can actually do anything proper.

I have a degree in computer science but to be honest most of the problems I have to fix are simple, just people being idiots – their mouse isn't plugged in when they phone up complaining it's broken, or the screen is switched off and they are irate about a 'blackout' losing their big project. But the money is good – I started on £30,000 – and the hours are regular, I'm done by 5pm on the dot every day, there's no work to take home with me, and people are usually pretty grateful for our help.'

WORKING LIFE: software designer Josh Benson works at a financial services firm in London

'For my job I code, make algorithms, design how websites look and how they are used. I meet clients and work out what they want in their software or site, and then make it happen. On an average day, I get to the office at 9, and have breakfast at my desk whilst checking my emails and tasks for the day. At 10, I have a quick meeting – it's called a stand-up – with my team mates to check what everyone is planning to do for the day. Then I start coding, attend meetings or give demos. At 12 it's lunchtime, usually followed by a game of table tennis or pool. Between one and 5.30, I continue with coding, designing, meetings and demos, then I head home. Generally I can switch off on weekends and evenings, but sometimes when a deadline is approaching we have to stay late or work weekends.

I got this job via a friend's referral after I graduated in computer science, including a year's work experience in industry where I worked as a software engineer. The most important skills are coding, of course, but also problem-solving, logic, teamwork – and working on being able to communicate with people in a language they understand. There's also a lot of admin stuff you have to do, and some things can be really dull, such as working on security requirements. Sometimes we have to deal with really difficult people, and if something goes wrong we're usually the ones who get blamed.

But overall I think my job is a perfect balance of work and play. The environment is fun – people tend to be themselves, and we can wear what we like. Money-wise, it all depends which industry and company you work for. I'm in finance and the salary is pretty awesome for my level, with great benefits. Most graduates start off with pay in the £30,000s, and I've seen tech lead jobs for more than £100,000 out there.

You can become a manager or tech lead within a few years, but it all depends if you want to go down the manager route. Some people can rise to the top as a technical expert, too, so there's no pressure if you just want to stick to coding.'

WORKING LIFE: Kate Morris is a software engineer at Moshi Monsters app firm Mind Candy

'My job basically means I sit in front of a computer coding all day, with occasional brainstorming meetings for new games and features. This generally involves about five people sitting in one of our colourful meeting rooms and throwing ideas onto the whiteboard. Someone might say, 'We need a popcorn mini-game since we're releasing a popcorn toy next month'. Then everyone comes together and throws out random ideas for a popcorn game. We'll write them all on the board and come to a collective decision on what ties in best with the whole game, what's fun, and what we can create in the time we have.

My company – and the industry – is a fun place to work. We get a lot of free food –breakfast and snacks, beer on Fridays, and even a Slush Puppy machine. No one wears suits, and we have AstroTurf, a slide, an arcade machine, a ping pong table, and karaoke on Fridays, with a massive annual summer party/conference somewhere fun (one year it was in Disneyland Paris). We also have stock options, a retirement plan, a ride your bike to work scheme, and a certain amount of money every month for any sports activities we want to participate in.

In this job, adaptability, hard work and a willingness to learn are the big skills: the industry is changing constantly, mostly because technology is doing the same.

The worst part of my work is fixing bugs, especially in code that isn't your own. You can spend so much time (even days) trying to fix one small bug and it usually turns out to be something really easy you just didn't think of.'

TRADESMAN: PLUMBER, ELECTRICIAN OR CARPENTER

AVERAGE STARTING SALARY – £13,000

ENTRY POSITION – Apprentice

TYPICAL WEEKLY HOURS – 40 hours

RECOMMENDED QUALIFICATIONS – NVQs in relevant trade

IF YOU LIKE THIS YOU MIGHT ALSO LIKE . . . engineer, surveyor, teacher

Working in 'the trades' – the traditional term for jobs that demand manual work and special training – has experienced a burst in popularity in the last few years. Why? Because it's an opportunity to work away from a traditional desk-and-computer role, using your hands to create something new, or fix a serious household or commercial problem. It's also much in demand: a dearth of qualified plumbers, for example, saw pay rates soar a few years back, leading Woody Allen to say: 'Not only is there no God, but try getting a plumber at weekends.'

For thousands of school-leavers, graduates and career-changers, there are clear benefits to working in the building trade rather than desk-work: some, working for bigger contractors, like the fact that at the end of their working day they can switch off and not have to be stuck to a BlackBerry/conference calls; others set up their own company and do have to cope with admin and invoices at the end of the working day, but find it a lucrative and rewarding career.

There's also a host of apprenticeship roles, and while they don't pay particularly well, they do pay while training you up – also known as 'earn whilst you learn' – which is in stark contrast to the debts run up by people seeking out other qualifications and degrees. Here are some of the options:

Plumber: the bulk of the job is installing and maintaining the pipes, boilers, tanks, radiators, etc. and to keep water and sewage flowing and heating working in a property. Other jobs might include fitting bathrooms, tiling, installing white goods like dishwashers, and emergency repairs. You could be working outside on a construction site, in schools, care homes, or in people's homes or offices – anywhere there's water – and you will need to be able to read and understand technical drawings and plans.

It takes an average of four years to train as a qualified plumber, securing an NVQ (Levels 2 and 3) in plumbing and domestic heating, and undertaking a work placement that will help you pass the practical elements of the course. An apprenticeship is another option, which usually takes two to three years. Newly qualified plumbers earn between £17,000 and £21,000 a year, rising with experienced plumbers to about £40,000 (an average call-out fee is £60–£120 an hour, depending on location), whilst those running their own firms with other plumber employees can earn considerably more. The hours are demanding – usually on the road before 7am and working through until 4pm or 5pm, followed by an evening of paperwork for the self-employed.

Electrician (a.k.a. spark): like plumbers, this trade has also suffered from a shortage of trained experts. There are a range of different kinds of roles, such as installation electrician (creating power systems, lighting, fire protection, security and telecoms systems in a wide range of buildings), maintenance electrician (checking these are safe and efficient), electro-technical panel builders (using IT to build control panels to run a large or complex building's electrical systems), electrical machine repairer and rewinder (working on electrical motors and other machinery) and highway systems electrician (installing and looking after street lighting and traffic light systems on the roads and motorways). Training-wise, electricians need a minimum of NVQ at Level 3 in a diploma such as electro-technical services or installing electro-technical systems, but again, apprenticeship schemes are common. Pay is similar to plumbers; first-year apprentices may start on around £8,000 a year and work can include overtime pay and bonuses.

Carpenter/joiner (a.k.a. chippy): the job involves making and fitting wooden fixtures, ranging from stairs or whole house and building structures, to smaller items such as cupboards and shelving units, sets for film and TV and the fittings of shops and restaurants. There are college courses in carpentry and joinery, or some chippies start as labourers or construction workers on building sites to get experience, or via apprenticeship schemes.

WORKING LIFE: Rick Green is a builder who also runs his own building firm in North London

'I've had many careers in my life, mostly desk jobs. This line of work evolved out of part-time work in which I was doing DIY and building jobs and has grown into my own building firm. It's a job that keeps me constantly challenged and interested. All of my training has been "on the job" – a kind of informal apprentice.

I generally wake up at about 6am, spend the first hour doing minor admin, responding to emails for quotes, etc. I'm then on-site from 8am until 5pm. This part varies the most – I might be doing building work, looking at quoting for new jobs, overseeing staff or getting more materials. I spend my evenings looking at prospective jobs, typing up quotes, searching for materials and planning the next day's schedule.

The top skills you need are excellent hand-eye co-ordination and the ability to focus in order to learn – and to learn quickly. You need to be flexible in the trades, as most days never go to plan and you have to be creative to find solutions to the constant problems, such as tools that won't get into the areas you need to work in, parts that don't fit together, or shortages in materials. If it makes you run behind schedule, that gets stressful.

I most enjoy finishing a job to the highest standard and taking pride in that work, and having a joke on site with the team. Most boring is the paperwork – and clients who need constant management, to a point where it stops you from doing the work.

There's a cap in your salary in this work because there's only so many tasks you can get through in one day – a reasonable salary for an experienced, independent tradesman is £30,000–£50,000. If you build it into a business, with lots of building staff, this can go much higher, but it also takes a lot of work. If you remain an independent tradesman you will be on the tools until you retire, and it is a physically demanding job. Or you can work for a building company, which is far less stress but there's also less growth potential.

Anyone considering this career should think about their long-term plan – think where you want to be in 5, 10, 20 and 30 years' time, both financially and at what level in your sector. Then work backwards to plan a route as to how to achieve it. Not everyone has the stamina or drive for this career, so that plan can also tell you if the work isn't necessarily for you.'

TRANSLATOR

AVERAGE STARTING SALARY – £18,000

ENTRY POSITION – Translator

TYPICAL WEEKLY HOURS – 30–40 hours (can vary)

RECOMMENDED QUALIFICATIONS – Degree with a postgraduate degree in translation. Fluency in at least one other language

IF YOU LIKE THIS YOU MIGHT ALSO LIKE . . . civil servant, spy, teacher

If you're a linguist and are keen to use your language skills, interpreting and translating careers might sound like a solid option. The only problem is, lots of people think the same – and supply far outstrips demand. The two jobs of interpreter and translator aren't as intertwined as you might think: the former involves translating one language into another orally, using speech; the latter focuses on written conversion. While freelancing means you can do both, some of the biggest employers of linguists, like the United Nations and European Union, separate out the roles.

Some translators and interpreters are 'only' fluent in one language beyond their mother tongue, although most do have more than one, which gives you more work opportunities. To work as a translator or interpreter for the United Nations, your main language must be one of its six official languages: English, Arabic, Chinese, French, Russian or Spanish; the UN also demands candidates know at least two other languages from the six well enough to translate into their mother tongue. (But some can still secure UN work if they have a relevant master's degree or their main language is either Arabic or Chinese.)

UN translators normally spend their first six months to two years being trained at United Nations Headquarters. They may then stay there or be transferred to offices in Geneva, Vienna, Nairobi, or one of the regional commissions in Asia, Africa or Latin America. Jobs at the EU demand fluency in one European mother tongue, a 'thorough' knowledge of English, French or German, and a third language from its 24 official languages.

Other important skills are flexibility and a willingness to accept work at short notice and potentially anywhere in the world, an interest in current affairs, research skills, cultural awareness, good public speaking, being calm under pressure and excellent networking skills. 'You will need academic qualifications (at least a First degree) to get into the profession – simply being bilingual or fluent in foreign languages won't usually be enough,' says one translator. You'll also need to be adroit at adapting writing style to different subject fields (e.g. an academic paper has a very different tone from a marketing press release), have good attention to detail, self-discipline (to work as a freelancer), good time management (all those deadlines!), a sense of curiosity and good concentration.

The main roles are:

- Translator – converts written texts (which could be anything from company reports or emails to journalism, non-fiction books or advertising) from one language to another.
- Literary translator – does the same but specifically with fiction; can be tougher as it's not just conveying the meaning but also the tone, mood, etc., of the original.
- Conference interpreter – usually working in pairs, this role involves live, simultaneous interpreting of speeches and debate at formal meetings or conferences, usually into the headphones of delegates.
- Public Service interpreter – simultaneous interpreting for bodies such as the police, courts, NHS, social services or local government.
- Liaison interpreter – mostly hired by corporates to simultaneously translate at meetings, foreign tours, factory visits or on the phone, etc.
- Lawyer–Linguist – qualified lawyers who are also linguists can secure this highly specialised work translating legal texts for international bodies.
- Subtitler – translating for film and TV subtitles.
- Language analysts – translating or analysing work in the security and intelligence services (see page 279).

Many in the industry have a post-graduate qualification, such as one approved by the European Master's in Translation programme from the EU, or a professional diploma from a body such as the Institute of Linguists or the Chartered Institute of Linguists. There are also a handful of paid training roles, like those run by the EU (tinyurl. com/EUlinguists).

Other freelance translators have secured work without extra study:

many sign up to translation agencies, which usually demand a test piece of translation, and may then offer corporate work or jobs for charities or other organisations. Freelance translators are usually paid per thousand words, at rates which could start at around £75 and go up to about £300. The long-term potential depends on how many hours the translator is willing to work, whether they have specialist knowledge in particular subject areas, and what type of clients the translator chooses to work with.

Jobs for the EU and UN are generally regarded as the top payers in the industry: translators for the EU start on €52,500 a year, and the most experienced and highly qualified can earn as much as €200,000 a year.

The two main professional organisations for linguists in the UK are the Chartered Institute of Linguists (ciol.org.uk) and the Institute of Translation and Interpreting (iti.org.uk). Both offer advice to newcomers.

WORKING LIFE: Simon Beswetherick is a freelance translator of French, Spanish, Catalan and Portuguese into English, working for clients including Survival International, Médecins Sans Frontières and UNESCO

'People sometimes think my job involves travelling around the globe, but in fact, I mostly work from home and do very little travel for work.

The kind of work I translate has evolved over the years, gradually becoming more specialised as I have gained more knowledge and experience in certain fields. Nowadays, I primarily translate in the fields of humanitarian aid, international development, human rights, law, culture and anthropology. I also work on marketing and business translations. Recent jobs have included a report on human rights in Mexico (Spanish–English), a series of videos about humanitarian activities around the world (French–English) and legal proceedings in a Brazilian corruption case (Portuguese–English). I most enjoy translating documents for NGOs [non-governmental organisations] and humanitarian organisations whose work I admire. I feel that in my small, invisible way, I am contributing to a positive cause in which I believe.

After I graduated with a First degree, which included modern languages, I spent time living and working in countries where the languages I wanted to learn are spoken (France, Spain and Brazil) and then undertook a post-graduate diploma in translation from the Chartered Institute of Linguists, while working in a translation agency. After gaining a few years' experience working as an in-house translator (I got the job after contacting translation agencies directly), I decided to go freelance. It gives me the freedom to choose which clients I want to work for, and to specialise. As a freelancer, it is definitely an advantage to work with several languages, as it brings in more work – and increases the variety of the work. With each new job I learn about a new initiative, crisis, innovation, dispute, etc., and I feel privileged to gain these insights.

Another of the benefits of the job is its flexibility – I'm able to organise my work hours to fit in with other personal or professional interests. Due to the flexibility of working as a freelance translator, it is particularly convenient for parents wishing to take time off work during school holidays; I estimate that more than half of professional translators are women.

On the flipside, being freelance means facing inevitable admin – bookkeeping, VAT returns, chasing up payments, tax returns . . . Yawn! Also, translations are often requested urgently. This may be because the documents are time-sensitive (press releases, humanitarian appeals, etc.) or because the translation stage of a project is often left to the last minute, as all the source-language documentation needs to be finalised first. I often make an effort to keep evenings and weekends free to make sure that work doesn't take over my life. Also, working alone might not be to everyone's liking.'

TV / FILM PRODUCER

AVERAGE STARTING SALARY – £94–£108 per day for a runner, £138 per day for a production assistant.

ENTRY POSITION – Runner or production assistant

TYPICAL WEEKLY HOURS – Variable

RECOMMENDED QUALIFICATIONS – Experience/student film

IF YOU LIKE THIS YOU MIGHT ALSO LIKE . . . journalist, online entrepreneur, publisher

Lights, camera, action! While the director, crew, actors or presenters focus on the creative part of a TV show or film, it's the producers who oversee the business side of a show, from conception to completion.

There are two main career paths for behind-the-camera work in film and TV: producer and director – although, confusingly, sometimes the roles are moulded into one and you see someone listed as a 'producer/director'. Production work involves looking after the business side of a show, doing things like securing funding and rights to scripts, and managing budgets. Directors, meanwhile, are usually responsible for the way programmes are made – managing the production process from deciding how and where it will be filmed to describing their vision to actors and supervising the post-production work.

Most producers and directors start off in the film or TV industry as a runner but then branch out: wannabe directors tend to work their way up via the third/second/first assistant director route to cameraman and director. Would-be producers, meanwhile, tend to rack up roles as researcher, production assistant, then assistant producer before becoming a producer and executive producer.

The work of both producers and executive producers involves running the behind-the-scenes action on every TV programme and film. Depending on the scale of a production (smaller ones will obviously have fewer people able to help out), other producer roles include coming up with ideas and pitching them to TV commissioners and film studios, reading others' ideas and scripts and potentially commissioning them, raising funding, talking to backers, budgeting and scheduling, recruiting a crew (major productions will have a casting director to find the 'talent' but on smaller ones producers would have to book guests, interviewees, or actors, too), organising shooting schedules, ensuring everyone sticks to them, maintaining regular contact with the director and finishing the production on time and on budget.

Major feature films and bigger-budget TV series will have teams of producers sharing these jobs, but smaller ones will see one person fulfil all the roles, and possibly even directing, too.

The media is still a tough industry to crack. 'Most successful producers get into the job by doing unpaid work experience for months or even years first,' admits one film studio producer. 'Or contacts – they're still crucial for getting that first job.' In both TV and film, lots of people start on the lowest rung in the studio, as a runner or production assistant, or as a researcher, and work their way up. It's a good idea to secure a placement on, say, a hospital radio station, university TV or radio station, or online broadcaster, to build up your experience and contacts. Qualifications could make it easier for you to break into this role, especially postgraduate degrees in broadcasting, but entry will usually require previous experience.

The fight to get into the industry could be good practice, though: a job as a producer is also competitive, high-pressure, and often involves long hours and travel. An average starting salary for production jobs is £25,000 to £30,000, rising to about £45,000 with experience and to as much as £80,000 for top producers. Depending on whether you go on camera or into a management role, there are many opportunities for career development.

THE LOWDOWN: anonymous film runner

'My uncle's best friend's cousin was working in post-production [editing] for one of the big studios in the US, and he knew someone over here, who got me my job as a runner for a low-budget film. That was after I'd tried, and failed, at sending out literally hundreds of emails to anyone I'd ever come across online, met at networking events, and so on, and heard nothing back. There are definitely a LOT of people who want to get a foot on the ladder as a runner, and a lot who fail or try for years and years.

My average day starts about 8am, running about getting the right actors and actresses ready, distributing drinks and food. Usually most people in production say thanks – it's like they remember their runner days – whilst the creatives ignore you, or moan that their drinks are too hot/cold/weak, etc. You just have to smile and move on.

Twice so far I've run to the loo to cry in secret. It can get quite depressing. The job is pretty thankless and doesn't really require me using my brain at all, so right now my degree in communications feels like a bit of a waste. The job is literally running all day – getting people through security to the set, getting them out again, taking people to and from make-up, wardrobe, etc. But I just have to remember that this is a means to an end.

The key is to be friendly and network and try to make as many contacts with as many people as possible – the whole point of this job is basically to escape it and climb the ladder to a better one.'

WORKING LIFE: Sara Benlow is a Sky News producer*

'After scouring the papers, internet and social media to look for stories and interviews that are coming up that day, I spend my first thirty minutes in the office researching the business stories and looking into any guests who we could use to develop a story. We then have a team phone call, where I designate the stories to other producers and say what we are looking for in terms of content – it could be a bespoke report, a wall graphic using the most interesting numbers, or asking our finance analyst to look into certain aspects of the story to find ways of relating large figures to real people. We discuss creative ideas for telling stories

---

* *name changed for anonymity*

– pictures we can use, for example, to visually represent the relationship between wage growth and inflation.

The rest of the day is fluid but often involves pre-recording interviews (which involves preparing questions, then timing and editing them for the show) and writing graphics and co-ordinating figures.

At 12.45 there is a live slot in which the programme is previewed, so I have to write what's called a tease – plugging the main stories – and cut images to reflect the show. At 3.30pm I write and edit the promo for the show, which plugs the main topics for discussion and the best guests. Throughout the day, I'm also tweeting new stories on behalf of Sky News.

That's how my day is planned, but new stories present themselves at any time during the day – whether it is through company announcements, world events or corporate gaffes. So we can change our stories, introduce new guests and send our presenter to a location to film something new if it suits. I'm often sent out of the office to produce a segment.

At 5.45pm there is another live tease for the show; after that, my job is to check all scripts for accuracy and spelling errors. We go live at 6.30pm, and when on air I am usually in the gallery [adjacent to the studio] in charge of breaking stories. If they break, we'll interrupt the show and come off a live interview to get the presenter to read the latest news. I have to make decisions and quickly, informing the director if there is a change to the rundown or a new piece of vision or a new graphic. I leave at 7pm when we are off air. I'm not usually connected to work in the evenings or weekends, but as I work for a 24-hour broadcaster it can be required at times. The next morning I review the audience figures and use this insight when making decisions about the next show.

I got my job following a master's in Broadcast Journalism at City

University. I pursued internship schemes at Sky News and Channel 5 News, then subsequently applied for this producer position while I was working there as a freelancer.

My favourite parts of the job are interviewing a range of important and interesting people and being sent to the heart of many developing stories. Meeting the Prime Minister, and bosses of FTSE 100 companies, is amazing. The office is fast-paced and dynamic, competitive and constantly moving.

My advice for anyone keen to crack the industry is to be driven; don't give up and keep on asking questions. Accuracy is essential in journalism, so check your facts and triple check your sources. And be thick skinned: a breaking news environment can often be stressful and pressurised.'

Dream Job: Zookeeper

Rosie Badger, 20, is one of the youngest lion keepers in the UK, working at Folly Farm zoo in Pembrokeshire

'The first thing I do every day when I arrive at the zoo is to put my wellies on, grab a radio and my keys, and check the lions through the window. Then I clean out the African Pygmy hedgehogs' hut, before going into the lions' enclosure. I do a head count and check they are all okay, then with another keeper I go into the lion paddock, check the electric fence and put out any enrichment, let the lions out of their house, and start cleaning it. There are also fossa, ocelot and tortoises in my carnivore section, so I start cleaning out one of their enclosures, too. At 11.30 there is a public talk, after which I carry on cleaning out. When that's done I give a talk on lions before making up the lion food, weighing out and cutting up beef or horse meat, clean the kitchen down and defrost frozen meat for the next day. Then I get the lions inside at 4.30pm as they are shut in every night. I then put the chains back on, check the electric fence, clean the windows and pick up any poo, before locking up the paddock and going home at about 5.30pm.

I got into zookeeping after leaving sixth form – I didn't want to go to university but wanted to continue my education, and do something animal-related. So I decided to go to a local college and study a foundation degree in animal science; I had to do 600 hours of work experience to pass my course, which I did at Folly Farm. Afterwards, I was lucky enough to get a job there. It's seriously competitive as there aren't that many zookeeper jobs – about 300 people applied for my job as a trainee keeper two years ago, despite a salary of between £12,000 and £16,000 a year. Most people have to move away to find work at a zoo.

My favourite part of the job is getting to feed and train the lions, and seeing their cute faces. The worst part? That has to be gutting chickens and rabbits for the carnivores. It's a very physical job, which keeps you fit, but you can't mind getting your hands dirty. People think the job is all about cuddling animals – it's not! It's a lot of cleaning and keeping up high standards of animal welfare. It isn't an easy job – there are early mornings and late finishings, and you're often working up to 10 days in a row. You have to be pretty dedicated.'

VET

AVERAGE STARTING SALARY – £30,000

ENTRY POSITION – Vet

TYPICAL WEEKLY HOURS – 43 hours

RECOMMENDED QUALIFICATIONS – Veterinary degree

IF YOU LIKE THIS YOU MIGHT ALSO LIKE . . . doctor, dentist, zookeeper

Or if you want to be posh about it, 'veterinary surgeon', because that's the full title of the job usually known as vet. But whatever you call it, the job is basically a doctor for animals – though some would say it's much tougher than being a GP as the average puppy or pony isn't great at explaining their symptoms!

Most high-street practices spend much of their time seeing small pets like dogs, cats, rabbits and hamsters, etc. However, all vets face a gruelling five or six years of training, learning about all types of animals, from the domestic to the exotic, zoo dwellers and farm animals.

An average day could include consultations, operations on sick or injured animals, diagnostic tests like X-rays and scans, vaccinations, advising farm owners and others on preventing the spread of disease, telling pet owners about diet and care, putting very seriously injured or terminally ill animals to sleep, neutering pets and other animals to stop them breeding, and dealing with the finance side with pet insurers.

Specialist vets may also be involved in checking up on the hygiene and standards in kennels, catteries, zoos, riding stables and abattoirs, etc.; some work around the country for the government, advising on and helping to limit the spread of animal diseases; others become specialist veterinary scientists working on new animal drugs or another kind of specialist, such as a veterinary cardiologist or dermatologist.

On top of that, there are lots of other jobs in the vet world (see below), while some practices focus on particular areas, such as specialist farm vets in rural areas, equine vets and small animal experts.

Becoming a vet is tougher than most people realise: only a handful of institutions – currently seven, including the Royal Veterinary College in London, and Bristol, Glasgow, Liverpool, Cambridge, Nottingham and Edinburgh Universities – can bestow the veterinary science or medicine degree, so competition is seriously tough. (There are also a number of overseas degrees which are approved by Britain's Royal College of Veterinary Surgeons, in Australia, New Zealand and South Africa.)

Degree courses usually last five years (six at some schools), and you'll normally need at least two As and a B at A level (or equivalent) in biology and either one or two subjects from chemistry, physics or maths, on top of stellar GCSE results. Some universities will consider applicants with vocational qualifications, such as the BTEC Diploma in Animal Science, with distinction grades. Some schools also offer that six-year course for students who do not have the required scientific qualifications.

Just as with medicine, vet schools also insist that applicants show evidence of their interest in and commitment to the subject – which means you'd better have a whole lot of work experience. If you're keen on this career, ask your local vet for weekend work or shadowing experience, or contact a farm, kennel or animal charity – it's important to prove you're adroit at handling animals, including livestock, and can show you're caring and confident with them.

Remember, too, that this isn't a job for you if you're totally obsessed with, say, horses but terrified of other animals: during vet school you work with a variety of species including cows, sheep and horses. 'There's something very glamorous about having your arm up the backside of a dairy cow. I'm so glad that chapter is closed for me now!' says one wry practising vet.

Pay-wise, the market rate for a new graduate is about £27,000, or about £30,000 in London. It rises by about £5,000 with experience, then hovers between £49,000 and £60,000 for senior vets. For specialists, pay can be considerably higher, while practice partners will take home a portion of the surgery's profits (which will depend on its location, success and number of patients) but also face the extra tasks of running the surgery's finances, invoices, PR work and recruitment.

Vets working in high-street practices will usually face regular hours, around 9am to 6pm, but there's almost always overtime, late shifts, on-call and weekend work, too. Vets working on farms, zoos and similar environments could work much more irregular shifts.

Another job in the vet surgery is the **veterinary nurse**, who provides expert nursing care for sick animals, as well as carrying out diagnostic tests, some medical treatments and minor surgical procedures (under a vet's guidance) and educating owners on maintaining pet health. The two routes to becoming a veterinary nurse are vocational training (the Level 3 Diploma in Veterinary Nursing, which is available on either a full-time basis or apprenticeship-style alongside a job in a practice), or a degree in veterinary nursing. The latter route can lead to extra career opportunities, such as research, the pharmaceutical industry and teaching.

WORKING LIFE: Nicola Wong is a vet at Medivet, a surgery in Harrow, London

'We mostly see canines, felines, rabbits and hamsters at my clinic. Generally the day begins at 9am, when I spend two hours doing consultations. It's usually 15 minutes per patient, on routine vaccines, blood tests or emergency situations.

After that, the rest of the day is spent doing routine operations such as neuters, dental work and lump removals, or more complex procedures such as MRI or CT scans, or keyhole surgery. Between all the consultations and operations, I try to find time to call owners with blood results – and slot in lunch. From 5 until 7pm, it's evening consultations. I often don't leave until after 7.30pm at least two out of five days a week in order to finish up jobs or deal with emergencies.

I usually work Monday to Friday, plus one in four weekends each month. But every year I have three weeks of being 'on call' for emergency home visits.

When I first started work, I found it quite difficult to detach, but with experience I've learnt to switch off – for my own sanity. You do get the odd case or two where you become very involved with an animal, and where you wonder, 'Have I done everything that I could have done?' On the odd occasion I've woken up at 3am suddenly remembering that I've forgotten to call this owner or send off this document, etc., so now I sleep with a notepad by my bed just in case.

My absolute favourite part of the job is doing a new puppy and kitten consult. I also love having a chat with pet owners, and getting to know them. Sometimes it doesn't actually feel like work when you have your favourite clients come in and you can have a good chat whilst attending to their little critter. Another thing that never ceases to amaze me is the range of foreign bodies that Labradors eat – from Lego pieces to lightbulbs. We have competitions amongst us vets about who can cut out the most obscure objects from these crazy dogs!

The worst part of the job is all the paperwork that we have to do for insurance companies. You must like people more than you like animals at times. I always remember a senior colleague telling me in the first week of work five years ago that communication is the key. There's no point being an amazing surgeon who knows every single bone in the body if you can't build a rapport with your client. Being a pet owner myself, I know that having a dog is like having a child, and entrusting someone with your child for the day is a big deal.

There's also huge job satisfaction – it sounds corny, but I had a four-week-old kitten recently who was hypoglycaemic and looked to be practically at death's door, but within a few hours of admission into hospital she was up and eating. Amazing things happen – every day miracles make you leave work with a smile on your face.'

APPENDIX ONE: THE CV

CV Clinic

Dragon's Den star and recruitment expert James Caan's tips for making your CV stand out from the crowd

1. Turn that piece of paper into a piece of you

Your CV will go into battle on your behalf against as many as thousands of other candidates' CVs. So make sure it reflects your skills: if you're a wannabe graphic designer, create something better than a boring black and white list; if you want to work in a bank, use the CV to prove how you'd make the institution money.

2. Don't just list

If your CV just bleats out your skills or work experience, it won't say much at all. Instead, describe what you learnt in particular jobs, extra-curricular activities, etc., and how they would help you excel in the role you're applying for. 'There is nothing more frustrating for an employer than reading something that is clearly generic and sometimes not even totally relevant to the vacancy,' says Caan. 'Adapt your CV for each job: it can be a simple case of adding in key skills that would be especially useful for certain positions, or talking about particular achievements that are more relevant. It can be a time-consuming process to tailor your CV a number of times, but when you weigh that up against the prospect of getting the job you want, it should be an easy decision.'

3. Short and sweet is best

You might think your Saturday job or experience studying for an esoteric degree is the most interesting thing in the world. Your future employer probably won't. The average employer has a huge sheaf of CVs to get through – and one study suggested the average employer spends only 6.25 seconds looking at a candidate's CV, scanning it for relevant keywords. So keep your CV to a maximum of two pages.

4. Error-free is crucial

As well as making sure your info is set out clearly and is easy to read, double and triple-check that it has no spelling, grammatical or factual errors – with address, email, phone number, etc., as well as qualifications. Ask at least one other person to read through your CV before submitting it – mistakes can be tough to spot in your own work. Revisit your CV every month or so to keep it up to date.

5. Cut the cliché

'There are certain words and phrases which always seem to crop up on CVs and the more employers see them, the less value they have,' says Caan. 'The whole point is for you to stand out from other candidates, so try to avoid the clichés which you know everybody else will use. Be creative with the way you describe yourself; you don't want to be seen as someone who is simply using buzzwords that they think employers want to hear. One of my recruitment businesses specialises in the digital, media and creative sectors, and many people believe video CVs will get more popular over the next few years. At the moment it is still a bit of a novelty, so provided it suits the role you are going for, it can add a unique quality to your application.'

6. Quantify your achievements

Pithy details go a long way. Stating, for example, that you boosted sales by 40 per cent in a year is better than saying you're a 'good salesman'; explaining you built a specific algorithm to solve a specific IT problem whilst at university is more interesting than stating that you're adroit at computing.

'Every member of an organisation, whether it's a sales director or a receptionist, can have their contribution measured in some form,' says Caan. 'It could be financial – you may have generated a certain amount of revenue, or made a certain amount of cost savings – in which case I want to know how much. It may be that you were in charge of managing a whole team, or were responsible for managing key clients – again, tell me how many. Attaching a number to what you have achieved gives me a greater idea of your value-add.'

7. Don't leave any gaps

A hole in a CV makes an employer suspicious, so any long periods without work should be explained. If you've been unemployed, try to indicate how you used it to your maximum benefit – perhaps volunteering or working on a particular course.

8. Add a winning summary

'First impressions count,' says Caan. 'Having a summary which succinctly and creatively states your experience, abilities and goals will give your CV a far better chance of being read further. It is particularly important that you do state what your career goals are in this section. Some people believe this is of no interest to an employer, as they are more interested in what you can do for them. However, I am personally always looking for people that are ambitious, so I certainly wouldn't be disappointed to see a candidate's future objectives stated in their summary. It tells me that they are driven and know exactly what they want.'

9. Special delivery

'About 95 per cent of applications are done online and there is absolutely nothing wrong with this,' says Caan. 'But what if you are speculatively applying for a company where there is no vacancy? An emailed CV may get ignored, or put on file but then forgotten about. Why not consider posting, or even hand delivering it? This is outside-the-box thinking and gives your application a far better chance of being seen by the relevant person. Fifteen years ago, somebody who emailed a CV rather than posting it would have grabbed the attention of a hiring manager. Now, it is very much the other way round.'

APPENDIX TWO: THE INTERVIEW

Preparing for an interview . . .

Start your preparations well before you're ironing your shirt or pulling on a suit. Research the company – what it does, what makes it different from others in the same industry, who the main competitors are, as well as the job itself. Go as deep as you can: read corporate blogs and Twitter accounts, look up the latest earnings reports, see where and what the boss has been saying.

Try to speak to past or present employees to find out more about the interview (your university careers office can help hook you up, even if you graduated a while ago, while social media can also be helpful). Consider potential questions you might be asked (see below – and, if you're going for a job in a large firm where others may have been through the process, then Google to see if anyone has reported back online) as well as your own responses. If you've got any gaps in your CV or have changed careers, be ready to explain your history. And prepare some questions to ask at the end of the interview – employers almost always ask if you have any unanswered issues and it sounds weak if you haven't got any.

If you haven't already done so, do a spring clean of your social media – employers almost always look at their candidates' Facebook, Twitter and other social media, and if your profile picture is you in front of 15 empty beer glasses, it doesn't look great. Or use the Social Sweepster app – it detects dodgy pictures and any swearing from past posts.

The day before, make sure you know how you're going to get there and exactly where the interview is, as well as what you're going to wear to cut down on-the-day stress. You'll usually want to wear a smart suit or business clothes – even dress-down firms can get dressed up for interviews – but obviously it depends on the firm; check any info you've been sent for specific instructions. Leave plenty of time to get there – aim to arrive at least 15 minutes before your scheduled slot.

Common interview questions

- What are your strengths and weaknesses?
- What do you know about our company?
- Why do you want to work here?
- What can you offer us that other candidates can't?
- If we offered you the role, what would you do in your first week/month/year?
- What would your friends or colleagues consider your best qualities?
- Why should we hire you?
- Where do you see yourself in one/five/ten years' time?
- Why did you leave your last job?
- Are you a good team worker/leader?
- How would you describe yourself?

Uncommon interview questions

- 'How lucky are you and why?' (Asked by Airbnb)
- 'What is the number of people travelling on the Tube per day?' (Asked by Barclays Wealth)
- 'How would you sell a fridge to an Eskimo?' (Asked by Harrods for a summer sales job)
- 'How many ping-pong balls fit in a Boeing 747?' (Asked by Goldman Sachs)
- 'If you were a pizza deliveryman, how would you benefit from scissors?' (Asked by Apple)
- 'Calculate the size of the disposable nappy market in the UK.' (Asked by Bain & Co)
- 'Are you more of a hunter or a gatherer?' (Asked by Dell)
- 'If you were on an island and could only bring three things, what would you bring?' (Asked by Yahoo)
- 'Do you believe in Bigfoot?' (Asked by Norwegian Cruise Line)
- 'How many square feet of pizza are eaten in the US each year?' (Asked by Goldman Sachs)
- 'If you were 80 years old, what would you tell your children?' (Asked by McKinsey & Co.)
- 'You're a new addition to the crayon box. What colour would you be and why?' (Asked by Urban Outfitters)

Source: Glassdoor

At the interview . . .

Each one is different – you could be grilled by a panel, or by one person; it might last ten minutes or a whole day or even longer; you might be doing group tasks with other candidates or just have a straightforward interview. Whatever you're facing, try to relax – take some time to think before answering a question so you can plan your response. If you think you've answered a question badly, it's worth asking politely for a second chance. But if the interviewer declines, try to put it behind you and focus on the next question. Be aware, too, that employers are increasingly asking exam-style questions that test your mental agility – there may be no right answer, they just want to see how your brain tackles a tricky situation.

James Caan's advice for acing an interview

Confidence – What really matters is how you project yourself and how you engage with the interviewer. If you've done your research, know that you can do the role and do it well, what have you got to be nervous about? It starts as soon as you walk into the interview – be aware of your body language; break the ice; use a cue from the room to start conversation, whether it be an award hanging on the wall or a family photograph on the desk, you can demonstrate your confidence in starting a conversation.

Smile, keep eye contact and draw the interviewer into what you are saying by explaining the value you have brought to other companies through specific achievements – but tell them as stories, not as a series of boasts.

Demonstrate how well you will fit into the company – The interviewer will be wondering 'how will he/she fit in here?', so your job is to work towards a specific objective in that interview to deal with some fundamental points:

- Have I done my research?
- Do I know enough about this company?
- Can I demonstrate my ability to do my work?
- Do I look the part?
- What have I done that demonstrates I am competent for this job?

If you have any gaps in answering these points, do more research ahead of the interview.

Go the extra mile – Consider what you might take along to the interview to enhance your presentation. This could be credentials, certificates, awards or reference letters. For me, I like to see examples of candidates' work, whatever the job. Bringing along a document that proves how you handle tasks in practice may only take a minute or two within the interview, but the overall impression you leave behind could be vital.

Ask killer questions – If you get to the end of an interview and almost all the questions have been asked by the person at the other end of the table, then quite frankly it is highly unlikely you will get the job. Not only does it make you seem to be lacking in confidence, but it gives the impression that you're not actually that committed to getting the job. If you really want to work for somebody, it makes sense to find out as much about them as possible – in particular, things which you can't glean from a mere job advert. Here are some questions you should be asking at every single interview:

- What are your short-, medium- and long-term goals?
- What's the culture like?
- What are the opportunities for progression?
- How will I be measured?

Ultimately, it is all about being confident without being too pushy. If you are good at what you do, have the right profile and are not afraid to get your name out into the market place, then you will stand a better chance of landing that all-important job when it does come along.

After the interview . . .

Afterwards, if you hear that you got the role – congratulations! If not, phone up to ask for feedback. Doing so can be scary, but it's common practice, you won't be the only one, and if you've made a mistake or a bad impression it's better to find out sooner rather than later and learn from your mistakes for the next one.